Shadows
and
Cypress

SHADOWS AND CYPRESS

Southern Ghost Stories

ALAN BROWN

University Press of Mississippi / Jackson

www.upress.state.ms.us

Copyright © 2000 by University Press of Mississippi
All rights reserved
Manufactured in the United States of America

08   07   06   05   04   03   02   01   4   3   2
⊗

Library of Congress Cataloging-in-Publication Data

Brown, Alan, 1950 Jan. 12–
     Shadows and cypress : southern ghost stories / Alan Brown.
          p.   cm.
     Includes bibliographical references and index.
     ISBN 1-57806-270-5 (cloth : alk. paper)—
     ISBN 1-57806-271-3 (pbk. : alk. paper)
     1. Ghosts—Southern States.   I. Title.

     BF1472.U6.B745   2000
     133.1'0975—dc21   00-021350

British Library Cataloging-in-Publication Data available

Contents

Chapter 3.—FLORIDA

Chapter 4.—GEORGIA

Chapter 5.—KENTUCKY

Chapter 6.—LOUISIANA

Chapter 7.—MISSISSIPPI

Chapter 8.—NORTH CAROLINA

Chapter 9.—SOUTH CAROLINA

Chapter 10.—TENNESSEE

Chapter 11.—TEXAS

*Chapter 12.—*VIRGINIA

PREFACE

The concept for this book had its origin in the research that I did for my first collection of oral ghost tales, *The Face in the Window and Other Alabama Ghostlore*. After recording stories from members of the audiences who attended a series of lectures I presented on ghost tales in 1992–93 for the Alabama Humanities Foundation, I began collecting stories from my own students at the University of West Alabama. After a year of collecting, it became apparent that I had far more stories than I needed for my book of Alabama ghost tales. Many of the stories that I could not use had come from students who lived in other southern states. However, simply having a source of southern ghost tales at my disposal was not enough to convince me that such a book should be written. My original reason for editing a collection of Alabama ghost tales was to fill a gap in the state's folklore by producing the first scholarly collection of oral ghost stories, and I applied the same reasoning before embarking on my next project. When I discovered while collecting books for my annotated bibliography that only one book of oral ghost tales from the entire South had been published—W. K. McNeil's *Ghost Stories from the American South* (1985)—I decided not only was there room for a similar collection but also that a single volume could not possibly do justice to the hundreds of stories that comprise Southern ghostlore. In addition, I realized that because ghost tales are still being told and generated by young people throughout the South, there were probably many new stories that had been circulated in the decade that had elapsed since the publication of McNeil's book.

After submitting the manuscript of *Face in the Window* to the publisher in 1994, I began working on my next book in earnest. I decided to search for stories from the same southern states that W. K. McNeil included in his book: Alabama, Arkansas, Florida, Georgia, Kentucky, Louisiana, Mississippi, North Carolina, South Carolina, Tennessee, Texas, and Virginia. Realizing that I would have to supplement the stories I had collected on my own, I applied for a research grant from my own university to finance my trips to various archives and libraries throughout the South. It turned out that the best source for oral ghost tales from the American South was the Library of Congress. Almost half of the stories included in this volume were collected by employees of the Federal Writers' Project, a subsidiary of the Works Progress Administration, between 1936 and 1941. Even though copies of these tales can be found in state archives, it made more sense to me to gather what I needed from one central location rather than travel to all the southern states. Still, in order to produce a representative collection of tales from all of the southern states, I had to look for other sources. Most of the tales I included from Virginia came from the Alderman Library because copies of the WPA stories from Virginia could not be found in the Library of Congress. I also had to look elsewhere for stories from Florida, Kentucky, Tennessee, and, surprisingly, Louisiana. Nineteen stories were taken from the Manuscripts and Folklife Archives of Western Kentucky University. The archives were an ideal source of oral ghostlore because they contains hundreds of folktales that had been collected by students from the folklore classes at the university. These stories, which have been recorded according to the accepted scholarly standards, are available to scholars for research. I also received a few ghost tales from the Ozark Folk Center of Mountain View, Arkansas. Fortunately, I was able to collect stories from Florida, Tennessee, and Louisiana from students and faculty members at the University of West Alabama.

Because many of the WPA interviewers paid little attention to such matters as comparative data or biographical information on the informants and sometimes even rewrote the stories they had collected, I gave preference to those tales that had been collected by trained scholars or by folklore students. For example, even though Mississippi produced more than a hundred WPA ghost tales, I opted to use tales that I had collected from people I knew from my hometown of Meridian, Mississippi. Nevertheless, a case can still be made for including WPA material in a scholarly folklore collection. Although some interviewers, like those who worked for the North Carolina Writers' Project, transformed what were originally fairly simple, straightforward texts into artistically complete works, quite a few WPA stories, like those collected from Arkansas, Georgia, and South Carolina, do reflect a concern for the dialect traits of their informants. Even those stories that have been rewritten are of value because they may be the only existing sources of eighteenth- and nineteenth-century folklore in certain areas.

Because my first collection of oral ghost tales was well received by folklorists, I decided to employ the same scholarly methods in the present volume. With the exception of the WPA tales, which are in the public domain, all the stories were used with the written permission of the informants. The stories that I collected were transcribed exactly as they were told to me in tape-recorded sessions. All of the grammatical errors and dialect traits common to southern states (for instance, the dropping of inflected endings such as -ing) have been preserved in the printed form. Although I reproduced most of the WPA dialect stories exactly as they were written by the interviewers, I did change the stories when a dialect spelling of a certain word did not seem to be warranted (for example, "sed" instead of "said" or "wen" instead of "when"). I also allowed my informants to dictate the organization of their stories. In some cases, for example, background information about a particular landmark is given in the end instead of in the beginning. Certain concessions were made for the general reader as well. All of the notes have been placed in the back of the book instead of at the end of the stories to facilitate reading. I also gave titles to the stories because storytellers do not normally attach titles to their tales. I added my own titles to those WPA stories that either did not have titles or that had very generic titles (for instance, "The Haunted House" or "A Ghost Story"). For the sake of balance, I have attempted to include approximately the same number of stories from each state (between fourteen and sixteen); however, some chapters are longer because the stories are longer.

Shadows and Cypress differs from *Face in the Window* in one very important way. The focus of *Shadows and Cypress* is much broader because I wanted to include stories that do not conform to the strict definition of "ghost story." There are some important southern oral traditions from other cultures that deal with supernatural figures and elements other than ghosts. The French inhabitants of Louisiana have produced some very fine werewolf legends that cannot be found anywhere else in the South. South Carolina's "plat eye" stories, which feature a shape-shifting creature that may or may not be the ghost of a human being, reflect the rich heritage of the Gullah influence. I also decided to include stories that dealt with prophecy, particularly those tales in which the appearance of a ghost or an angel portends a tragic occurrence, such as death.

I was pleasantly surprised to find that Alabama is not the only state in the South that still has a thriving oral tradition of ghost tales. Ghost stories are the most popular type of folk tale that is still being told, a fact that is supported by the large number of current collections of ghost tales from individual states that have been published in the past few years. The large number of tales that I collected from young people between the ages of eighteen and twenty-one testifies to the continuing popularity of ghost tales and to the emergence of a new genre—urban folklore—which includes tales set in the present or the recent past that are believed to be true. Frequently, but not always, these stories are set in cities or small towns.

The advances that have accompanied the emergence of the New South have obliterated many of the "lonely places" that have been the conventional settings of ghost stories. While it is true that young people still seek out these remote areas as the locales for parties and "make-out" spots, it is a fact that the typical setting of a southern ghost story is gradually changing, moving from the woods and the fields to college dorms and office buildings. Therefore, any genuinely comprehensive collection of southern ghostlore must include the stories being told on high school and college campuses as well as those that are conveyed in the more traditional rural settings by elderly residents. The inclusion of old and new texts in the same volume is becoming a feature of the most recent volumes of oral ghost tales, such as John Burrison's *Storytellers: Folktales and Legends from the South,* Docia Schultz William's *Phantoms of the Plains,* and my own *Face in the Window.*

I am grateful to everyone who assisted me with this project. Gregor Smith, the archivist at the Julia Tutwiler Library at the University of West Alabama, provided invaluable assistance with tracking down obscure collections of oral tales. Another librarian to whom I owe thanks is Patricia M. Hodges, manuscript and archives coordinator at the Folklore Archives of Western Kentucky University, for helping me locate and photocopy ghost tales from Kentucky. Needless to say, I could not have finished the book without the cooperation of the staff in the Manuscript Department of the Library of Congress. The folktales provided me by W. K. McNeil, folklorist of the Ozark Folk Center, were equally helpful. I would also like to thank Dr. Ed Roach, provost of the University of the West Alabama, and the research grant committee for giving me the funding required to complete this project. Dr. Tommy DeVaney from the University of West Alabama gave me the stories and photographs that make up the bulk of the Tennessee material in the book. Finally, I am indebted to my daughters Andrea and Vanessa for helping me with the photocopying and to my wife Marilyn for assisting me with the proofreading chores.

İntroduction

In an article entitled "The Ghost Theory" that appeared in the *Oxford American* (October/November 1996), Marc Smirnoff said that he arrived at "The Ghost Theory" after polling twenty southerners from a wide variety of backgrounds and discovering that they all believed in the existence of ghosts: "Simply put, the Ghost Theory reveals a distinction that has hitherto been unvoiced: Southerners believe in ghosts; Northerners do not."[1] While the recent publication of books such as Beth Scott's and Michael Norman's *Haunted America* (1994) and Dennis William Hack's *Haunted Places: The National Directory* (1996), as well as many regional collections of ghostlore, refutes this sweeping generalization, it is a fact that southerners love to tell ghost stories. Indeed, the South is and always has been a haven for the collector of ghost tales, as the size of this volume's annotated bibliography demonstrates.

The idea of "the South" is problematic at best because of the various overtones of meaning. Simply defined, the South is the thirteen states that made up the Confederate States of America during the Civil War. Arriving at a concise geographical or cultural portrayal of the region is much more difficult. The popular view of the South as consisting of cotton fields and swamps completely ignores the region's other topographical features, such as the mountains of Appalachia, the plains of Texas, and the pine forests of Mississippi, Alabama, and Georgia. Likewise, the folkways of the South also defy any attempt to pigeonhole them into a specific category. The influence of Afro-Americans, the French, the Spanish, and other ethnic groups is indelibly etched in the culture of the South. However, the wave of British and Scotch-Irish immigration in what is known as the backcountry region of the United States had the greatest impact on the manners, customs, and mores of the South. These early settlers immigrated from the border country between Scotland and England. This border region included the following counties: Cumberland, Westmoreland, and parts of Lancashire in the far north of England; Dunfries, Wigtown, Roxburgh, and Berwick in southern Scotland; and Derry, Down, Armagh, Antrim, and Tyrone in Ulster.[2] The distribution of surnames collected by the first U.S. Census of 1790 indicates that more than half of the population of the western parts of Maryland and Virginia, North and South Carolina, Georgia,

Kentucky, and Tennessee came from Scotland, Ireland, and northern England. Other ethnic minorities also inhabited the backcountry at this time, but their numbers were relatively small.[3]

As a result of the arrival of thousands of borderers into the southern highlands, many cultural traits that have become closely identified with southerners actually had their origin in England, Scotland, and Ireland. Southern dialect, which is commonly called southern highland or southern midland speech, was referred to before the Revolutionary War as "Scotch-Irish" speech. Typically, the regional dialects of the Appalachian and Ozark mountains, the lower Mississippi Valley, Texas, and the Southern Plains substitute *shet* for *shut*, *hit* for *it*, *he-it* for *hit*, *far* for *fire*, *eetch* for *itch*, and *nekkid* for *naked*. Certain vocabulary words common to southern highland speech, such as *scoot* (slide), *nigh* (near), *fixin'* (getting ready to do something), and *honey* as a term of endearment also originated in the dialect of the Scotch-Irish immigrants.[4]

The strong family ties that are so important to many people living in the backcountry recall the clans of the border country. The clan system, which spread rapidly throughout the southern highlands, occasionally led to disputes between families, the most famous of which is the feud between the Hatfields and McCoys.[5] The belief in magic, witchcraft, and wizardry was also transferred to the southern highlands from the borders of North Britain. People living in the southern highlands differed from their counterparts in New England, though, in that their magical folkways were never institutionalized in the church or legal system. For the most part, magic in the backcountry took the form of homespun superstitions that were employed to control worldly events.[6]

To a certain extent, the violence that permeates the lore of the South, including the tales contained in this book, has its source in the principle of *lex talionis*, the rule of retaliation. Under this principle, a good man had to defend his personal honor by wreaking vengeance on the offender. The overriding purpose of the rule of retaliation was to maintain order, but it also fostered a climate of violence, similar to that which existed in eighteenth-century England.[7] Although the regional culture of the southern highlands has definitely evolved somewhat over the years, the primary traits of the border culture survive to this day in the lore of the folk.[8]

Even though the borderers exerted the most pervasive influence on the culture of the twelve southern states, other ethnic groups also made important contributions to that aggregate of folkways that is known as "southern culture." When the first Spanish, French, and English explorers made their way through the American South, they encountered an assortment of Native American tribes, the most prominent of which were the Creeks, Chickasaws, Choctaws, Cherokees, and Seminoles. All of these tribes exerted a powerful influence on the lore of the South.[9]

The plantation system introduced the African-American influence into the southern United States. According to the 1860 census, the slave population in the South was so dense that in some southern states, it equaled and even surpassed the white population. In Alabama at that time there were 435,000 slaves; in Arkansas, 111,115; in Florida, 61,745; in Georgia, 462,198; in Kentucky, 225,483; in Louisiana, 331,726; in Mississippi, 436,631; in North Carolina, 331,059; in South Carolina, 402,406; in Tennessee, 275,7129; in Texas, 182,566; and in Virginia, 490,865.[10] The vast numbers of slaves in the South, living in close proximity to the whites, ensured that some cultural sharing would take place. South Carolina's most distinctive folk beliefs derive from the Gullah culture on the coast. Descended from slaves who had previously belonged to the Bantu and Angola tribes, the Gullah dialect is a variation of the language spoken by the people of Angola.[11]

The French influence in the South was most strongly felt in Louisiana, which LaSalle claimed for France on April 9, 1682. However, French settlers did not move into Louisiana in large numbers until the expulsion of the Arcadians from Nova Scotia. Between 1760 and 1790, more than forty thousand Arcadians made southern Louisiana their home. Their descendants, today's Cajuns, form the majority of Louisiana's French stock.[12]

The Hispanic culture is most evident today in the lore of Texas and Florida. Although Spanish explorers had been trekking through Texas since the early sixteenth century, Spanish settlers did not really come to Texas in large until the order of Franciscan monks embarked on a spiritual conquest of Texas and began setting up missions where people could be protected from Indians with the heavily buttressed walls.[13] The Spanish influence in Florida first arrived with the founding of St. Augustine by Pedro Menedez de Aviles in 1565.[14] The Spanish-speaking inhabitants of Cuba have also left an indelible mark on the state. Although the Cuban population of Florida surged after the influx of an estimated 500,000 refugees who fled that country soon after Fidel Castro rose to power in 1959, Cubans have lived in Florida ever since Spanish slavers visited the area just before the arrival of Ponce de Leon.[15] Because the Bahamas are only fifty miles off the eastern coast of Florida, descendants from slaves brought to the islands by the British have been immigrating to Florida since the nineteenth century.[16] The South has been so heavily impacted by the folkways of people from different ethnic and national backgrounds that only a very uninformed person would ever speak of the area as an area of cultural unity.

The migration of different groups of people to different parts of the South also accounts for some of the variation in Southern ghost tales. French settlers transported the "Loup-Garou," or werewolf, from the hills of France to the bayous of Louisiana. The Gullah people living in South Carolina brought with them their tales of the plat eye, a horrible, ghostlike creature that tormented people walking out at night alone. The Bahamian immigrants in Florida created stories dealing with the practices and beliefs of Obeah, a voodoo-like religion of African origin practiced by blacks in the British West Indies. The English pioneers who made their homes in the Appalachian Mountains entertained themselves at night with traditional stories about spectral dogs and cats, ghostly women in white and headless revenants who disturb the sleep of unsuspecting visitors to a haunted house. The Hispanic inhabitants of Texas concocted tales of spirits condemned by God to walk through the rooms of abandoned adobe dwellings because of their failure to fulfill a promise to pay a priest a certain sum of money for prayers. The Native American influence surfaces in stories about white wolves that escort the souls of the dead to the afterlife. The black experience in the South manifests itself in the tragic stories of mistreated slaves who haunt their masters. Taken as a whole, all of these multicultural influences make up what we refer to as southern folklore.

Even though southern ghost stories can be found in many collections, very few of them are presented in their original form, probably because they have been recorded in an artificial setting. In his introduction to *Storytellers: Folktales and Legends from the South*, John Burrison explains that the folk element of many of the published tales is lessened because, in a tape-recorded interview, they are "removed from the social and physical stimuli that would normally have triggered their telling."[17] Consequently, few of the "book" tales retain the flavor of the natural context of the storytelling event. The dissatisfaction with the end-product, combined with a desire to make the stories more appealing to a general audience, may explain why so many collectors have succumbed to the temptation to rewrite what they had heard and recorded.

For the older tales at least, it may be impossible to reproduce the original contexts of the storytelling event because they no longer exist.[18] Ray B. Browne attempted to do just this in his book *"A Night with the Hants" and Other Alabama Folk Experiences* (1977) by including a transcript of a folk storytelling session. In this session, the storyteller interacts with members of the audience who comment on his performance and ask questions.

One can argue that it is the element of audience participation that lies at the heart of a folk performance, not the location of the event. In the following transcript from a storytelling session recorded on October 14, 1993, in Coatopa, Alabama, between the interviewer; two elderly black sisters, Bessie Spencer and Alice Armstrong; and a sixty-year-old white woman, MacGregor Smith, one can see how the participants play off each other as they introduce their own stories:

INTERVIEWER: Have you heard of a place called Conky Bayou? Josh [Horn, the sisters' father] said he saw a headless horseman there.

ALICE: I was told now that they was having a revival at Christian Valley [a church] 'cause I used to walk up and down that road going to work at night. That was supposed to be a haunted street down there at Christian Valley. And my great-grandfather claimed that—I don't know what man it was; I never will know—said they was comin' from the church and this no-headed horse come buckin' up the road. So instead of them lookin' back, they ran, and this horse, like, ran after 'em. So they all jumped in the bushes and covered themselves up with leaves and branches. Then one of them say, "There he go! There he go!" But there was two of them. They was headless horses. And they say every time—I think they claim that every time somebody died at that church, they would have a ghost. They would come back in a ghost fog. And these no-headed horses just ran on by them and ran on down the road.

MACGREGOR: What church is that?

ALICE: Christian Valley.

MACGREGOR: Oh. It's on the road to Belmont.

ALICE: You turn right off at the store, and there's a sign that tells you it is Christian Valley.

MACGREGOR: Who is supposed to have gotten killed down there?

ALICE: I really don't know. But they say people got killed all up and down the road. But you know the trees used to bend all over the road. I don't know why. I used to walk down there and look up and see all these trees against each other along the road like that. And I always wondered why that road was made like that. Those trees were bent over there. But I think some men was fighting and killing [each other] by those trees on the road there.

BESSIE: Papa said one time he was comin' down the road there and he see these big red eyes and this tongue, this big, black dog with this tongue hangin' out of his mouth, you know, and he says, "God! Here come de dog!" Papa said he took off runnin', and when he got home, he yelled, "Open dat gate! Open dat gate!"

ALICE: That place just ain't right. Do you all believe in haints? Do you believe in ghosties?

MACGREGOR: Well, I think I heard one one night in my house, so I guess I do believe in them.

ALICE: Some people thinks that it just your imagination, but I don't think all the time.

MACGREGOR: People in my house heard the same thing I heard, and I think it was my brother-in-law that had just died. But it wasn't scary. We weren't scared.

ALICE: Well, Bessie, you used to think your mother was in our house, didn't you?

MACGREGOR: When my mama died, you couldn't go into that room, and she'd pull that door shut on you every time. You couldn't keep that door open.

This session is typical of the type of storytelling events that currently take place in college dormitories, at family reunions, and around campfires in that each storyteller develops tidbits of information from the person who spoke before (as in Conky Bayou, Christian Valley Church, supernatural beings, belief in ghosts, ghosts of dead relatives). The contexts may have changed—the blacksmith shop and the general store are no longer gathering places for tale-swappers—but the dynamics of storytelling have not.

The basic functions of oral ghost tales have also remained fairly constant down through the years, even the ones that were not generated in a genuine storytelling sessions. First of all, ghost tales, like all legends, tend to mirror the fears and anxieties of our times.[19] In many of the humorous ghost tales, the terror generated by lonely, out-of-the-way places is dissipated by a logical explanation for the phenomenon. This is certainly the case in "The Haunted Cemetery," a tale told in Meridian, Mississippi, by Fonda Rush on December 12, 1995:

I have a great ghost story that my Daddy used to tell me. It's not really a ghost story, but we didn't realize it until we got to the end. He was originally from Kemper County from a community called Pleasant Grove. Back when Daddy was in high school in the 1930s, people from Kemper County came down to school in Center Hill, which is in Bailey, and Daddy was manager of the basketball team, and he had a brother a couple of years younger than him, and they would always come to basketball. School buses at that time used to go out and pick people up from basketball games at night, but because the bus was from Lauderdale County, it would only take Daddy and them to the Lauderdale County line, and they had to walk. It wasn't a long way. If it were inside the city, it would be only a few blocks to their house.

On this particular night, they had to pass a church's graveyard, and it had gotten late by the time they dropped everyone off. And you know how we'll get these foggy nights around here. They had to go by the cemetery, and they eased around. They'd always go on the other side of the road, and as they were going around the cemetery, they could see a white movement in the cemetery coming closer and closer to them. Being teenage boys, they got scared. They ran up to their parents' house. And they got there, and they started telling my grandfather about the ghost in the cemetery. And my grandfather, being the strict Methodist that he was, said that there was no such thing as ghosts. And they kept saying that there was this ghost in the cemetery. So he [the grandfather] loaded them up in the wagon, and they went down to the cemetery, and when they got there, their grandfather saw this white movement, and my grandfather started to think, "Oh my gosh, there is a ghost!" It was moving around in the graveyard, and you could barely see it in the mist and the fog. As it got closer, though, they began to realize that a white mule had gotten out. But that's one of the stories that my Daddy used to tell. It's probably the first ghost story that I have a recollection of.

Supernatural tales such as this one that present an unnerving experience in a humorous light serve as a kind of folk therapy in that they provide balance for the mind.[20]

Even the ghost tales that cannot be explained away connect us to our world and restore our sense of order if the supernatural explanation reflects a human motive.[21] This is particularly true of stories in which the revenant has returned to right a wrong or to protest the immoral actions of the living. A good example is this local legend told on June 24, 1996, in Livingston, Alabama, by Ginger Glass, an English teacher from Dixon Mills, Alabama:

> There's a trailer right close to my house, and the trailer's been there for as long as I can remember. It's a very, very old trailer. About twenty or twenty-five years ago, there was a family living there. A brother and a sister got into a fight one day over a set of car keys. She told the brother he couldn't have 'em and ran out the front door of the trailer, and the brother got mad and got a shotgun and shot her in the back, and she fell on the ground, and he walked up and shot her in the head and killed her. He was put in a mental institution for only seven years, which scares me because now he's livin' over there. They did a lobotomy on him.

But anyway, the family that lives there still—the man that killed her's living in back of the trailer. And they say that on nights when it rains, they can hear her ghost comin' through the trailer, and she'll go into his room and try to drag him outta the bed on his feet. And one of the uncles lives there, and he comes fishin' at my grandmother's place a lot, and he says they'll wake up in the middle of the night, and he [the murderer] will by layin' in the middle of the floor screamin', "Don't get me, Delores! Don't get me, Delores!"

The moral lesson that is implicit in this tale—the warning against committing an act of domestic violence in a fit of rage—elicits our loss-of-control anxieties.

The message of the next tale involving the desecration of an Indian burial ground shows what happens when one intrudes upon the spiritual world. This story was told on June 24, 1996, in Livingston, Alabama, by Mary Gilmore, a history teacher from Gulf Shores, Alabama:

Gulf Shores Middle School and Gulf Shores Elementary School were built right adjacent the state park on eight acres of land that was donated by the Meyer Foundation, and the Meyers are a very generous group of people. The areas that could not be cultivated and used they have donated to churches, and they did give eight acres to have a school built about fifteen years ago, and since then, about four or five other buildings have been added on. When the gym building and four classrooms were added, all kinds of problems occurred. It was as though this particular part of the school was never going to be built. All the footings would be washed out. One calamity after another kept occurring. And jokingly, people would say, "Well, it's probably part of the old Indian burial ground which we knew was somewhere in the state park, but no one but a small group of people knew exactly where, and finally, after many, many delays, the building and the four classrooms were complete.

Tales like this one are moral fables that guide the listener along the "straight and narrow" pathway. In this case, it is society, not an individual, that has committed sacrilege and is suffering the consequences. Although the listener may not totally understand what happened, he or she experiences a kind of catharsis by being given an interpretation that is at least halfway satisfying on a moral level.[22]

Of course, some ghost tales appear to have no explanation, especially those that deal with extremely violent crimes. The folklorist Thomas E. Barden feels that the appeal of these unsettling tales lies in the truth that they reveal about ourselves: "The moral messages of murder and violence stories are peripheral; it is the anxiety they invoke that is central. What holds us spellbound is their graphic proof that violence and cruelty dwell in our fellow human beings and, therefore, potentially in us."[23] Stories that focus around the murder of small children, like this story told by Eileen Isaacs to Ollie Frasier, a WPA worker from Fort Smith, Arkansas, are particularly disturbing on a deep psychological level:

> A house on 46th Street in Fort Smith, Arkansas, is said to be haunted. A member of a family that formerly lived in the house related the story [to me]. After the change was made, the family who bears credit for the story was seated in the kitchen. A boy called his sister to see his gun which was behind the door in the bedroom. Just as he reached for the gun, the cries of a baby were heard. The children and their grandmother heard the cry. But they heard no noise. The sound seemed to come from behind the door. The story is told that a baby was killed there by his mother, and its spirit returns at regular intervals.

The absence of a motive in tales like this is intriguing, not just because of the mother's ability to override her maternal instinct, but also because of what it says about human nature: that all parents, at one time or another, may have become angry or frustrated enough to seriously harm their children.

Although the purposes of the supernatural legends may differ, they all have one element in common: they invoke our inherent uncertainty about death. Not surprisingly, religion, which originated, at least in part, as a response to the questions people have had about the hereafter, is frequently an important element in these stories, especially the tales containing an embedded moral concerning an individual's reward, or punishment, in the afterlife. The following tale told by Mrs. Lenore Kilgore of Big Laurel, Virginia, to WPA worker James Taylor Adams in 1941 includes a strong warning against blasphemy:

> I've heard Uncle Sam tell the awfulest tale about Old Ran Hubbard. He said Old Ran lived on Critical Fork of Guesses River when he died. That's been fifty years or more ago. He had been a very wicked man, but on his death bed he was converted and requested that the Bible be buried with him. Now most all the neighbors objected to putting the Bible in the coffin with him, saying it was a sin to bury the Word of God. But Old Ran had said bury it with him, and here in this part of the country when a dying person makes a request, it is carried out. So they finally placed it in his hands on his breast and buried him that way.

Well, it went on for a few weeks and Aunt Pop, that was old Ran's wife, had a log-rolling one day. Old Ran had cleared up a new ground before he died, but hadn't rolled the logs off of it. So all gathered in to roll the logs off of Aunt Pop's new ground. The had made one log heap right close to the house, and that night after most of the people had gone, someone stepped out and come running back in the house pale as death and trembling all over. Said he'd seen something out there in the log heap that was burning in the yard. Uncle Sam said that him and Grandpa Roberts, who was Aunt Pop's brother, went out and some others that had stayed for supper and to talk a while, and sure enough as plain as they ever seen anything in their life, there was old Ran Hubbard right there in the rolling flames with his Bible in his hands. They watched it for a long time, and it was still there till they went to bed or went home. Everybody believed that it was a sign that old Ran had went to hell and was reading the Bible in the flames of torment.

Only a small percentage of ghost tales have an actual theological basis; many more tales end with a moral, and they can be said to be primarily educational in purpose in that they are told to promote conformity to accepted standards of behavior within a community.[24] However, even those tales that have no implicit message still qualify as philosophical treatises to the extent that all ghost stories are meditations on death.

Of course, purpose is not the only way in which ghost tales differ. The differences in content are, to some extent, dependent upon the geographical location of the tale. The mysterious swamps of Louisiana, for example, served as an ideal locale for the "fifolet" stories involving strange balls of light that are reputed to be the souls of unbaptized children but in actuality are probably balls of "swamp gas," or methane. Many of the ghost tales from Florida, especially those dealing with headless apparitions, grow out of the apprehension fisherman feel when confronted by the immensity of the ocean on dark, foggy nights. The dark, foreboding limestone caves of Kentucky and Tennessee were ideal settings for the nefarious activities of social outcasts like Kate Batts, the infamous Bell Witch. Other caves, like the one in the Great Smoky Mountains National Park, inspired stories about children who get lost and are transformed into spirits doomed to wander the dark recesses forever. The pine forests of the Appalachian Mountains gave rise to tales about "haints" lying in wait for travelers foolish enough to travel the lonely roads through the woods at night. The plains of Texas generated tales of mysterious lights that could be seen hovering over the ground far off in the distance. The rural settings of many southern ghost stories capitalize on the fear many people must have felt living in the middle of nowhere, miles away from the nearest house or town.

All ghost stories can be distinguished by the type of narration, which frequently impacts upon the length of the tales. Swedish folklorist Carl Wilhelm on Sydow devised the notion of "active" and "passive" bearers of tradition. Active bearers, he says, make a concerted effort to keep a tale alive, whereas passive bearers can recall fragments of a tale if asked to but do nothing to keep it alive.[25] One can easily detect the difference between the two styles of storytelling in Reverend Methane's lively rendition of the classic ghost story "The Golden Arm" (story 104) and George Macro's version of the ghost that haunts the Kappa Alpha House at Mercer University—"The Haunted Fraternity House" (story 47)—in Georgia. Naturally, it stands to reason that tales that recount the narrator's personal experience will probably be longer than those that the narrator has received second-hand. Compare the difference in supporting details in Ray Jordan's account of the night he spent in a haunted library—"The Ghost in the Library" (story 13)—and Wes Hutchinson's story of a female ghost who carries a lantern, recorded in Livingston on January 12, 1995: "This lady's son was in the Civil War. He went off and fought and was killed. Her husband went and looked for him. Finally, he too was killed. And every night she'd walk the trails through the woods and through the swamp lookin' for them. And she died din' that. And they say when you're down there real late at night on certain nights, you'll see her walkin' around with a bucket in one hand and a lantern in the other. You can make it out as a woman, but you really can't make out facial features. This is in Monroe County, Alabama." Obviously, Ray Jordan is more of an active bearer of tradition because the enthusiasm with which he tells his tale is infectious. One could add that a mark of an active bearer of tradition is that he narrates the story as if it really happened to him.[26]

Contrary to popular belief, southerners do not all speak the same dialect. The Cajun dialect of Louisiana and the Gullah dialect of South Carolina are just two examples. Therefore, any genuine collection of southern folk tales must account for linguistic differences. The stories contained in this book reflect the editor's attempt to present an inscribed record of the original oral performances. Ideally, a folklore text becomes "the basic source, the pure stream, the inviolable document of the oral tradition. It comes from the lips of a speaker or singer and is set down with word to word exactness by a collector."[27] However, creating a reasonable facsimile of what one has heard is not as simple as Richard Dorson has made it sound. Admittedly, tape recorders have made transcription somewhat easier. Noted anthropologist Dennis Tedlock believes that tape recorders are much better than the notebooks used by early collectors of folklore, such as the WPA field workers, because it preserves not only all of the dimensions of the speaker's voice but other features of the performance as well: "The information on the tape is not limited to what the voice sounded like at the moment it left the lips. Even the performer's bodily movements are in evidence, affecting the sound of the voice as the head moves with respect to a microphone that was not tied around the neck. Also on the tape is evidence of the remarks or movements of an audience (including the mythographer), along with evidence as to whether the performance took place indoors or out, whether seasonal birds or insects were singing, and whether there was a violent wind or thunderclap."[28] When one considers all of the other paralinguistic features of narrative performance, such as rate, length, pause duration, pitch contour, tone of voice, loudness, and stress, the task of transcribing an oral text becomes even more daunting.[29]

One does not have to have spent very much time studying folklore before he becomes conscious of the implications in the way the speech of certain regional, social, and ethnic groups has been represented or misspelled.[30] The transcriptions in this book were guided, at least in part, by the research of Dennis Preston. His statistical analysis of 203 articles that appeared in volumes 83 through 92 of the *Journal of American Folklore* indicated that what folklorists choose to respell "most often turns out to be that which strikes them as nonstandard or unusual. . . . Folklorists find 'folk speech' in performances that contain language noticeably different from their own or from their notion of the standard."[31] Preston admonishes the ethnographer against showing regular phonological differences that depart from what he perceives to be Standard American English "unless such differences are important to the discussion of the text or a complete understanding of it. If that is the case, a phonetic transcription, narrow as the point to be made requires, is the appropriate strategy."[32]

In order to avoid falling into the trap described by Preston, I followed, to the best of my ability, four of Edward Ives's guidelines for the preparation of transcripts from taped material:

1. For material not on the tape, use inserted brackets.
2. If you can't understand something, leave it out.
3. Omit such interview comments as *sure, yeah.*
4. Avoid eye dialect (e.g., *wuz* for *was*).
5. Use ordinary punctuation; don't overuse exclamation marks.[33]

Ives concludes his chapter on transcription with a basic rule that has guided me and other collectors of folklore: "Get everything down that is on the tape. Don't record what you think the informant meant to say; put down exactly what he did say, without correcting grammar, usage, or sentence structure."[34] With Ives's basic rule in mind, Dennis Preston contends that the ethnologist should not omit hesitation phenomena (e.g., "uh"); tag questions (e.g., "you know"); and false starts and corrections (e.g., "The house is supposedly—my great-grandfather died there").[35] I retained these expressions because I have found that in many cases, they reveal the narrator's emotional state, especially anxiety or fear, as he tells the tale. Other markers indicate the age of the informant, such as the word "like" in "And we were, like, totally afraid," which was uttered by a teenager in a story collected for this book. As William Bascom points out, prose narratives from different groups of people differ according to style and manner of delivery; consequently, singling out these traits is another way of identifying the age and background of the speaker.[36]

Admittedly, the WPA narratives included in this book violate many of the rules I tried to follow in my own transcriptions. B. A. Botkin's *Manual for Folklore Studies* told field-workers to make every effort to record each story's "source, history, and use, in addition to the past and present experience of the people who kept it alive."[37] However, because many of the field-workers were students, bank tellers, clerks, newspaper reporters, and aspiring writers, they were not skilled in the techniques of collecting folklore. In fact, most of the training they received consisted of written guidelines from the Washington Office, advice received from fellow field-workers, and their own experience.[38] Not surprisingly, then, many WPA narratives were heavily rewritten and edited for content. Transcriptions of narratives provided by African-American informants contain many more dialect transcriptions than those from whites. Rather than completely rewrite the WPA material to match my own transcriptions, I removed eye-dialect (*laid* instead of *layed*) and regularized punctuation and spelling (e.g., *ev'y* instead of *ev'vy*). I also added apostrophes to those words in which a letter had been dropped (e.g., *an'* instead of *an*).

Finally, southern ghost tales can be differentiated by placing them in categories. The method most widely accepted by folklorists of labeling an oral ghost narrative as being of a certain type is through the identification of motifs within the tales. The tales in this collection were inventoried for the occurrences of words relating to the setting of the stories. The count revealed that the word *house* was employed in sixty-two of the narratives—approximately 30 percent of the total. Old, dilapidated houses are conventional settings for ghost stories; it is surprising, therefore, that there were not more "haunted house" stories in the collection. When the informants were specific about where the ghost appeared in the house, the word *bedroom* was used in twelve of the narratives. Because the night appears to be an opportune time for seeing ghosts, it stands to reason that they would show up in the bedroom. Only one ghost appeared in the kitchen, and no ghosts made an appearance in the basement or cellar. Houses were not the only haunted places in these stories. Six of the stories featured "college ghosts," which haunted dormitories and administration buildings. Considering the age of many college buildings, one expects many of them to have a tragic history. Ghosts seem to prefer spiritual places, a fact that may account for the sighting of ghosts in churches. Ghosts were also seen in three narratives featuring theaters, all of which were very old. Hospitals were the settings of two of the tales. The words *city hall* and *office building* were mentioned once. The fact that ghosts are gradually moving out of houses and into other buildings reflects the gradual urbanization of the South.

The physical features of outdoor settings were also inventoried. In twenty of the stories, ghosts frightened people along lonely country roads; in fifteen of these tales, the individuals who saw the ghosts were traveling alone. Ten of the narratives were set in cemeteries, which are certainly conventional places for seeing spirits. The only other out-of-the-way place where ghosts were seen is bridges (twice).

Stories can also be classified according to the types of ghosts that scare people. The ghosts were overwhelmingly female, with forty-two citations; males were mentioned twenty-four times. Two of the female ghosts were identified as witches. Three of the male ghosts were identified as boys, and four of the female ghosts were girls. Sixteen of the ghosts were headless, an element of ghost tales that the English and Scotch-Irish settlers brought to this country with them. Not all of the ghosts in this book are human, including, interestingly enough, one of the headless revenants, a horse minus its head. The rural settings of most of the stories accounts for the appearance of dogs (five), cats (five), cows (three), horses (two), alligators (one), wolves (one), and opossums (one). One would expect that as the South becomes more urbanized, cows, horses, and wild animals will appear less often in oral ghost tales. The country or forest settings also explains why fifteen of the narratives featured ghosts as balls of light, which are often identified by more objective observers as swamp gas, or methane.

A third way of categorizing ghost stories is the reason for the manifestation. The overwhelming number of ghosts (thirty-two) show up for no apparent reason, a category that William Lynwood Montell devised for his book *Ghosts Along the Cumberland*.[39] The second largest group included those spirits who cannot rest in their graves, either because they were murdered (eight) or because they committed suicide (seven). Two restless spirits returned because of the theft of a body part. Five ghosts informed the living of the location of hidden or buried treasure. Twelve of the ghosts appeared to warn people of impending doom or to comfort and reassure them. Eight ghosts returned either to complete unfinished work (three) or to reengage in their earthly activities. The reluctance of ghosts to depart completely from this life accounts for the haunted rocking chairs (two) and haunted spinning wheels (two).

The pivotal historical event that has shaped the development of the South for the past 130 years—the Civil War—is one of the primary elements of southern ghost stories that distinguish them from ghost stories gathered from other parts of the country. With the exception of the Battle of Gettysburg and a few other battles, most of the fighting in the Civil War took place in the South, and the war's terrible effects have manifested themselves in every aspect of southern life—including its folklore. Many Civil War stories survive to this day in the form of family folklore, tales that have been handed down from one generation to the next. A prime example is "Knocking Spirit" (WPA) (story 187) from Virginia, which serve as reminders of the indignities southerners suffered at the hands of the Yankee invaders. A similar story, also passed down in the same family through the years is "Uncle Issue's Treasure" (story 187), a North Carolina tale that again records the cruelty the Yankees imposed on civilians but also demonstrates the ingenious methods southerners devised to protect their valuables. Of course, conventional ghost stories have also emerged from the conflict, such as "The Haunted Rifle" (WPA) (story 182), which deals with a haunted object that is taken into a home. The impact of the Civil War on the average southerner is just now beginning to wane, a fact that is substantiated by the large number of young people who no longer harbor a grudge against the North. Consequently, the Civil War does not seem to have nearly as great an influence on the ghost stories being told in high schools and colleges today, except for those storytellers who identify the ghost of an unknown person with the statement, "It could have been a soldier, I guess."

The sad legacy of slavery is another major distinguishing element of southern ghost stories. It is interesting to note, though, that most of the stories featuring slaves do not stand as condemnations of slavery. A good example is "The Screaming Woman" (story 74) from Kentucky, which is actually more of an indictment of miscegenation than of slavery itself. Another Kentucky story, also from a white informant—"The Unseen Feeling" (story 69)—is actually a fairly conventional haunted graveyard tale, although the narrator does make the statement in the beginning that owners thought of slaves as being "[not] much more than possessions." The almost complete absence of references to slavery by black informants in the WPA stories can be attributed to the fear of reprisal from a white interviewer who might be offended by references to the cruel treatment of slaves by their white masters. A notable exception is "Buck's Visitation" (WPA) (story 31) by Adeline Buries, an ex-slave, but even this story omits any direct reference to the horrors of slavery. In fact, the story showcases the generosity of the master in giving a house to a slave, and the slave's loyalty and respect for white people by giving the ghost's treasure to the relatives of the owner of the house. Ironically, the only WPA ghost story that actually does touch upon the mistreatment of slaves is "A Haunted House" (WPA) (story 122), the tale of the return of the spirit of a slave named Samba after his murder at the hands of his master's drunken son. Surprisingly, this tragic tale ends on a humorous note as the notoriously slow-walking slave gains a little speed in his stride after he has become a ghost.

Although this collection does not provide an implicit answer to the question, "Why do so many ghost stories come from the South?," one can infer several reasons after having read the tales and the notes. As was stated before, southerners love to talk, and ghost stories engage the listener's attention and emotional involvement to a degree that no other type of folktale can match. In addition, the Bible Belt that stretches across the entire South has produced a deeply spiritual people who have always been somewhat skeptical of coldly scientific explanations for the mysteries of the universe. Most important, though, the South's tragic past has provided countless accounts of misery and suffering that have been transformed through various retellings into little memorials of belief in the value of human life and the eternal persistence of the human spirit.

1. Tony Early, "Ghosts in the Mist," *Oxford American*, Oct./Nov. 1996, 4.
2. David Hackett Fischer, *Albion's Seed: Four British Folkways in America* (New York: Oxford University Press, 1989), 621–22.
3. Ibid., 634.
4. Ibid., 652–53.
5. Ibid., 668.
6. Ibid., 714–15.
7. Ibid., 765.

8. Ibid., 629

9. Oliver LaFarge, *A Pictorial History of the American Indian* (New York: Crown Publishers, 1956), 26.

10. United States Historical Census Data Browser (http://fisher.lib.virginia.edu/census/).

11. *South Carolina: A Guide to the Palmetto State* (New York: Oxford University Press, 1941), 45.

12. *Louisiana: A Guide to the State* (New York: Hastings House, 1941), 41–42.

13. *Texas: A Guide to the Lone Star State* (New York: Hastings House, 1940), 37.

14. Michael Gannon, *Florida: A Short History* (Gainesville: University Press of Florida, 1993), 3–4.

15. Ibid., 133.

16. Gustavo Antonini, "Bahamas," *World Book Encyclopedia*, 1988.

17. John Burrison, *Storytellers: Folktales and Legends from the South* (Athens: University of Georgia Press, 1989), 17.

18. Ibid., 17.

19. Jan Harold Brunvand, *The Vanishing Hitchhiker: American Urban Legends and Their Meanings* (New York: Norton, 1981), 2.

20. Ray B. Browne, *"A Night with the Hants" and Other Alabama Folk Experiences* (Bowling Green, Ohio: Bowling Green University Press, 1977), xvii.

21. Thomas E. Barden, *Virginia Folk Legends* (Charlottesville: University Press of Virginia, 1991), 23.

22. Ibid., 23.

23. Ibid., 22.

24. W. K. McNeil, *Ghost Stories from the American South* (New York: Dell, 1985), 15.

25. Carl Wilhelm von Sydow, *Selected Papers on Folklore* (New York: Arena, 1977), 12–13.

26. McNeil, 5.

27. Richard Dorson, *Buying the Wind* (Chicago: University of Chicago Press, 1964), 1.

28. Dennis Tedlock, *The Spoken Word and the Work of Interpretation* (Philadelphia: University of Pennsylvania Press, 1983), 4.

29. Richard Bauman, *Verbal Art as Performance* (Rowley, Mass.: Newbury House, 1978), 20.

30. Dennis Preston, " 'Ritin' Fowklower Daun 'Rong: Folklorists' Failures in Phonology," *Journal of American Folklore* 95 (1982): 306.

31. Ibid., 306.

32. Ibid., 309.

33. Edward Ives, *The Tape Recorded Interview* (Knoxville: University of Tennessee Press, 1980), 95–98.

34. Ibid., 98.

35. Preston, 309.

36. William Bascom, "The Forms of Folklore: Prose Narratives," *Journal of American Folklore* 78 (1965): 7.

37. Barden, 7.

38. Ibid., 6.

39. William Lynwood Montell, *Ghosts Along the Cumberland: Deathlore in the Kentucky Foothills* (Knoxville: University of Tennessee Press, 1975), 93.

Shadows
and
Cypress

CHAPTER ONE

ALABAMA

✝

I. THE MUSIC CRITIC

This house is an early 1900s [structure] as far as we can determine. There was a big house on the lot before that one. I don't know what happened to that one. And before that, there was a stagecoach inn or stagecoach stop on that site. I don't know the dates of that either.

But as near as David [my son] could remember, it was probably the spring of '93, and he had been stayin' in the house, like, for a month or so. He said it was probably in the middle of the day. And he was in the livin' room cleaning—vacuuming—and the livin' room and dinin' room and bedroom behind it were kind of a shotgun. You just go straight through. He had a tape player set up in the bedroom and had a tape on and had it turned up real loud so that he could hear it over the sound of the vacuum. And he said all of a sudden, he's up there cleanin' and dancin' and probably singin' along with the tape and all of a sudden, the tape starts draggin'. He said it stopped almost to the point of talkin' real low and deep. And David told me that he had always felt like the house had a presence there of some kind. He has always felt like it.

And so he starts back through the livin' room and dinin' room, and he's sayin,' "Okay. Okay. I'm comin'. Don't be angry. Don't be upset. I'm comin' to fix it!" And the livin' room and dinin' room are open. There's one big room with a big archway between 'em to kind of separate 'em. And just before you get to the bedroom, there's a door to the left that goes into the kitchen. And he said that when he got to that kitchen door, something stopped him in his tracks—just stopped him there. And he said, "I just froze." He said, "The hair on the back of my neck literally stood up." He's very matter-of-fact about it. He said, "Going by the door, I literally froze in my tracks, and the hair stood up on the back of my head, and I stopped dead still and turned to the left and looked into the kitchen."

And he said he saw a woman, kind of a cloudy vapor kind of thing, and yet he could give details about her. He said it was not a distinct outline like I see you, but all the features were there. She had light-colored hair, and it was piled up on her head in the Victorian style. She had on a white blouse with the high collar of the Victorians, the long sleeves, a light-colored skirt. He said he didn't think the skirt was white, but it was light-colored. She was standing with her arms straight down, and her fingers laced together in front of her. And he did not get the feeling that she was angry or distressed, but he felt that she wanted the tape turned down. Yet he said it was almost a warm feeling, a feeling of reassurance that he knew exactly what she wanted. She wanted that tape turned down. He says there was no anger or deep emotion involved. And he said when all this was going on, "I was not conscious of any other surroundings. I do not remember the tape player at all during this interval. I did not hear anything else, including the tape." He knew exactly what she wanted, and he said while they stood there looking at each other was probably no more than five to ten seconds. And it's as clear in his mind as if it were a conversation with you or with me.

When I asked him about her disappearance, he said she was there, and then she wasn't there. It wasn't as if this cloud blew away or anything like that. She was just there, and then she left. But he said even after she was gone, he turned down the tape and went into the livin' room. He still had this feeling that there was still a presence here, but it wasn't a threatening kind of presence, and he didn't rush out to the house where I live and tell me about it. I mean, it was something that came out some time later. He said, "Oh, I saw a ghost over at the house at Sumterville." He was twenty-four at the time. We're not talkin' about a kid with a big imagination.

My family owns this house. It was my grandparents' home. It [the ghost] could have been his great-grandmother. She died on August 17 when he was three weeks old. She never saw him because she was pretty much in a coma. She was in the hospital when he was born. My mother, though, says there was also a Miz Randall lived there, and there was another old lady [whom] my grandmother and her husband kept. She didn't have any family, and it could have been her.

2. THE BOYINGTON OAK

For many years, I taught fourth grade Alabama history in Mobile, and Mrs. Mac Roberts used to take my children on a tour downtown in the Church Street Cemetery where the Boyington Oak was located. It was on the tour, and they had a wonderful bright caretaker at the cemetery. He would entertain us for hours. His name was Julian, and he knew that I worked with his children and that I would be bringing another group over there in the summertime. He had his own version of what had happened to many people in the cemetery. It's been a long time since anybody's been buried in this cemetery. It's downtown behind the library.

One of the stories he told was about the Boyington Oak. Back in the 1880s, there was this man, a printer, I believe, who was sentenced to be hanged for murdering his best friend. He said that he was innocent and an oak tree would grow from his grave, and it did. And there was a placard on it [the tree] for many years, and it [the tree] stood for a long time. Of course, the people who said he was innocent probably put acorns in his ears.

Many years ago on Sunday afternoons, they would have a Joe Kane parade which would end with a picnic inside the cemetery, and I would climb that red brick wall into the cemetery and sit on the graves and have a lunch. People would walk around and tell all kinds of stories about people who were buried there. They said if you looked inside some of the graves, you could see the bones. They also said that a local fraternity wanted to do something charitable, so the boys decided that it would be easier to clean the cemetery if the tombstones were out of the way, and when they got through, they put them back where they thought they fit.

The oak tree was actually just outside the brick wall. That's because they would not allow him [Boyington] to be buried in that cemetery. I've also been told that with some of the recent developments down that way, it [the tree] has been destroyed. I really can't believe that the historical society would let that happen.

3. THE GHOST IN WEBB HALL

I guess you know that Webb Hall is haunted. And I had a personal experience with a ghost there. This happened two years ago. I stay late after work a lot, and on this night, I was here all by myself. Sometimes, I'm the last person to leave the building.

Let's see, we were on daylight savings time. It was probably 7:00 or 7:30. I think it was in the spring. I got to the point that I was quitting for the day. Security had already been around. They come by, of course, to verify [that] all the doors [are locked]. And to report if there is anybody in the building and they turn off all the lighting in the hallways and the stairwells. Now, if you've been in my office, you know that there's a short hall outside of my office that runs right next to a long hall. We got one security light at the far end of this hall and nothing back here and nothing on the side hall. Well, in that side hallway, there's nothing there except two bookcases. And the opening to the hall is a door at the end. And, you know, I just locked the door and went out. Didn't bother to turn on any lights. I really didn't feel like I needed anything. And when I got to this door here in the hallway, off to my right where there's nothing there except the corner of the building, I heard a rustling that sounded for all the world like a woman in multiple petticoats like you would have had in the early part of this century or the late part of the last century. When I heard that, I got out of there. I went through the door and turned a light on quick. There was nothing there. Within the next two weeks on three different occasions within here [my office] working late, I smelled perfume.

This [building] is the third version of Webb Hall. The other two burned, and I think there was an even earlier version than that. The last time it was rebuilt was 1913 or 1914. It's a noisy old building. When it was rebuilt, there was no steel available, so all the framework was wood. It makes a lot of noise, particularly at night.

4. GHOST CHILD

We had just moved into the house that we live in now. We found through a title search that my husband's family is off by about three or four generations of being the original builder and owner of the house, and we thought that was interesting. And my son was two, and there were hardwood floors in the house, and I would set him down. One day, I heard footsteps. I thought he had gotten out of his crib and was having himself a good old time in the front of the house. I went in to check on him, and he was still in the crib. I had thought that he was too young to pull this "in-out" thing. And it went on for several weeks. The house was about two thousand square feet. [It seemed as if] he [the baby] could get into something at one end of the house, and you wouldn't know what was goin' on at the other end of the house. I said to my husband, "He's too young to be sneaking out of his bed," and he looked at me somewhat strangely. He wasn't quite sure what to make of it. He wasn't quite sure what he was hearing because I hadn't said anything about any ghosts.

One day, I put Hunter [the baby] down for his nap. He [my husband] thought he was up, and it didn't even occur to him that this [a ghost] was what he was hearing. It was like a child running down the hall. He mentioned that he'd heard it, and I think this was the last time we'd heard it. We never did find out what the sound was, and we never did see anything, but it sounded like a child with hard-soled shoes.

5. The Head of the School

I teach at Riverside High School in Northport, and you go out the back door of Riverside, go about fifty feet, and you're at Matthews Elementary. At one time, they had just one big school there—Tuscaloosa Training School. It was a wooden building, had a tin roof, and in 1957, the school was destroyed by a tornado.

Well, the tornado hit in the middle of the day while school was in session. And all the kids at Tuscaloosa Training School went to the basement. One of the teachers after they had counted heads to make sure all the kids were there told the principal, Mr. Matthews, that some of the kids weren't accounted for and that she was afraid they might be upstairs. So he left the basement during the tornado, and they never saw him—he never returned to the basement again.

And after the storm, the same day and later that afternoon, the storm was over, and everyone was clearing out. The building was pretty much ripped apart. They found his body in the rubble of the building, but his head was unattached—his head was gone, and apparently, what they think happened was that a sheet of tin from the building—you had to go outside the building to get to the basement—they thought a sheet of tin had severed his head. Well, they found his body. They found some tin not too far away with some blood on it. A few days later, some students or some neighborhood children found his head in a tree. And it's documented that that's where his head was found—in a tree a few days later.

Of course, there are two schools built there now where there had been one school. The children in the neighborhood would not go between the two schools at night because they say if you walk between there at night, you can see his eyes staring at you from the pine tree, and supposedly, he had big bugged-out eyes, and you know how some people's eyes are always sort of glossy, and you can see his eyes from the trees. And if you go around the school at night, you can hear his footsteps in the hallways where his body is looking for his head. and the kids that live in East Circle over there by that area will not go between the two schools at night. This happened in 1957. There are newspaper accounts of the tornado destroying the school and of the head being found in the tree. If you go to East Circle and ask, every kid there can tell you that.

6. LEEHAVEN

Editor's note: Leehaven is an antebellum mansion that is currently being used as a deer camp in Marengo County.

Well, we've had several experiences [at Leehaven]. Some of them are—you know, we've had lights turn on and off. We've had car alarms turn on, and I thought I heard her [the ghost of Miss Bessie, the former owner] talk to me. It just happens all along. There's been two of us that have experienced the ghost. For example, the other day—I guess, last week—I was standing on the porch, and the old man who doesn't believe in the ghost who's been down there for years [the caretaker] said, "Are you going to stay here tonight?" And I said, "Not with this damned ghost in the house!" and the minute I said that, my car alarm went off. My car alarm has never gone off like that. Then two days later, I was standin' out there talkin' to somebody else over at the skinnin' rack, and I said somethin' about the ghost again, and my car alarm went off again.

And now I have not experienced her in the house. One of my friends had an experience in the house. He came in the house with his children, and the lights wouldn't work. He then went upstairs, and finally a light worked, and then the alarm all of a sudden goes off. Then he turns all the lights on, and part of the lights turned off, and [it] finally scared him so bad he left, and as he left, the alarm went back on.

So that's basically what's happened down there. But I guess her name was Bessie Ferguson. And there's a lot of stories about her. I don't think how she died is true. We've been told that she had Dalmatians, and she came home one night, and the Dalmatians killed her. But I don't think that's true. Other people said she died of natural causes. A lot of the black people down there won't come near the house. They're superstitious of the house. The story I've heard is that they've seen her outside. They've seen her with her dogs. You know—stuff like that. There's a lady that works in one of the gas stations [who] will not even come in and clean the house anymore.

That's pretty much what the story is. My wife had a bad experience too. She was in the house cleaning up, and she got mad at me because I was walkin' around, and she kept hollering at me, and I wouldn't come, and she looked outside, and I was outside. And I hadn't been in the house. And it was just her and I down there. So she got real scared. She won't go back in there.

7. HAUNTED HOMESTEAD

My father died when I was nine and a half years old. I heard him tell things, but I wasn't old enough to find out years and places. These are some of the things he told me.

Grandpa's folks were pretty wealthy, and they lived in South Carolina. He got to loving Grandma when she was only twelve years old. For some reason, Grandpa's folks thought she was below him, so they disinherited him.

I've heard Grandpa say [that] when he did marry, his father told him, "Mike, I'm gonna disinherit you, but the law says I've got to give you five dollars."

"Well, if you've got to give me five dollars," Grandpa Mike answered, "I want it put in a five-dollar gold piece, and I'm gonna split a stick and sling it to hell!"

Well, when Grandpa Mike got married, he took his wife, one ox, a two-wheeled cart, and her folks gave her a bed, a pot, a coffee kettle, and an oven to bake bread in—and a gun. That's what they had when they started out. I think he was about twenty.

After that, he just rambled. He never did stay nowhere but just a little while at a time. When he came to a place he liked that was thinly settled, he'd build him a cabin and settle. Then the first feller that came along and wanted to buy it, he'd sell it to him and go some place else. Then he'd just load his belongings and move on until he found another place he liked.

The country was all thinly settled with houses abut twenty miles apart. So he'd just go on until he found him a nice level place he liked, and he'd build him a house.

I heard Grandpa say his mother said [that] one evening, they were driving through a little town when a fellow stopped them and asked Grandpa where he was goin'. He said, "Well, I'm just traveling. I was thinking about if I found a place that suited me, I'd make a crop."

"Well," the fellow said, "I'll tell you what I'll do. I've got a place up there, and if you'll stay there and make a crop, I'll not charge you no rent. I'll let you have it free."

"What's the matter with it?"

"Well—it's hainted."

"I'll look at it."

So the fellow went with them and showed them the place. When he had seen it, Grandpa said, "I'll stay here, and I'll make a crop." The fellow went back to town, and they unloaded their stuff and put it in one of the rooms. By that time, it was about dark.

Well, the fellow had just got out of sight, and they had just got their stuff in the house when people began praying and crying in the house and going up and downstairs dragging chains. People would come and draw water, but you'd go out to find them, and they wasn't there. Grandpa cut him a big old stick, and he went all over the house, a-cussin' and a-huntin' them people—jus' a-huntin' and a-cussin,' while Grandma lay there scared nearly to death. But he never found them

They never was there. Every night, Grandpa'd take his stick, and when those people started their moaning and their drawing up water and they're going up the stairs, he'd walk all over the house huntin' and cussin,' but they never was there.

Grandma wanted to leave, and every day she'd beg him to go, but Grandpa wasn't scared of nothin', even haints, and he said, "I told that feller we'd stay a year and make a crop, and we will."

So they stayed there and made their crop, and they left. Grandma never was so glad to get away from a place in all her life.

8. THE VANDERGRATH HOUSE

The old mansion is out there by the Nissan dealership on Greensboro Avenue. I don't know the family's name in the Civil War days when [the Vandergrath House] was built. By 1900, it was the Vandergrath House because Robert Vandergrath grew up there and invented the Vandergrath generators in the 1930s when he was an adult and a well-known physicist. Given that, he would have been a child there around 1900 or so.

Did you ever meet my first wife, Jeannie? When I was in graduate school, she worked for a publishing firm that published *Antique Monthly* magazine and one of the arts magazines, and it [the Vandergrath House] was their corporate headquarters. And a lot of them had stories about hearing things in the house. There was a secret tunnel that nobody ever found that supposedly ran to the river where they hauled the bales of hay in the riverboats. And a lot of the workers talked about working there late at night and hearing things. My wife—the one story she told [was that] she was in the hall on the second floor. And the only thing that was in the hall on this side of the hall were the bathrooms. And two of these bathrooms were right near her desk. She was up there typesetting late one night and all of a sudden heard the water start running in the bathrooms. Nobody had walked by her desk. She got up, and when she opened the bathroom door, the water quit running. Just as she started turning the doorknob, she heard the water go off. She looked up, and there was nobody in there.

A lot of other people there had stories that were just about as unexplainable. But for about six months, the last person out would turn off the lights and lock up the door and leave, and the cops would see lights on and call the owner of the magazine and say, "There are lights on in the mansion." The man in the office would go in, and nobody would be there. He'd turn off the lights and leave, and a few hours later, he'd see the light on again. And this went on for about two or three weeks, and the cops would say, "What's goin' on here?" Then they finally caught some of the homeless people in town who had figured out how to get in through the basement window. But there was certainly no homeless person in [there] when [Jeannie] heard the water runnin'. There were several other stories like the water story when it could not have been a bum off the street.

9. GINSENG ANGEL

Uncle John Holland sold ginseng and other roots for part of his livelihood. Ginseng was worth quite a sum of money in those days. Well, Uncle John went up to Island Creek Cove to camp and dig ginseng. He had been there for several days and had planned on staying a couple more. One night, he woke up and felt that somebody was watchin' him. He sat up, and there on the other side of his campfire was a woman dressed in white. She jest walked back and forth, back and forth.

Well, Uncle John got up and built up his fire and sat the rest of the night. As soon as the day broke through, he got his self on out of that cove.

He says that he is convinced that somebody of ill intent was a-watchin' him. The lady was an angel sent to protect him. He says he was spared a robbery and even death. Uncle John always used his story to warn us if we ever seen an angel to act quickly in what we felt we should do, lest the harm come to us.

10. The Ghostly Noise

My daddy wouldn't like it that I'm tellin' ghost stories about his house. My brother will verify it [this story] though. It was built in 1950 in Wilcox County. We were in another room. Jimmy [my brother] was, like, in the third grade, maybe. He played with little soldiers, the kind you line up. He had a little Alamo fort and had another tin fort with plastic soldiers. It was back in his room. He'd line 'em up and have battles, but he never left 'em standin'. You know, he was never goin' to walk out of the room [and leave the soldiers standing]—he'd kick 'em, if anything. He was not into neat things, you know.

Anyway, my parents were entertainin' that night, and they were out by the swimmin' pool. We were in my room lookin' out the window at them, you know, instead of bein' where we were supposed to be, which was, like, two bedrooms over. It was one of those houses where you have to go through one bedroom to get to another. So all of a sudden, we heard this big noise. We were all three of us in the house—my sister and brother and I—and everybody else was outside. So nobody else was in the house. We could see 'em out at the pool. And it was this gigantic [makes noise with her tongue]—a noise. But, of course, we didn't go back there. We ran straight out of the house to the pool. Daddy made us go back in, and we told him what happened, and he didn't know what the noise was, but he went there and checked out the room, and there wasn't any—person— back there. So he made my brother, crying, go back to his room. My sister snuck back there later in the night because she felt sorry for him. I didn't. I didn't want to go back there. But all the little men were lined up in rows just as neat as you'd want them set up for a battle. And they definitely were not left back there like that.

It was the second time that some kind of noise like that came. The first time was in my room. We were all in the kitchen playin' dominoes, and we went back there when we finally got up enough nerve. My parents went out that night, and we were with a baby-sitter. I mean, there was nobody back there, and there was no way to get back there. I mean, you would have had to come through us to get back there or back out. There was a table that we used—you know, it was a child's table, but not like one of those child's tables today. It was one of those heavy tables made out of mica and steel. It was turned upside down with all of my dishes just everywhere. It wasn't a gust of wind that turned the table over.

11. THE GHOSTLY VOICE

Well, my mother tells me this story. This story was told to her by her mother. And I guess she got it from her mother. But the time in which this happened was soon after the end of the Civil War. My grandmother who had told this story initially—her family, or her mother's family, was named Ramsey. They had a large plantation in a community called Giles, a small area between Giger and Scooba. The homeplace is still standing there, as a matter of fact.

This happened to—I guess he would be my great-great uncle. His name was Thomas Ramsey. He fought in the Civil War. All male children of age went to the Civil War along with him. So the story goes that he returned from the war. He had met a young lady named Mary. My mother did not remember the girl's last name, but Mary was engaged to marry my great-great uncle, Thomas Ramsey. Mary lived in Scooba with some close friends of the family, because her father had died in the Civil War, and her mother had died shortly before. So she was staying with some friends of the family. Anyway, she and Thomas were engaged, and her next of kin lived in Pensacola, Florida. So about two months prior to the wedding, she traveled down there to prepare for the wedding. I think the plan was that she and her closest friends would come back up for the wedding.

Well, one night, Thomas Ramsey at one o'clock in the morning heard tapping on the window in his bedroom. And it woke him up. He sat up in bed, and he heard a voice was just as clear as day that said, "Mary has just died," and nothing else beyond that. It upset him so that he couldn't go back to sleep. He got up and paced the floor and walked up and down the hallway. It really bothered him, obviously, because he was completely sure that it wasn't a dream, and he was pretty sure he was awake when he heard the voice.

So after breakfast, he was so alarmed and so concerned and so bothered by it that he asked one of the workers to saddle his horse as soon as he finished breakfast because he was going to ride into Scooba and send a telegram to Pensacola, just to ease his mind. Well, as soon as his horse was saddled, he mounted up and was ready to leave the place, and another rider met him coming in with a telegram himself. And the telegram read that Mary had died the night before at one o'clock of typhoid fever.

My family—we're not a very superstitious bunch. My grandmother, my grandparents, you know, these were well-educated [people]. I've got some kinfolks who were kind of loony, but these folks weren't. I believe this to be a true story.

He heard the tapping on the window. And it sounded to him like the voice came from outside, but the window was closed. He told that story to my grandmother, and she believed it. If she didn't believe there was some validity to it, she would never have told my mother.

12. Miss Farris's Ghost

Miss Farris was the first lady that owned this house many years ago. My great-grandfather—this is his home that we live in—Rudolf Leland Hilton. His father was a drummer boy at Shiloh. And, uh, also that part of the family came over after Napoleon fell at Waterloo. They're a very colorful crowd. Very unusual. Very aristocratic. Anyway, they bought this house in 1927. He moved here from Farnsdale. The plantation was over in Farnsdale. He was an agent for the railroad, and they were supposed to move up North somewhere, but his wife backed out at the last minute, and they ended up buying this house.

Miss ——— died a year or two ago at the age of ninety-eight, and she saw Miss Farris's ghost, who owned this house at one time. She was with a young man, and they were both in their teens. It was about 1900—somewhere around there. And they were walking up the hill going to a dance or something late one afternoon. (My father told this story too. He would be about ninety if he were still alive). But anyway, she walked out the front door, and they [Miss Farris's ghost and the boy] walked around the corner of the house and up toward the garage. My great-grandfather built the garage, but there used to be an old kitchen behind the garage. She hasn't been seen in recent years.

The young man who was with her was, I think, the son of the last overseer on one of our plantations. And he was with her, and they were both reputable people. She [the woman who saw the ghost] went on to become the postmistress here and a pillar of the community. And she continued to tell this story all her life—that she saw Miss Farris. I think the young man who was with her went on to become a constable. And she had on a long, flowing, white gown, and she walked out the front of the house. [The woman who saw the ghost] was a registered nurse and a postmistress, so she was not a wild-eyed person at all. Up until I saw Papa, I thought that stories like this one was just folklore.

I believe this story because of the person who told it to me.

13. The Ghost in the Library

I believe the date was April 11, 1995. And I had just returned to Livingston. I had been gone about six quarters, I guess. And I used to know Becky that closes up the library. She works in data processing, and she closes up the library every night. And I hadn't seen Becky since I left, so I came back, and I was going to surprise her that night, and I thought the library closed at 12:00, but actually, it's 11:00, so the lights started goin' off, and I started getting my books and my backpack. And I stood up. I was in the back corner of the library downstairs, and I stood up, and Becky was just walkin' out the door, and I said, "Becky!" And she turned, and she looked at me, and she couldn't see me, and she walked right out the door. I finished putting everything in my backpack, and I ran to the door, and she was driving off, so I thought, "Okay, I can go out one of these exits," but I didn't want to set off any alarms or anything, so I thought, "Well, I can call campus police." I was studying for a sociology test the next morning, so I though, "Well, heck, I'll just stay here another thirty minutes and finish this up, and then I'll call campus police."

So I sat down by the circulation desk, and I was tryin' to study, and I kept hearing little sounds. And at first, it wasn't something out of the ordinary. It got so loud that I finally—it was pretty unbelievable—it got so loud, and the sounds were no longer just building sounds, but they were sounds of pages being flipped, books being slammed shut, bookshelves being bumped. Those kinds of sounds. I knew I had to go, because I knew I was the only person in that library so anyhow, it was a real scary thing, because I knew I was the only person in there. So I started putting everything together, and at that point, I felt something, and I realized I wasn't in the library alone. It wasn't just fear, because I was pretty fearful, but it was also something else. And it—I could just feel it. I was really scared at that point. I wanted to run right out the door, but I couldn't because it was locked. And having been in the Marine Corps, I thought to myself, "I can't be worried about this. I just can't be afraid of this."

So I could feel this whatever it was and kind of sense it in a way. I knew where it was without seeing it, and I could feel it without touching it. And so I went into the office, the rear office of the library where I could kind of feel it, and when I walked in there, I think I was just about ready to faint, because I was fearful. I could feel this presence or whatever it was.

Anyhow, so as I'm standing there, I could feel this. Where it was going, I could just sense it. It was then that I just really realized that there was something here. I mean, this is something. There is something else right here. And as I realized that, something just walked right on by me. It felt like something was right by me, and that was when my hair almost fell out. I realized that there was something there, and when I realized it, something walked right on by me. And there was a really cold breeze that went by with it, and then it went by again, and then it just kind of settled in a bookshelf there in the office, and I just was in tears. It was scary. I couldn't assimilate it in any way. What was really weird was that I was not so much in awe of this thing as I was trying to understand it. When I reached that point, for about five seconds, I felt that all my dead ancestors and relatives were there in that room. And I could feel all of them and within five seconds, they were gone. I was there, the realization was there, I could feel it, and it was gone. And I was back to one-on-one with whatever this was.

And so my fear kind of subsided, and I was able to walk out of the office and leave that "whatever-it-was" and make the phone call to campus police. And every time now when I go back in the library, I cannot help but to—I'm always looking. I'm always trying to explain what happened.

A few weeks later, I went back in the library. I sat down in the same place I was when I got locked in. And I'm sitting down there during the day, and I don't know what happened, but a book fell off one of the bookshelves there, and I remember thinking, "How in the world did a book fall off the bookshelf like that?" And while I was putting it back up, I looked at a picture of a woman, and I immediately went, "If that thing had a face on it, that's it right there." Anyhow, I asked the librarian whose picture this was, and she said that it was Hazel Stickney's picture and that Hazel had died of cancer, I think it was, when she was thirty-nine. From the very beginning when I felt it, I knew it was a female. And when it walked by me twice, it was like somebody wearing a dress. Whenever a woman walks by in a dress, you feel a little breeze down here, and that's exactly what it felt like.

14. The Haunted Shack

The legend of the Indian girl near our camp house on the Warrior River [which] we moved into about twenty-five years ago is really real to me.

The site is located near Old Lock 5 on the old Judge Green property. This location is between Demopolis and Greensboro. Very soon after we set up our vacation home, our two young daughters—Betsy and Sally—and their little friends—Robin and Tracey—came trompin' across the field behind the camp house luggin' a too-heavy stone that accidentally had been used by Indians to pound corn into meal or somethin' like that. It's still at Sally's house now. We also began findin' arrowheads.

It came as no surprise that we started hearin' the legend of the Indian girl. The beautiful young Indian maiden who lived on the bank of the river. As the story goes, the Indian girl had a baby which she loved dearly. The baby was taken away from her, and until this very day, you can hear her soft, sad wail, sayin', "I want my baby! I want my baby!"

There was once a shack or outhouse buildin' on the edge of a field. The children loved walkin' the dirt road after dark, and there was a large group of children belonging to the nine families who had several places on that dirt road. And when they would get to that spot, they would run and scream. I had an eerie feelin' when I went past it too. But the shack is long rotted away. The feelin' is still there when you pass the spot where it used to stand. It seems like the cry [of the Indian maiden] comes from that spot. I believe that the spot where the old lean-to once stood is the very spot where the Indian girl sat and cried for her dying baby.

15. THE BEAVERS' HOUSE

The Beavers' House is in a little town called Cuba next to the Alabama-Mississippi state line, and the road that it's on is a dirt road still. And at the time Ms. Beavers lived there, it was called "Cotton Patch Road." I don't know why, but the name has changed throughout the years. But she, as I remember, was part of a family of children that grew up in the house, and the siblings married, and the maiden sister, Ms. Beavers, stayed there in the house that she had grown up in. And she never was afraid, was my understanding, and it being a small town, even though now it's located fairly close to the interstate, which has brought some interesting crimes in throughout the years, nobody worried a great deal about crime touching them in a small town.

But there had been some prisoners escape from Leavenworth Penitentiary in Kansas, and they were military prisoners and had been trained in the Vietnam era—or were veterans of the Vietnam war—I don't know. They had Green Beret training, and one of them had connections in Sumter County. After they escaped, they began to make their way back South, although authorities apparently weren't sure where they were going. They were described as sociopathic. They killed for pleasure as they made their way South. They didn't get anything from some of the killings; it was like a sport. So when it was recognized that they were in Sumter County, people got extremely—and I think, justifiably—paranoid. They [the townspeople] carried weapons openly in vehicles. People would walk dogs with shotguns cradled in their arms. And Ms. Beavers played the organ at the York Presbyterian Church—a little town near Cuba. And on Sunday night, with knowledge that these men were in the woods somewhere in Sumter County, all the little old ladies in the church said, "Oh, Miss Stacey, don't go home. Come in with us." And she said, "Oh, they're not going to bother me. Nobody's going to bother me. I'm way out there. They won't find me!"

Well, unfortunately, the next morning when they couldn't get Ms. Beavers to answer the telephone, somebody went to check, and she had been left dead in the foyer of the old house with her throat cut. They had not hurt the dog, but they killed her and stole her car. And the criminals went back into the woods, lived off the land. They [the police] had expert tracking teams that were called. And they said, "We know these men. We're not going to sacrifice our dogs." And they [the prisoners] stayed in the county for a while longer and began to make their way back where they came from or another location, and they were all killed at a roadblock.

Ms. Beavers died intestate, so there was disagreement as to who should get what and how the estate should be settled. So there was an auction of the house and its contents. And the Munozes—he [the husband] was adopted by his stepfather; he's not Hispanic—they now live in the town of Cuba. It gets very confusing when you start talking about the Munozes. They had not been married too terribly long and did not have any children at the time, and they thought that this was the ideal house. The Munozes fell in love with the house and bought a few pieces of the furniture but left the integrity of the house just as it is.

The first thing that happened was they had been living there for some time, and it's like a lot of the old houses around here. You heat the part that you live in, and you don't heat the part that you don't. So they didn't have the bedroom heated and had a lot of quilts. Linda Munoz remembered waking up and feeling snugly down inside the covers on a cold winter's night. And she realized that she smelled honeysuckles—they have a distinctive smell, especially in the spring. And she thought that she was dreaming. She woke up, and she smelled the honeysuckles very distinctly. She thought that was extremely strange.

She mentioned it to Charley the next morning and also told Mrs. Brock, who was Ms. Beavers' sister. She mentioned to Mrs. Brock the smell of the honeysuckle, and she said, "Oh honey, that was Stacey's favorite fragrance." And it spooked Linda because traditionally, we love our ghost stories, but we don't believe in them. Linda said she thought about it, and she hadn't imagined it. [She was convinced] that she very clearly smelled the honeysuckle.

Well, some time after that—we have a traditional party at the house singing "Waltzing Matilda"—there's a scroll on the piano bench with all the words on it so that newcomers cannot feel left out. So we had done a rousing rendition of "Waltzing Matilda" on the grand piano. And it was one of those clear, beautiful nights. We'd go up on the planter's walk and look at the stars. They also have telescopes for stargazers. But we had—at that time, our children were small—our son was getting tired, so we said, "We'll just go on home."

The next morning, I called Linda to see how long the party lasted, and she said, "You're not going to believe this." I said, "Did Stacey put in an appearance?" And she said, "I don't know." They had an antique sewing cabinet—it was a little, horizontal cabinet. It was an upright cabinet close to the piano. And she said they had all started up the stairs to the attic, and they had gotten about halfway up the first flight of stairs when there was a "Kaboom!" like something had fallen. And she said it was so loud. The children were downstairs in a room but not in a hall, and she said it scared her so badly. She said, "Something's fallen on the children!" So they went right on down the stairs, and this antique sewing cabinet that had belonged to Ms. Beavers—all four legs at one time had just come out from under it, and it had sat down flat on the floor and not disturbed anything—didn't break the glass on the front. The children were nowhere around when it happened. And it wasn't that a leg collapsed—it wasn't that it [a leg] fell out. It [the cabinet] just fell flat. And we don't make as lightly as we did about the incident as we might have if we didn't know about Ms. Beavers.

16. BILL SKETOE

Bill Sketoe was in the Confederate Army, and his wife was pregnant, and she lived in Newton, Alabama. And he wanted to come home to see if she had had the baby, and if the baby was doing okay. So he went AWOL, and when the Confederate Army caught up with him, they hung him under the bridge in Newton. And he was kinda tall, so his feet still drug the ground, and it made a hole. You can still go there today and see the hole. And if you try to cover it up with sand or whatever, you come back the next day, and the hole's still there. And you can go and put trash in it, and somehow, it gets cleaned out by the next day.

I've seen the hole, but I've never put trash in it the next day. They named the bridge after some judge. There used to be an old bridge where the new bridge is now. We always heard this story when I was in elementary school, and I've lived there [in Newton] all my life. All my family knows the story.

CHAPTER TWO

ARKANSAS

✝

17. YELLOW EYES

[These stories] probably [occurred] from around 1910 up to around the mid-forties. I think the ones that come from the two sides of the family differ a little. The ones from my mom's side of the family, the Tolberts, the favorite one of her stories, I like because it happened twice—the story about the eyes. I guess they would have been yellow or something. This would have been probably the early to mid-forties. This was in White County, Arkansas, probably southern White County. Some cousins of hers were walking home from church one night, and they were a very excitable family anyway—that might have something to do with it. But anyway, they saw the eyes following them. They must have been traveling low because the girls were afraid they were going to get up their skirt-tails. So they started running down the road and went back to Aunt May's house, my Great-Aunt May, and said that they had seen the eyes.

The other incident—these always seemed to happen in groups with these girls; these were the Ray girls—they lived in a big farm house, and the group that Mom was in [was] in another room, a bedroom, I guess. They were talking, and the Ray girls were in another room, playing the piano and dancing. And Mom said that she was afraid that they were going to knock the door off the wall [because] they came through the wall; [they had seen] the eyes again looking through the window outside with them. So they ran into the other room. I always liked that one [story]. It was very funny, the way Mom told it. These girls were very excitable and were always into something.

18. DEATH OMENS

Grandmother Bradley tells the story about [how] her mother died when she was very young. And she [Grandmother Bradley] was a very little girl, and they didn't think she knew what was going on. But she said that she heard the clock stop in the living room, and about that time a lady came out of the bedroom and took her out of the house. Because her mother—she didn't really know that [that she had died]—but she knew that the clock had stopped, and when they came back to get her again, they said, "Your mother has died." And she asked what time it was, and they told her, and she said that that was the time that the clock had stopped. And that would have been—I think that they might have been living in Upper Wyatt County at that time in the hills. She was born in 1907—that probably would have been the early teens perhaps. She was a very little girl. It was probably before the war anyway.

And there was another when her daddy died or her mother died that they heard the rushing of wings. They heard something come out from under the house and take off in flight. They couldn't see it. She never said it was like a big bird. And Grandmother Bradley never interpreted any of her stories. She just told them. That was the way it happened.

19. GHOST LIGHTS

This is in the general area of Prossit, Arkansas. It's right above the line where Arkansas and Louisiana join. It's maybe forty miles above the line. It's a little small town. Kind of one of your backwoods southern towns. The story behind the light is that back when they were puttin' the railroad that went in part of Louisiana, one of the workers got killed. His head got chopped off by—I'm not exactly sure what happened. But he carried a lantern. He was carryin' a lantern. And the story goes that he's lookin' for someone's head to replace [his own head]. And that's the basic story behind that.

I've had a personal experience with this one. One night, it was me, the boy I was seein' at the time, his little sister, and two other males crammed into a Ford F-150 pickup. We thought we were goin' to find the light. So we drive out there, and we drive and we drive and we're thinkin,' "Are we ever goin' to get there?" We get lost twice tryin' to get to the railroad tracks where it's [the light] said to be.

Well, we finally get there, and we've all scared ourselves half-dead, you know, talkin' about it. And we get out and we say, "Let's get out and walk around." So we get out on the tracks. And me and his little sister—she's twelve and her name is Sissy; her nickname is Sissy—we start walkin' down the tracks. The boys are in the opposite direction from us on the tracks. They're on the other side. And I looked up. Somethin' caught my eye. I looked up again, and I didn't see anything. I thought, "Well, it's just my imagination playin' tricks on me!" All at once, Sissy said, "What's that?' She said, "Look!" I looked down the tracks, probably—Oh! I have no idea how far—it was probably a very good distance. Then we could see a small light. Sissy said to me, "It's just your imagination."

Well, we can't watch it, so we call the boys on over there. Then we were all in a tight group watchin' it, and we watched it til it seemed like it was down. I thought, "No, Michelle, you're imaginin' things." I looked at my boyfriend, and I said, "What did you see?" "I see a movin' light. That's what I see!" We all ran back and got in the truck. It was an older model, and the emergency brake never worked. Never. And that night, that emergency brake held. And we—it was muddy out there, and we almost got stuck tryin' to get out, 'cause the tires were spinnin' 'cause the brake was on. And he popped the brake, and we skidded out of the area. It was very, very scary!

20. THE NEGRO SOLDIER (WPA)

It was about midnight that I heard a sound as someone walking on the back porch. I got up thinking some neighbor was at the door. In the bright moonlight I saw a tall Negro soldier in uniform standing on the steps. As I stepped to the edge of the porch, the soldier turned his back on me and started walking towards the north fence. A very few feet from the fence, he stopped and turned around facing me and pointed to the ground and made a mark with his foot. He then turned facing the north and walked directly through the fence. This frightened me so badly that I ran into the house.

The next morning, I went out into the yard where I saw him standing and where the mark should have been. After digging in the ground, I found a small, round plate, about the size of a fifty cent piece which must have belonged to this soldier at some time. Since then, I have never been bothered.

(I will give you the metal as proof of my statement).

21. Night Visitor (WPA)

When we moved into this house, my husband was working at nights, and I was alone. Night after night, I could hear noises as though something or somebody was coming through the front door. I laid in bed and trembled with fear. The third night, the house would shake and tremble, and I felt as though someone was in the house. I laid with one foot on the bed and one foot on the floor when I felt something press on me, nearly smothering me. I screamed and jumped up and ran to the front door, which was locked. I was so frightened I could not get out for some time. I sat on the front porch the rest of the night.

The next day, I got a mule-shoe and nailed [it] over the front door points down. Again that night, I had the same trouble. My neighbors said I should have a horse-shoe. The next day, I got one and nailed it up instead of the mule shoe, and since then, I have never been troubled.

22. Ghostly Playmate (WPA)

When I was about five years old, I saw a ghost. During the following three years, this ghost was a regular visitor to our house, which was located, at that time, eight miles southwest of Pine Bluff. I can remember that after we had eaten supper, my sister and I and other children from the surrounding farms would play "I Spy," and this ghost would come out and play with us. We could see her peeking around the corners when we started to play.

She was a Negro woman, about forty-five years old. She had lived in the neighborhood and had died about a year previously. Depending upon the size of the children playing, she would appear as a young girl, a middle-age woman, or an old woman. We all ran usually when she came too close to us.

Now, in those days, country niggers always took in people passing by and sometimes kept them for days. Following this custom, we took in an old Negro woman. She stayed for several days, and during that time, the ghost was always hanging around. One afternoon when the folks were going to the fields, the old woman asked my mother to let me stay with her as she was not feeling good. My mother agreed to this. As soon as the folks left, however, the old lady found a long stick and asked me to go down in the swamps with her. We spent the long afternoon in the swamp, poking holes in the ground every so often. Finally, she took me back home and went off by herself. We never saw her afterwards.

I am sure that the ghost had been trying to tell my mother or father where money was buried, and when they could not, or would not, understand her, she told the old Negro woman where it was and how to find it. I think the old woman found it and went on to where she was going.

23. ZEB'S GHOST (WPA)

Years ago when I was a young man, there was an old building on the corner of Fifth and Ringo Streets known as the Zeb Ward home. For years after the death of Zeb Ward, no one would live in the house, which was furnished throughout. I was working with some white boys when a wager was made that I was to sleep one night in the old house alone. Should I do this, the following morn the white boys would meet me at the front door at 6 o'clock with the money.

I went to the house after getting permission and went to bed. Sometime after midnight, Zeb Ward walked through the room and out the front door. Later, he returned and stood in front of the fireplace and looked towards me as though to say something. I waited for what seemed like an hour, then [I] raised up and started over to him as I did not believe that it was a ghost I saw, but when I hit the floor, he just faded away. I had very little fear, for the vision was so natural that I could not believe that I had seen a ghost. The building later burned and was rebuilt and is now an apartment house.

24. THE ANGRY SPIRIT (WPA)

My wife had spirits come to her for three months for money. The spirits had told her that money was buried on the place and wanted to tell her how to find it. So she and me took a rod and pushed it into the ground. We then got back from the rod. It quivered and come up out of the ground. We never did find any money.

Then the spirit set de house afire. Spirit his name was Brown. Every time my wife come home, the house was all tore up. She told de spirit to go back whar he come from. She was tired of him messing up her house.

So de spirit broke all her windows about twelve o'clock that night. He threw a file through the window and almost hit a woman visitor. It broke the molasses jar. When we had stood that for awhile, we moved off to Altheimer, later to Tucker.

After that, I never had any more window glass in de house, just nailed boards or tin over the windows. Spirits did not come any more after that. Before he left, he shook the bed springs every night for a while and gave the old lady a ride.

25. Spectral Escort (WPA)

While we were living in Conway, Arkansas, my brother came home from work one night very much excited and told us that he had seen a ghost. He said that a ghost in the form of a woman joined him at Cannon Church and walked to the railroad tunnel. He tried to touch her, and she would move just out of his reach. He talked to her, but she would not answer him. When they reached the tunnel, she disappeared. Everyone in the family told him that he just imagined it, but he swore that it was real.

The next night he came home and told the same thing, and the next and the next. At last my sister and I and our friends said we were going to meet him and come home with him and see if we could see what he had been seeing. This we did, and sure enough, when we passed the church, the shadowy form of a woman joined us. We would talk to it, but it would not answer. If we reached out to touch it, it moved over just out of reach. If we ran, it ran; if we walked, it walked, and it always stayed near us. When we reached the tunnel, it disappeared. As long as we lived in Conway, this ghost continued to escort us from the church to the railroad tunnel if we were passing that way at night. And so far as I know, it is there until this day.

26. The Cattle Rustlers and the Lady (WPA)

Several years ago, Charlie Kilgore and his gang of cattle rustlers made it pretty miserable for the cattle owners in Bradley and Drew Counties. They were very bold and had the reputation of not being afraid of anybody or anything. One night while in Drew County, they camped in a two-story vacant house that was said to be haunted. They had heard many weird tales about the place but thought that there was nothing to them. They added that they were going to sleep in the old house.

After eating the evening meal, they sat around and talked until very late, teasing each other about "haints." At exactly midnight, there was a terrible noise upstairs. It sounded like a lot of chains rattling. Everyone was awakened by the noise, and all eyes turned to the stairs. Just as the clanking of the chains stopped, a beautiful woman appeared at the head of the stairway and walked slowly down the steps to the foot of the stairs, turned and looked at the rustlers long and hard, as if to say, "Why are you trespassing in my house?" Then she turned and disappeared up the stairway. Not one word was said until the ghost had disappeared. Then the rustlers lost no time getting out of that place.

Mrs. J.R. Wilson told this story as it was told her by Alfred Garrison, who was being held by the rustlers and was present during these events.

27. GHOSTLY CHURCH SERVICE

Down in Boggy Bay, there was an old house. It stood there for many years. Many people had died there. Both old and young, good and bad. It was said that no one could ever stay there because of so many ghosts.

One dark, rainy night, a colored preacher and a deacon was traveling through this old open field and spied this old house. They thought they'd stop and spend the night, so they went in. After a while, the preacher started preaching. [Then] the ghosts started marching all in white robes; lights began to shine, big fires rose in the fireplaces. Still the preacher kept preaching: "God gonna set this world on fire." The deacon started to run, but the preacher said, "Hold on, Brother." The preacher stopped preaching. The deacon got his hat to take up collection. When he started the collection, every ghost in the house was gone.

28. HUNGRY GHOSTS (WPA)

While living in Poplar Bluff about fifteen years ago, I lived at Dr. Crow's home with his widow. There was another set of people living in the house—three families were living there at the time. One lady bought several gallons of blackberries and made jelly and jam of them. Later, she went away to visit her sister. When she returned, she found the lids off the jelly and jam jars and some jam used out of the jars. She could not account for this and was very much surprised and alarmed about how it could have happened as the doors to the cupboard and to the rooms were locked.

The following day, the wash woman came to the house, and Mrs. Eakin before giving her the washing told her what had happened. The Negro woman said, "It was these white folks dead come back because they were hungry and done come and took dat jelly and jam like they pay visits to a house where they want something." Mrs. Eakin gave the jelly to the Negro wash woman and moved from the house.

29. THE DANCING SPIRITS (WPA)

Yes ma'm, there sure is such a thing as spirits being restless and coming back here! Not long ago, about two years ago, one of my girls went to see her sister over at Forrest City. She didn't stay but one night. She told me after she went to bed, she went to sleep for awhile. Then she thought she could hear dancing and a little low humming like music away off, and it seemed to be right over her room upstairs. She couldn't go back to sleep for hearing those feet dancing, some heavy like men and some light and easy like women's slippers.

She got up early and went into her sister's room to ask what in the world that racket was. Her sister said, "I forgot to tell you that you'd hear that. It's hants, spirits of people what died dancing up there. Two men was killed, and a woman died out dancing, just fainted away, and was dead before the man she was dancing with lay her down." This was a big old two-story house, and when the town was pretty rough a long time ago, it was a dance hall and whiskey house upstairs. My daughter left that day and went over to her brother's to stay her visit out. She said her sister might get used to hants and not mind them dancing, but she couldn't stay in dat bed another night, and she didn't.

30. THE NEWTON PLACE (WPA)

The spring of 1908, we lived at Hillsboro. The Newton Place there was said to be haunted. Mr. and Mrs. Newton were very wealthy and died, leaving their son Louie and their daughters to live in the house alone. Louie and several of the daughters were grown. One evening just about dark, they came down to the evening meal and found a note supposed to have been written by a spirit under one of the plates. No one besides the family ever knew what was in that note, but they left the house that night and would not live in it again.

They had a number of Negro servants, and one of the men who helped to catch the chickens told that while he was up in the tree catching chickens—it was the custom in those days for chickens to roost in trees instead of having houses for them as we do today—that he heard someone walking and talking in the attic and that someone upstairs pushed open a blind and looked out at him. When that happened, he came down out of the tree and didn't catch any more chickens.

Everyone was afraid to live in the house because of tales circulated about it, but at last, the Newtons found an old German couple who were not afraid, so they hired them to live in the house and take care of it. This old couple allowed my father to keep his stock in the pasture.

One evening after a rain, brother Albert was taking the mules to pasture. It was dusk and a cool evening, so there was a fire burning in the fireplace in one of the downstairs rooms. The firelight was dancing on the wall, and brother saw what he believed to be real live children standing on the walls. He turned the mules in the pasture and just flew home to tell the family about it. He truly believed he was seeing ghosts that he had heard so much about.

The next afternoon, my sister and I went to call on the old German lady. While there, we told her what brother Albert had seen, and she laughed and invited us in to see the life-size portraits of the Newton children.

31. Buck's Visitation (wpa)

Away back in war days, I knew a man who talked to a spirit, and it talked to him. When we lived in Alabama, there was a haunted house on a white man's place. For a long time, nobody couldn't live in that house 'cause of the spirits walking around in it.

One day, the white man it belonged to told one of his slaves, Buck Jones, he'd give him that house for his own if he could live in it. Buck said, "I shore will try, Marse Jason, and I thank you, too." The white man laughed and said, "Buck, I think you better save your thanks 'cause I don't think you'll stay there more than one night." Buck said he was going to live in dat house, but he went by hisself first to see if he could stay and find out something about the haunt that wouldn't let people sleep there. He said he remembered his mammy told him if he ever saw a spirit to ask it what it wanted, and that's what he was going to do.

So that night pretty soon after he lay down, one of the double doors opened right easy. When he got up to shut it, she couldn't see anything nor couldn't feel any wind what might have blowed it open. He shut it and locked it and just as soon as he got back on his pallet—he just took him two quilts and a pillow from his home to sleep on that night—the same door come open again. That time, he could hear somebody walking in stocking feet. He remembered what his mama told him, so he said, "What in the name of the Lord do you want here?" Then he could see as plain as my hand before my face a big tall man standing there right in the door with his right-hand stretched out to him. He said again, "What do you want?" In a whisper clear and plain, the ghost said, "When I died here ten years ago, I left my money buried here, and I want my children to have it. Will you get it and divide it amongst them?" Buck said, "Yes, sir! I sho' will." Then the spirit told him right 'zactly where to dig by a big cottonwood tree in de horse lot, and there he found a wash-pot of gold and silver.

Buck sent for the chillun of this white man who used to live there. They all come to see what the man could be wanting them for. He told them about seeing their papa and about the money. All of them took a part of the money and give Buck some too and went back to their homes. Buck went that very day and brought Mendy and the chillun to the house and said, "Dis is goin' to be our home, 'cause dat spirit is satisfied now and won't come roaming around here any more." He never did see it again. Yes, sir! Him and his folks lived in that house till he died, an' he lived till he was 'most a hundred.

He told me, "If you'll just ask a spirit what it wants, it will tell you every time."

32. THE HAUNTED BED (WPA)

When my grandmother died, she told me not to let anybody sleep on her bed. It was a high fine feather bed. For ten years, I didn't. Then I let my wife sleep on it. Then we got a bed of our own. When we got a bed of our own, we decided to use grandma's bed and room for guests.

One day, a friend of ours came to see us and planned to stay over night. We said we would sleep on Grandma's bed and let her sleep in our bed.

She said, "No, I can sleep on your grandma's bed just as good as you can. I don't believe in no ghosts."

She gone in it but it worked out from under her. Finally, we heard her walking about in the room and went to see what the matter was. She said she was convinced. We changed beds with her and everything went off all right. That bed never would do anything to us, but it worked out from most everybody else we put in it.

33. Skeleton Hollow (WPA)

In the hills of the Ozark National Forest, there is a long hollow which leads towards the Buffalo River. It has the name of Skeleton Hollow and is said to be haunted, so few people take the lonely trail through it, especially at night. The skeletons of two men were discovered in this trail almost fifty years ago, and since that time, the spirits of these two unidentified men are supposed to hang about the spot where they were murdered by an unknown enemy.

However, settlers in the county at the time think they know who the murderer was, but as he was never apprehended and punished, and the murdered men were never identified, it's popularly believed that the ghosts must remain in the Hollow, where the tall trees add to the ghostly appearance of the long ravine.

In the early 90's, a peddler came to the Big Flat community. He was considered pretty queer from the first—he refused to share a room with anyone, he went armed all the time, refused to tell anything of his past life except that he had always been a peddler and a wanderer and had no home. People in the area doubted this; they believed that he was hiding from something. After a while, he started living in a cave; he quartered his donkey close to the opening of the cave, and he slept back in the darkness. He didn't welcome strangers who stopped at the cave, but when it was necessary to give them shelter, he took their guns from them and kept them close to himself during their stay. His own gun was double-barreled—one barrel a shotgun, the other a rifle.

One day, some travelers down the hollow trail came onto two skeletons—one skull showed that it had been shot with a shotgun, the other had a rifle ball hole in it. When there began to be some talk of the skeletons and suspicion pointed to the peddler, he disappeared from the cave and wandered on to some unknown location. The skeletons were unidentified.

Some believed they were officers in search of the peddler, but this theory seemed doubtful. They were strangers in the community, and no one ever asked any questions there about them. Many of the old-timers believe they were cronies of the peddler who knew about his money and that they had come to ask for their share of the booty.

CHAPTER THREE

FLORIDA

✝

34. THE FISHERMAN'S GHOST

I'm pretty sure that this happened at the end of his [my father's] senior year of high school or afterwards. He and one of his friends were out on a double-date. They had two girls with 'em. They [his friend and his date] were in the back seat of his car, and he was in the front seat with his girlfriend sittin' beside him. They was drivin' down a coastal road, right along the coast. There was marsh grass on both sides of the road. Marsh grass gets a foot-and-a-half or two feet tall. And since then, they've put houses in over there. It was fairly foggy—I don't think it was too dark. Anyway, they were drivin' at a pretty good speed, and, uh, there was a guy dressed in yellow, like the old yellow slicker suits that you think of fishermen being in. Didn't have a hat or anything, but he was headless. And as soon as they passed him, they turned around as fast as they could and got back there, and he was gone. And there was nowhere for him to go. There was just marsh grass on both sides of the road.

At the end of the road, there's, like, a little Junior Food Store or somethin'. It's a Junior Food Store now, but it used to be, like, a corner food market or somethin'. They told the attendant about it [the ghost], and he said it happened all the time. This happened in Ochlachee Bay. Right on the end of the Ochlachee River. It's a good-sized river. It runs all the way from Georgia down to Florida, and this is the Bay area. All four of 'em in the car saw it. He [my dad] said that as soon as he saw it, he looked at his friend, and his friend was lookin' at him. It was just a man in slickers. It's a fishing community. I don't know if there's a story behind it or not.

35. THE GLOWING EYES

It's [this story's] something that happened on the Sewanee River in the early 1900s soon after my grandparents got married. This was around 1906 or 1916. Anyway, my grandparents used to live on the Sewanee River. In fact, they owned a store up there. They used to like to sit out on the front porch at night and watch the sun go down. One night, they were sitting on the porch, and two glowing eyes appeared over the fence post. My grandmother said, "What the hell is that?" And my grandfather sat out on the porch again, and sure enough, the two glowing eyes reappeared over the fence post, and this time there was a little noise with it. My grandmother said, "I wonder if it's the ghost of one of the old Spaniards looking for his gold." There are a lot of old Spanish and French cemeteries around there.

Well, the third night, they sat on the porch again, and this time, when the glowing eyes appeared, my grandmother ran inside and got my grandfather's shotgun. He said that he shot the blasted thing right between the eyes. He was sure he'd killed it. Now my grandfather was a crack shot, and if he said he hit the thing between the eyes, he probably did. They ran over to the post to see what he had killed, but there was nothing there. My grandparents were so excited that they went into town and told all their friends and neighbors about shooting the glowing eyes. And everyone was sure that something bad was going to happen on account of it.

Well, they were right, because the next morning, my grandparents looked out their bedroom window, and the whole fence had been torn up. Even the fenceposts were removed. My grandfather ran out to inspect the damage, and he saw where somebody had dug a hole where one of the fence posts was. The hole was empty, but you could tell where a cooking kettle or a wash tub had been. It's a good thing that my grandfather didn't see whoever did this, because there sure would have been some shootin' goin' on around there.

On the same day that this happened, one of the town boys disappeared. He came back ten years later with a brand new car and a new wife. My grandfather accused him of digging up the gold, but he [the boy] claimed that he had left the day before the fence was tore up.

This happened not far from Branford. Branford is as far as the [Spanish] vessels could navigate. It [Branford] was an in-land seaport. There are still a lot of Spanish around there. There is even an old mission. This is one of those missions where the monks don't talk to each other.

There is a lot of that sort of [supernatural] thing around here. My dad's side of the family is a bunch of seers. One day, my dad told my mom, "Don't go to work today. Someone's coming, and you don't want to meet them." Well, later on, they found out that my mom's aunt had died, and her uncle had gone to her job looking for her.

36. OLD JOE

This story takes place in Wakulla Springs. It's sort of a tourist area now. They've got glass-bottom boats. They've got the area as pristine as possible. They've got wildlife and all this kind of stuff. They have a restaurant. And in this restaurant they have this gigantic stuffed alligator named Old Joe. And the story about Old Joe is he was supposedly gunned down in the swamp by Ma Barker's gang. And I don't know if Wakulla Springs was a tourist attraction at that time or not. But the story goes that they got in the boat and were drunk and had those old tommy guns and went out there and saw this thing. I mean it was just a monster; I forgot how long it was, but it was twelve or fourteen feet. Something like that. And he really had a personality—you know, Old Joe.

So they went out there that night. And they were drunk and everything. And saw this alligator and just tommy-gunned it to death. And the next day, of course, it was found. And it was just such a character around there, such a legend, almost, that it was taken and stuffed and set up as a showpiece in the restaurant. And of course the story is that Old Joe—the spirit of Old Joe—is still out there in that swamp area at Wakulla Springs at night. He has been seen because no other alligator around there has reached those proportions. And supposedly, he still haunts that area out there. Whether or not there's any truth to that, I don't know, but it is a good story. I don't know if the restaurant had a name or not. It was just part of Wakulla Springs. I've seen the alligator. He's just a monster. You can't really see the bullet holes because of the way the alligator's skin is.

You really need to talk to Raymond Rushing. He was born and raised here [in Sumter County]. So if anybody would know anything like that [ghost stories], it's him. He lives in town on Highway 28 going toward Demopolis.

37. THE HAUNTED CONDO

Maria de Gutsens is probably our most famous ghost. There was a hospital here called the Mercedes House. It was a house, a very large house, that had belonged to a cigar manufacturer named Gotto. And his wife was named Mercedes. And anyway he donated the house when he moved back to Cuba. [It was] a hospital for the Cuban poor. And she [Maria] was the matron that ran it for many years in the '20s and '30s primarily. And the house is a large house—two story. It has a porch around it. And the story is that she walks there at night. People wake up in the room, and she's taking their pulse. The building is a condominium now in Key West. That [the haunting] seems to be a selling point now.

There's a whole bunch of ghost stories that have happened here in the past few years. There's a guy who runs a ghost walking tour in town. Some of his ghosts are more figment of imagination than anything though. But she [Maria] is long-term. She's been around for years.

38. THE HAUNTED DORM

This story takes place at the University of Florida in Gainesville. I heard this from people. My brother goes there. It occurred in one of the dorms. Their story was that there was a girl who was sleeping in her room. And her roommate had went out for the night. She [her roommate] came in about 4:00 or 5:00 in the morning. And she didn't turn on the light or anything. She just walked in and went to take a shower. When she went back in the room, she flipped on the light, and her roommate was dead. And on the window was written in blood, "Aren't you glad you didn't turn the light on?"

It's supposed to be that before that, somebody had committed suicide in that room during exam week. So it's supposed to be that girl's ghost who killed the girl and wrote on the window.

39. GHOST STORY

In May of 1969, I went to Daytona Beach, Florida, with eleven other girls who are very good friends of mine. One night, another girl and I and two guys from Daytona went out to a real swampy place to find the light. The story was well-known by everyone we asked about it. The place is real spooky with trees covered with moss completely covering the overhead of the narrow road. There is a casket factory out there, but no other buildings or people except the light. And no one knows what it is. It is always off in the distance. Our friends told us that everyone who had tried to chase it had been killed in accidents. So we didn't try to chase it, but we certainly did see it—with our headlights and without them.

40. The House on Otter Creek

One of the spookiest places in my hometown [of Lynnhaven, Florida] was an old abandoned house near Otter Creek. Otter Creek is in Bay County that runs into Washington County. My grandmother and grandfather lived right around the block from the old abandoned house. When we drove by or walked by, we would see a light on or even someone looking through the window on the second floor. We walked around, you know, like in the afternoon or late afternoon or whatever, and we'd hear footsteps or something and people talking inside the house. It sounded like two ladies talking, but we didn't stick around long enough to find out. And then one day during the daytime, me and my uncle and my brother went up there—we had a little metal detector or whatever—and we looked inside the house, and we saw half glasses of water. The place was clean. It didn't look like it had been abandoned for that long. We would find little baby strollers around the house with the metal detector. An old tractor was sitting outside the house and a bunch of old tools. We would never really mess with anything.

My grandmother used to tell us stories about noises she had heard and about the people who once owned the old house, which frightened me and my brother. My grandmother didn't really talk to my brother and me about the house until our teenage years. One day, I started asking her about the old house. I also told her about what we had seen up until that point. She began to tell us about the noises she used to hear, noises like screams that didn't sound like any male scream she had heard before. It was like a woman in excruciating pain. When walking by the house, she said she heard footsteps and two women talking. When these events occurred, no one lived in the house and hadn't for at least five years.

When my grandmother began telling us about the past owners, me and my brother were already quite frightened. She told us a couple lived there, and they really didn't get out of their home very much. They were like hermits and very strange-acting people. Once when the creek flooded, my grandmother stayed the night with them until my grandfather returned from out of town. That night in the house, she said she could hear things moving around the room. When she opened her eyes to see what it was, a human figure ran out the door. My grandmother vowed she would never stay there again.

41. GRANDMA'S HOUSE

This story took place around the Bay County area near the coast. I used to live with my grandmother on my father's side, and the house is supposedly haunted, and I really believe it, you know? My uncle would tell me stories about how he would come in and set his guitar on the coffee table, and it would start playing. And we thought it was just him, you know, really tired and stuff. But he tried it again the next night, and it started doing it again.

And some of my aunts had said that they would be in their room and, like, somethin' would grab their leg or somethin'. And they would see figures all over the house. My brother once said that he was sleepin' in the room, and he looked up, and he saw some figure that looked like my father. The figure had a beard. He didn't think much of it until the next day. The house is supposedly—my great-grandfather died there, on my father's side.

Like I said, we didn't really believe it, [but] we started playin' with the Ouija Board one night. And we were asking the basic questions—"How'd you die?" And it said, "From cancer" or something. And we asked him what his name was, and he said his name was Hutch, which was my grandfather's name. We were asking questions, and we asked if there were any other spirits in the house. And he said, "Yes. Sure." And he told us the names. And we were askin' it just little questions, and then my grandmother came in, and she told us to get the thing out of the house because she didn't like it. And we were, like, "Well, since he knew you, why don't you ask him something that me and my brother wouldn't know?" So she asked him the name of somebody's wife, and it told her. I didn't know, and I know my brother didn't know. And then she started asking it all kinds of questions because she finally got interested in it. She'd go, "Who did this?" And it'd give her the name of people in the family, you know.

And this was all stuff we had never heard about. So finally, it spooked me, so we quit doing it. This is my grandmother's house in Lynnhaven.

There was one time that my grandmother said she woke up, and she looked beside her bed, and there was, like, a figure squatting down. And then she didn't think much of it. She kind of denied it and wouldn't say she saw it. And then she said that she thought it was a sign that something was going to happen to somebody. Two weeks later, my grandfather died. That was her father-in-law. He lived there for a couple of years. He was in a walker. And everyone that's ever stayed there has said that they've seen something. I can get you a picture of the house.

42. THE ROCKING CHAIR

[This house] was down Blue Springs Road in Youngstown. It's like an old wooden house in the middle of a field. It didn't look like anybody'd lived there for a long time. The windows were all boarded up. The door was boarded up. It looks like, not a plantation house, but more of what you'd call an A-frame. And there's a rocking chair on [the porch]. And the rocking chair would always just rock, and we thought it was the wind or something. My brother and a bunch of his friends went to see what it was, so they went up to the porch, and the rocking chair was still rocking. And they stopped it. And I thought it was a hoax, you know, just the wind [rocking it]. But there really wasn't that much wind that day, so they didn't think that much about it, though, and when they turned to go, the rocking chair started rocking again. They got out of there fast!

43. LADY IN THE RECLINER

I was coming home one night. I had stayed out till maybe 11:00 or so. I was coming home, and my grandmother comes to the door. She is kind of in a walker now. She walked to the door, and she let me in, and she started walking around her house. This bothered me, you know? I said, "What are you looking for?" She said there was a lady sitting in the recliner, like, watching T.V. I thought, "You're crazy!" You know? And she goes, "You see her there? You don't hear her movin' around?" She said it was like someone watching over her.

She used to say that she could hear music coming from the back hall. I said, "What kind of music was it?" She said it was church music, like

"Amazing Grace." Something like that. She'd ask me some days, "Do you hear the music?" I'd say, "I don't hear the music, Grandma."

44. The Will-o'-the-wisp

(WPA)

Them will-o'-the-wisps is somethin' to see! Or that's what we calls them. I've 'eerd me aunt speak of them many times, but I haint never seen none. She claim they'd come rollin' outten the 'ills at the height of them turrible hurricanes, and they'd come down the hillsides in the form of great fire-balls. She useter say that they'd come so closet to the 'ouse that she was shore they was gonna hit. Then they'd burst and disappear. I ask 'er what caused them, and she claimed it was the foul air from the graves of our people up in the 'ills, and I reckon it was.

Mr. Harding, 'e's claimed 'e's seed them too. 'E seen them at sea one time when 'e got caught out with a sponge boat. The boat was in a turrible fix; the decks was awash and loaded with sea weed what had been flung up. The mast was gone, and the boat was listin' turrible, but it was then when 'e seed them balls of fire. 'E claim they come outten the sky from nowhere and soared right toward the boat. Then they burst and disappeared just before strikin'. We don't know what caused it out there at sea, but I reckons it was jest the storm.

45. Kunjured Nigger (WPA)

Yes, I knowed that niggers 'ere in the United States practice kunjure. They shore can do it, too!

You know I got a nigger woman friend down 'ere who told me somethin' like that about what 'append to a nigger man that she knowed in West Palm Beach.

You know, niggers is nice, especially this one what I'm tellin' you about right now. They can be the best friends anybodys got, and people 'ere treats them terrible, it's pitiful. They cheats them so 'ere. They gets treated much better over to the Bahaymees. But to get back to this 'ere feller what this nigger friend of mine told me about.

'E was sick all the time and couldn't get well. 'E kept goin' to doctors and takin' medicine, but it didn't 'elp none. After it 'ad gone on for a long time, 'e decided 'e was sick from somethin' beside ordinary things, and although 'e claimed 'e 'hadn't no enemies, 'e figured 'e'd been kunjured. So goin' to a soothsayer among 'is own people 'e soon found out what was wrong, and it was this. The feller 'e told 'im to go 'home and shake the sheets o 'is bed, and when 'e did, 'e would find a snake, 'e told 'im to take the snake out and 'e would get well. Well, accordin' to what I was told, 'e done that very thing, and shore enough, there was the snake. So he took the snake out, and then 'e got well.

46. Bottled Magic (WPA)

Well, oncet in a while them obeah tricks follows us 'ere to Riveriera. I mean folks 'ere in Riveriera practice them tricks on folks around 'ere.

You know, there's one magic what will make you blow up and bust. It's funny and of course it don't work at all, but niggers and children's is shore afraid of it. What 'appened not long ago was jest this, and it was done by a woman 'ere; a neighbor of mine, who come from Bahaymees too. She's a-little-by-the-head, so it hain't no wonder she done what she did. We was embarrassed to death, but it didn't make much difference 'cause she went right on doin' it.

You see, we went to a funeral of another of our neighbor's, and just as the last dust was bein' put to the grave, this 'ere neighbor of mine reached down and cotched up a pinch of the dust and put it in a kerchief. Like I mentioned before, we was shore embarrassed, but there warn't nothin' nobody could do about it.

You see, this 'ere trick of takin' grave dust is a real old one, 'cause when they gets the dust, they put an English sixpence down in the little hole from which they took the dust. This is to pay the grave fer what they tooken. They then put the dust in a bottle, take the bottle to the sea and catch water from the ebb tide. When this is did, they cork the bottle tight and hang it in a tree or place it neck down in a field from which somebody 'as been stealin'. If anybody goes into the field to steal where one of these bottles is or swipes from a tree where one is 'angin', they'll blow up and bust shore as life. Or that's what niggers and children's thinks. But believe you me, they shore do leave them alone. Sometimes they put those 'ere little blue lizards in the bottle too to make it seem more real, cause 'e stretches and swells up so nice after 'e's been soakin' in thet salt water fer awhile.

CHAPTER FOUR

GEORGIA

✝

47. THE HAUNTED FRATERNITY HOUSE

The fraternity Kappa Alpha at Mercer University in Macon, Georgia, was the old frat house—the old president's house, a historical landmark. And they say—not just them, a lot of different people—say that the daughter of the president (I believe it's a fact) that she hung herself in the bedroom, which is the left-hand window facing the street. And it's—I'm almost positive it's a fact. All kinds of people come runnin' out of there. They don't even like to have their pledges stay there overnight or anything just because it's so spooky. They hear things—footsteps, visions in the windows. Not visions, but the upper torso. I think there are some accounts of doors closing. But [it's] really, really interesting. And some very good friends of mine are in that fraternity, and they don't make up things like that.

48. GHOST HORSE (WPA)

Once when my daughter dat's teaching at Paine College now was a baby, I was goin' 'long de road to my sister's house. Us was livin' in de country at dat time, down in Elbert County, and us had to go thoo' a long road dat had a lot of trees on both sides. Dese trees made de road real cool, and most folks laked to travel it in de summertime. I had two of my chillun wid me—one was 'bout 5 years old, and de other 'bout 7. Dey was walkin' 'long 'side me playin'.

When us got pretty close to my sister's house, I heared a hoss comin' 'hind us gallopin,' and I stepped out of de road to let him pass. A few minutes later, I heared de hoss pass me wid de saddle cryin' and ev'ything, but I ain't seen nothin' 'til yet. I could even feel de wind from him when he passed jus' lak you would any other hoss, and I heared him goin' on up de road in front of me, but I still didn't see nothin'.

Atter he had done gone on up de road, I axed my oldest chile why did he git out of de road. I wanted to see if anybody had heared de hoss 'sides me. He said he got out of de road to let de hoss pass, but he said it must have stopped 'cause he never did see it. I was satisfied den it was a ha'nt 'cause I knowed I warn't de only one who had heared it. I've had plenty of s'periences lak dat since. My chillun laughs at me when I tells 'em, but I knows dere is sich things as ha'nts.

49. Ghost Dog (WPA)

I was 'bout 10-years-old when I seed my fust ha'nt. Ma had sont me and my sister to de spring to git some water. Us was livin' in de country, and de spring was a good piece from de house.

Dis night, it was real dar, and on our way back from de spring, us heared a noise. It sounded lak something draggin' on de ground. Us heared dis noise jus' as us got to a tree standin' in de road. It sounded right 'side us. When us looked to see what it was, a dog was standin' by de tree wid no head. De dog was 'bout three feet high and jus' as white as snow.

When us seed him, he skeered us so bad us started runnin' and runned all de way home. When us got dar, us had wasted all of our water. Right atter us seed de dog, us looked back, but de dog had disappeared. It disappeared jus' lak you might turn a light out.

50. The Man in the Field

(WPA)

Some folks say dere ain't no sich things as ha'nts, but I know it is. I have seed 'em in more ways dan I have fingers and toes. The most 'citin' one of all was one I seed jus' 'fore I married.

Us was livin' 'bout a mile from any other fambly and right 'cross de road, in front of our house, was a real large field, and right in de middle of dis field was a bunch of woods. Dey would have cut dese woods down, but dere was a real good spring in 'em, and dey let de woods stay dar to help keep de water cool.

I never will forgit one mornin' in de spring I seed a man plowin' in dat field. Dis field hadn't been wukked for more dan 15 years, but dis mornin,' I seed a man plowin' out dar near de woods. You could even see de ground bein' plowed up jus' as plain as day.

When pa come home for dinner, he seed de man plowin' too, and he thought it was a cousin of ours. He told me to take a coat over dar to my Cousin Jack Knox. I took de coat and went on over in de field, but when I got dar, I found de field hadn't been plowed at all, and de man dat was plowin' had disappeared. I went back to de house and told pa dat Cousin Jack Knox warn't over dar and dat de field hadn't been plowed at all. He come to de door and looked over dar, and he seed dat de man had gone and sho' 'nough, de ground hadn't been plowed.

Dat got next to Pa 'cause he didn't even finish his dinner. He went in a room by hisself and sot down. 'Bout a half hour later, he come and told us he knowed who dat was plowin' dat field. He said his pa had been killed over dar 'round 15 years ago, and dat he was plowin' over dar in dat same field when he was killed. He said dat was his Pa us seed out dar plowin' dat day, and dat was de fust time anybody had ever bothered wid dat field since my grandpa was killed.

51. JULIANNA'S SPIRIT (WPA)

Me and a gal by de name of Julianna Crawford was playmates when us was chilluns. She died when she was 'bout 22 years old, and at dat time, I was 18. She lived 'bout a half mile from us, but us all got water to drink from de same spring. Us had a spring closer to us dan dat, but us didn't use it for nothin' but washin' and feedin' de cattle. Dis spring us drunk from was on de other side of Julianna's house, so us had to pass dar to git to it.

'Fore she died, us used to go to the spring together. Whenever any of my family had to go, us allus stopped by her house for her to go 'long wid us. me and her allus enjoyed goin' to de spring together 'cause us got a good chance to talk widout bein' 'sturbed, and 'sides, us had to pass by de farm dat de boy lived on dat she was 'gaged to git married to.

When Julianna died, nobody couldn't believe it. She tuk sick one week and died de next, and ev'ybody thought it was a shame 'cause she was so sweet to ev'ybody. But dis evenin'—it was 'bout 4 o'clock in de day—when us was comin' back from de spring, I seed Julianna goin' up de road in front of me wid a bucket of water on her head. I knowed she was dead, but she could be seen so plain 'til anybody would have thought she was still livin'.

I walked real fast to try to catch up wid her, but de faster I walked, de faster she walked. When she got to her house, she turned in de yard and went into de house jus' lak she allus done. She was so real 'til ju's had to stop in her house when I got dar and axe if she had really come in. 'Course nobody dar hadn't seed her, but her Ma said she had seed de same thing I had seed a heap of times. She said Julianna could be seed 'round de house real often.

One reason I knowed it was a ha'nt I seed was 'cause as soon as I seed it, every bit of my hair stood up on my head, Dat's one thing dat allus happens when a ha'nt comes 'round you. You have cold chills dat run all over you, and your hair stands up straight on top of your head. I have seed 'em all kinds of ways wid and widout heads. I have seed 'em real small when you first seed 'em and later dey git so big you can't even go 'round 'em. But you see a lot more of 'em in de country dan you do in town. I don't know why dat is—you sho' can't say it's on account of de lights in town, 'cause you kin see ha'nts in de broad open daylight.

52. The Good-Time Gal (WPA)

A gal was goin' out on a party wid some fellows who peoples thought warn't quite de kind of mens she should go wid. 'Course, she had done dis so much 'til folks had started callin' her "Good-Time Gal." She had several fellows, but one of de boys was in love wid her and told her dat she would have to let all de other mens alone if she was goin' wid him. But she didn't stop runnin' wid de other fellows.

So one night, he axed her to go out for a ride wid him and said dey would go to a dance later dat night. He had planned to kill her, so he carried her way out in de country by a cemetery and parked de car. De gal was dressed in a pretty evenin' dress. She thought dey was really goin' to a dance dat night, but dis fellow tuk her in de cemetery and kilt her.

When dis happened, it was 'bout one o'clock on a dark night. 'Fore he kilt her, she got 'way from him and runned out in de road, which was de public highway. He ketched her and carried her back in the cemetery. Atter dis gal was kilt, de boy went on back to his house, just lak nothin' had happened. And if it had not been dat dis gal come back as a ghost nobody would have knowed dat dis boy had kilt her.

But ev'y night atter dis gal was kilt' round dis same time, she could be seed dressed in a evenin' dress. She would run out and stop ev'y car dat she seed passin' and beg 'em to take her back to town. One night, a man picked her up and 'fore he could git in town, she had disappeared. Several more folks passin' seed de same gal and picked her up, but evvy time she disappeared 'fore dey got to town.

Peoples began to wonder at dis new 'sperience, and two mens 'cided dey would go out and see what was all de 'citment and trouble dat de people began to talk 'bout. Dey got some folks to show 'em de spot whar de gal appeared, but when dey got dar, dey never seed nothin'.

One rainy night 'bout a week later, dey went back, and just as dey reached dis spot, a gal runned out in front of deir car and begged 'em for a ride. Dey picked her up, and one of de mens axed her her name, and she told 'em. She told 'em dat a man was tryin' to kill her. Dey axed her whar was she goin,' and she said to a dance, but just as before, she had disappeared when dey reached town.

De next' mornin,' dey had mens to go out and search de cemetery and de woods close by. Dey found a funny lookin', newly-dug grave in de cemetery, and dis gal was buried in it wid de same evenin' clothes and ev'ything. She had been kilt and buried in dis cemetery. Ev'ybody was so s'prised to think of a dead pusson leadin' 'em to her own grave.

Later on when dey got back to town, dey found out dat dis was de same gal dat had been missin'. Den dey went and got de boy dat dey knowed was in love wid her and axed him 'bout de killin'. At fust, he said he didn't know nothin,' but when dey locked him up in de room wid her for a whole day, he was glad to tell de truth. He told ev'ything 'bout it and said dat when he was locked in de room wid her, she had 'most choked him to death. Ev'ybody b'lieves dat is de reason he told ev'ything 'cause 'til den he had denied ev'y question dey had axed him.

53. The Ghostly Banjo Player (WPA)

Once a long time ago, dere lived a man in Columbia County. Dis man used to play for dances, and evvyone knowed he was a good banjo player and would try to git him to play for 'em. One night when he was playin' for a party, some mens was dar drinkin'. It was a very dark night, and de moon was not shinin'. De house was very brightly lighted wid oil lamps.

Dese mens dat had been drinkin' started a argument, and from dat began to fight. De man dat was playin' for de party tried to stop 'em. He tried to part de mens dat was fightin,' but one of de mens fired a shot, an' though he didn't mean to, he kilt the banjo player. He fell daid right in de midst of de fight.

Atter dis, de folks dat was livin' dar moved 'bout a half mile down de road. Dis happened on a Sadday night, and evvy Sadday night 'fore dese people moved, dey could hear a banjo playin' jus' 'fore de time de man was shot, but he never played atter de time he was shot.

Atter dese peoples moved away from dis house, nobody else moved in. One night, a strange man who had jus' moved in de neighborhood was passin' de house. Jus' as he got close to de house, he seed a bright light in de house and heared a banjo playin'. So he and his friend 'cided dey would go in to de dance dat was bein' given. Jus' as dey stopped deir mules and got out of de wagon, de noise stopped, and de lights went out. De house got very dark, and not a soun' could be heared.

De mens looked at each other, knowin' somethin' was wrong, and one said, "Let's git away from 'round her." Dey went down de road further whar dey knowed somebody lived. Dey axed 'em 'bout de house and tol' 'em how de lights went out when dey got up to de steps.

Dese peoples tol' 'em dat ev'y Sadday night when de moon warn't shinin,' dis light could be seed and de banjo heared. And dat was de reason peoples wouldn't stay in de house.

54. The Ghost in the Well

(WPA)

When us lived in de country, people had parties 'mos' ev'y Sadday night. Dese parties was usually given in empty houses so dey would have room 'nough to dance. At dese parties, dey always had plenty to eat an' drink, an' folks would attend 'em from miles 'round. Mos' times, if dey was given at one place dis Sadday, de next dey would be given at another little town 'bout five or sometimes ten miles from dar.

One Sadday night at one of dese parties, while sittin' at de table eatin' and drinkin,' a man by de name of Jimmie and another man named Tom got in a big fuss, an' while dey was fussin', Tom's brother come in de room, listened at de fuss awhile, den he turned 'round an' went an' got a pistol from somewhar. Atter he got dis pistol, he slipped in and got under de table and shot Jimmie in de stummick, killin' him instantly.

Atter he was kilt, dey let him lay dar on de floor 'til de next' mornin'. Dey didn't 'low you to move folks 'til de sheriff got dar, dat is, if de person was kilt. You could move him if he warn't daid and you was takin' him to a doctor tryin' to save his life. Well, dis man lay dar all night, so you see, he had bled all over de floor 'fore he was moved.

Sometime atter dat, a fambly wanted to move in dis house, but dey didn't want to move in wid all dat blood on de floor. So de peoples who owned de house had dose boards took up wid de blood on 'em and put 'em in a old well in de back of de yard.

Dere was a road dat runned by de well, and 'fore de well went dry, peoples travelin' would stop dar and git water. It was on de right side of de road. But anyway, one night when us was passin' dis well, us would call Jimmie jus' to see if he would come. Us had heared so many peoples say dey had seed him when dey passed, and us wanted to see him too. So us called and called but didn't see nothin'

When us got 'bout a mile down de road and looked back, dere was a real little white kitten followin' us. My sister, who was younger dan I was, wanted to wait and git him to take home wid her. Us all stopped to wait for de kitten, and when us stopped, de kitten stopped too, and as far as we went, dat little kitten followed, but when us got to our gran'ma's house, he warn't nowhar.

On our way back, atter us had gotten 'bout a half mile down de road, us seed de little kitten followin' us back. Dis time, my brothers and all of us tried to ketch him, but when us got close up to him, he got bigger dan a dog. It scairt us so bad dat my little sister 'veloped heart troubles from it. Us had to carry her all de way home from dar and us lived more dan two good miles.

When us got home and tol' Ma an' Pa 'bout it, how us had seed him go back in de old well, dey tol' us dat if us hadn't tried to ketch him, he never would have scairt us lak dat. Dis Jimmie was a good man and was crazy 'bout chillun, but you jus' can't bother ha'nts.

It's a strange thing, but he never tried to scare de folks dat moved in de house. You could hear more peoples dan a little talkin' 'bout dey had seed Jimmie las' night, but he never tried to scare none of 'em. 'Course, atter dat, de peoples who was livin' in de house put kerosene in de well and tried to burn up dose boards.

55. THE SPECTRAL COW (WPA)

Late one afternoon, I was on my way home from town. Dis was 'fore dey put 'lectric lights on Pine Street, what is now Linden Street. It was very dark 'long de street, and I was 'most to a house whar a old 'oman had lived. Dis 'oman used to sit out on de sidewalk ev'yday and was always watchin' flowers dat she had planted 'long de walk in front of her house.

'Fore she died, she tol' her husban' to watch her flowers and not to let peoples walk over 'em. But her husban' was a kind ol man and never runned de chillun lak his wife had done. Dis old 'oman had been mean an' hateful. So atter her husban' didn't sit outside and watch de flowers like she did, people's began to tromp over 'em.

I was on my way home, and jus' as I reached dis spot, I seed a big cow layin' in de path. I had to walk out in de street to git 'round de cow. Jus' behin' was a man on a bicycle. He rode through de place I had gone 'round. I knowed de man, and I stopped him and axed him if he seed de cow. He said, "No," dat he didn't see no cow. He axed whar was de cow, and I pointed to de spot I seed de cow in. De man walked back to see whar de cow was and said he never seed it. Den he called me to show him whar I seed it. I walked to de spot I had gone 'round, and I didn't see de cow I had walked 'round. De man den axed me if I was 'fraid to go on home and went wid me.

When I got home, he said he wouldn't scare me for nothin,' but what I had seed was not a cow; it was a ha'nt of dat old 'oman who had died and was so crazy 'bout her flowers. I 'mos' fainted when he tol' me I had seed a ghost. An' from dat day to dis, I had never walked Linden Street by myself at night.

56. THE BECKONING SPIRIT

(WPA)

When my husban' died in 1908, it 'mos' worried me to death. I worried and worried 'til atter a while my son wanted me to go away. I went, but I never stayed. I wanted to be back as near my husban' as I could.

I was livin' on Watkins Street, right 'cross from de cemetery, when my husban' died. Ev'y night, I would go out on my porch and sit for two or three hours, watchin' over dar whar he was buried. An' ev'y night, he would stan' over his grave and wave a light dat looked lak a lantern to me. He always did dis as if he was tellin' me to come on over. I knowed it was him 'cause I could see him as plain as day.

He kep doin' dis 'til I showed him to my son. Den my son didn't want me to sit on de porch no more. He said, I was goin' out dar jus' to see him. I stayed off de porch for 'bout three weeks, and one night jus' as I was 'bout to go to bed, I heared him call me jus' as plain as if he had been livin'. He called me three times, "Alberta! Alberta! Alberta!" De fust time he called, I thought it was jus' my 'magination and I kep' on undressin,' and he called me two more times. I never answered him 'cause it's a bad sign to answer your spirit or de dead.

I didn't go out de fust night he called me, and he called me sev'ral nights atter dat. And den one night, I was feelin' a little bad and went to bed early. Jus' 'bout de time I was restin,' somebody knocked on de door hard. My son was takin' a bath, so I had to git up and go to de door. While I was puttin' on my shoes, de knock come again. I hurried to de door, but when I opened it, nobody was dar. I looked up and down de street, but I never seed nobody in sight. Den I happened to look over in de cemetery, and I seed my husban' wavin' dat light for me.

I went back in de house and shut de door and went over to de window to see if I could see him still or if he would stop atter I lef'.

Sho' 'nough when I got to de window, I didn't see nothin'. Den it come to my mind dat it was my husban' who had come an' knocked at my door. Atter dat, I didn't set on de porch no more; he come ev'y night and knocked at de door or at de window, and if he didn't do dat, he would call me. He started worryin' me so much 'til my son 'cided to move. Atter us moved 'way from down dar, he never worried me no more!

57. THE REJECTED LOVER (WPA)

Once dere was a man dat was in love wid my sister. My sister didn't want to go wid him. So she tol' him dat he needn't come to her house no more 'cause she was already keepin' company wid another young man. He was heart-broken over dis and went on dis way for three years, den he tuk down sick. He got lower and lower an' at las' he died.

'Bout two months atter his death, she passed 'long de road whar he used to live. It was fust dark and people was out ev'ywhars. Right in front of his house, she heared a growlin'. She thought it was a dog, but when she looked back, it was a cat. So she said to a man she was meetin,' and who had heared the growlin' too, "I thought dat was a dog tryin' to bit me." Atter she seed it was a cat, she warn't so worried, but when she turned and looked, it had sot down in de road.

So she started off walkin' again, and it began followin' her jus' a-growlin'. When she got to a store dat was 'bout six blocks from de place she seed de cat, she stopped dar to git somethin' for her dinner, and de cat stopped too. But it went under de store.

De cats dat b'longed to de peoples in de store began to run and climb up on de walls in de store, and de dogs dat b'longed dar started barkin' at him. So one of de dogs runned him from under de store and hemmed him up, and dis cat slapped him down. De dog runned out yelpin'. De cat walked away from de store and down de street de way it had come, and on back to de house whar it used to live, den walked on back in de yard and disappeared.

Two or three men who was in de store followed him all de way jus' to see what he would do and whar he was goin'. My sister was so scairt, she wouldn't even stay at her house dat night.

58. Let de Whiskey Alone

(WPA)

Way back in slavery time, dey would let de slaves go to town and buy deir own wood. So a man got up a load of wood and carried it to town and sold it for two dollars. Atter he sold his wood, he bought hisself some whiskey and him and his friends drunk some out of de jug, and den he tied it to the couplin' pole of his wagon.

Night ketched him in town, and on his way home, 'bout a mile from town, he heared a noise and looked back for his whiskey, and a man was sittin' on de wagon. He tuk his whip and popped it back at de man to make him let his whiskey 'lone. When he looked again, a big steer wid big eyes and large horns was a-sittin' back dar.

Atter he seed de man change to a steer, he got scairt and stopped his wagon. A cemetery was right up de road. When he got back to his wagon, he never seed nothin'. He was too scairt to pass the graveyard. So he poured de whiskey on de ground and jumped in de wagon to drive as fas' as he could. Den he looked back, and a big shaggy dog was lappin' up de whiskey, which was dryin' fas' in de sand.

His mules began to run 'way and acted as if dey was scairt too. Atter he got de mules settled, he went on and come to a creek. De mules began to pull back and wouldn't cross de bridge. So he got off de wagon to see what was wrong, and a mule was standin' in the middle of de bridge widout no head. He tuk de jug dat de whiskey was in, off de wagon and sot it down in de road and lef' his mules and runned all de way home, which was 'bout ten miles from dar. When he got dar, he was out of breath. He couldn't tell what was wrong wid him 'til de next day. He never did buy no more whiskey ater dat when he went to town.

Dis man had always been crazy 'bout whiskey, and ev'ybody said dat dere was a brother of his who had tried to stop him from drinkin' so much. He never drunk so much dat he would cut up in any way, but he would have so much in him that when he went to church, he would sit dar and go to sleep. He had a brother who had tried to stop him from dat, and he kep it up. Dis brother died, and ev'ybody said he come back and scared him to make him stop drinkin' so much whiskey.

59. HAUNTED ORPHANAGE (WPA)

About ten years ago, the matron over the boys at the Shiloh Orphanage died, and I became matron there. There was a woman who had two girls and three boys. She lived so bad until her husband quit her, and therefore, the children was put in the home. She came to see the children often. Finding them under good care, she began to visit me every time, talking about she needed work. Finally, she went to the head matron and asked her to give her some work. She had been trying to learn how to dress hair, so she asked the matron to let her dress the girls' hair, and she wouldn't charge anything because she wanted to have some heads to practice on.

The matron gave her the privilege of dressing the girls' hair. So the first day, she worked until late in the evening. I always served supper. After supper, I thought she was going home, so I told her good night and went on over to the boys' dormitory. About ten or fifteen minutes afterwards, she came knocking on the door, calling me. I went to see what she wanted, and to my surprise, she wanted to spend the night with me. I let her stay, but I felt like she should have stayed with the girls after working with them. I offered her the bed in the living room, but nothing would do her but to sleep with me. I didn't want her to sleep with me, especially after I found out that she was trying to undermine me out of my job.

Anyway, I let her sleep with me. I always slept in the room where the matrons was supposed to sleep, but the last matron that was there before

I went there, the one that died, her bed always sat in the same place where I had mine, but this woman didn't know it. I never shut my eyes the whole night. About twelve o'clock that night, the dead woman opened the window and came in. She slammed the window behind her and walked all around the room. I was wide awake, but I didn't hear nothing, neither did I see anything. She got the pitcher of water and began pouring it in a night pot I had in the room. After she had finished pouring the water, she came over to the bed and stood. Finally, she went under the bed, and that's when this woman, who was spending the night with me, began to holler and raise sand, just as if she was going into fits, telling me that someone was under the bed. I told her that no one was in the house, but she said, yes, there was, because she saw them when they went under the bed.

She kept up so much noise I got up to turn on the light, but she said, "Don't turn on the light because they will kill me." She begged and begged, but I wanted to see what was in the house. I looked under the bed, all in the hall and everywhere anything could hide, but I couldn't find a thing.

The woman was tremblin' like a leaf on a tree. After that night, she never did want to stay with me any more. I never did see anything, but I'm surely was glad it happened because it kept her from pestering me any more.

I knew the woman had been coming back and walking around there because the children had mentioned it several times, but I didn't want them to be scared, and that's why I never told them what it was. I never did see or hear nothing, but even the head matron had seen a woman dressed all in white going in the building late at night, and I knew it wasn't me, but the dead matron coming in and out.

60. The Weaver Woman's Return (WPA)

Durin' dis time, dere warn't many lights out dis side of town, and you could see hants real good. You could be walkin' 'long any time and see somebody walkin' in front of you, and when you'd git to 'em, dere wouldn't be nobody dar. I has seed pretty dogs and cats and tried to take 'em home wid me; den all of a sudden, dey would disappear, But I'se not 'fraid of 'em; I s'pose it is 'cause I was raised in de country whar you seed 'em mos' anytime. I knows if you points at 'em, dat will make 'em mad, and den dey will run you sho' 'nough, but other dan dat, dey will not bother you 'less it's a mean pusson lak de Weaver 'oman.

Pore ol' man Weaver dried up, and 'most los' his mind from dat 'oman worryin' him [after she died]. He finally had to sen' for his son and his wife to come and live wid him so he could have company all de time. He said when he was in dat house alone, she caused all kinds of trouble, but atter his son and his wife and chillun moved in wid him, he got a little bit peace. Atter de ol' man died, nobody had any more trouble wid her. Ev'ybody said dat was all she was atter, and as soon as he went to her, she was satisfied.

Ol' man Weaver's son and his wife said dey seed her and heared her moan the night 'fore de ol' man died, but dey wouldn't never tell him 'bout it. Dey tried to make him think it was his 'magination, but dey knowed it warn't. Dey thought at one time dey would have to move, but dey hasn't seed or heared her since de ol' man died. Dey is still livin' in de house now.

61. ROAD GHOSTS (WPA)

One night, years ago, I seed a man wid no head on him. I was comin' down Battle Row wid my little grandchile. But I warn't skeered of him at all. He didn't have no head on him or nothin'.

Den another night, I was on my way home from near Milledgeville Road. I was comin' out 15th Street, and I had a handbag in my hand, and jus' as I got near Sunset Avenue, I seed dis man. He was turnin' out from Sunset Avenue and come walkin' right behind me. I warn't 'fraid of him 'cause I'm not 'fraid of nothin' but bull frogs. I'd walk a mile to git 'round a bull frog.

But when I seed dis man, I thought he might grab my hand-bag, so I changed hands wid it 'cause he was walkin' on de right-hand side of me.

Dis man followed me all de way home to my gate. It was 'bout ten o'clock at night, and when I turned in de gate, I looked 'round to tell him good night, and I never seed one thing. I had thought he was a ha'nt 'fore I got home 'cause I had tried to talk to him. I axed him whar he lived and what his name was, but he never said a word. Den I axed him if he was deaf, and he still didn't say nothin'.

CHAPTER FIVE

KENTUCKY

✝

62. THE WITCH'S CURSE

One time way back in the colonial days in Kentucky, there was an old woman who lived way up on a hill all alone except for her little baby and two great big black dogs. Her husband had been killed in the war. The people in town had always been very suspicious of the old woman. She never spoke to anybody and would never have visited anybody. One time, a great epidemic came. I forget what kind, but anyway, it was really bad. The children were dyin' every day. Finally, one old woman (usually known as the village gossiper) told her best friend that the old woman on the hill had caused it. The tale spread everywhere. Everybody believed it—even the preacher, and he was always right. He suggested that they go up there and settle things. After all, their children were dying. So they did.

The woman was so scared when the townspeople started marching up the drive that she ran and hid in the smoke house, but she didn't have time to get the baby. The people were real upset because they couldn't find her, and they figured she was hid in the house someplace, so they just set it on fire. The old woman came running out of the smokehouse screaming that her baby was in there. She cursed them and told them their grandchildren and great-grandchildren would pay for their terrible crime. She ran in the house to get her baby, but it was too late, and they both died in the fire. When they died, the big dogs started barking so loud that the people slashed their throats.

But the story did not end until years later when the old lady's prophecy came true. One of the ladies of the same town and a grandchild of the preacher was out beside of the house making soap, and her baby was lying on a blanket in the sun back behind the house when the mother heard the baby scream a terrible scream. She ran behind the big house, and there were two great big black dogs eating her baby alive. Other incidents of the same kind were reported for some years afterward.

63. HEADLESS HUSBAND

One time, there was a man who had worked on a railroad crew for years and years. He kept growing harder and harder of hearing until finally, he was almost totally deaf, but he kept on working.

One time, he was working on a track when an unscheduled train flew up the tracks behind him. One of the old niggers hollered for him to get out of the way, but, of course, he couldn't hear him. The train hit him and completely cut off his head. It rolled down the bank into a big pond. There were twenty-five men tried to find his head in it, and even though at least ten men saw it roll in there, they couldn't find it. But they just buried him without a head.

Then on the night he died one year exactly later, his wife woke in the middle of the night, and there was a noise in the room. Then she saw it. Her husband's favorite rocking chair was rocking, and in the seat laid his head. But that's not all. It had great big golden ears.

64. THE GHOST OF VAN METER

I heard this story from some acquaintances of my parents one night. My father is an engineer, and they were talking about construction of some buildings, such as Van Meter Auditorium. Supposedly, the contractor who, the first contractor of Van Meter Auditorium had trouble laying the foundation. He would pour the foundation, and it would fall through into the caves; as you know, Western Kentucky is undermined by a series of caves. As his finances ran out, he bankrupt, and he had no place to turn; he committed suicide by throwing himself into the pit, foundation, whatever you want to call it, of Van Meter Auditorium. And he is supposedly the Ghost of Van Meter.

Now, another contractor took over the contract and successfully constructed Van Meter Auditorium. The administration of Western Kentucky

University moved into Van Meter Auditorium, and it was also used as a theater. And during this time is when the Ghost of Van Meter began to appear in the form of doors being locked and being found unlocked, rooms being in, ah, shambles, chairs being turned over, papers reshuffled, files missing, and one thing that stands out. Custodians would lock the front door of Van Meter, and they would come around to check again, say, at midnight, and they would be unlocked. There was no explanation for it. No one had a key but them. Who could unlock it? Why should they be unlocked? When they started to have play rehearsals in Van Meter, one night Dr. Woods seemed awfully upset because a blue light floated out from under the stage out of the vents under the stage. The chandeliers would shake, the chairs would rumble, the curtains one night fell down, and it got so bad no one would stay in Van Meter after the sun went down. They couldn't even have play practices. They had to practice in the afternoons. And one night, a young technician, light technician, was up in the scaffold up above the stage adjusting lights, and the blue light came out—the blue haze came out. Let's call it that. And he was so frightened he lost his footing and fell to his death to the stage. Well, naturally, his head and bones and everything was crushed. After that, blood, supposedly the stain, kept coming up through the floor, and they couldn't get rid of it. They tried everything. They sanded the floor. They used everything you could think of on it. As you know, recently Van Meter has been, ah, renovated—whole new floor and stage, everything—but the stain is still coming up through the floors. And that's the Ghost of Van Meter.

65. PARKED LOVERS' STORY

One time there was this guy and this girl, and they were really in love, and so one Saturday night when they were out together on their date, and they decided that they wanted to be alone out in the woods somewhere. So they went driving on this long country road way out in the woods. And it was really dark. There wasn't any stars in the sky that night. And so about the time the boy was getting ready to kiss the girl and really start loving her good, they all of a sudden heard sketch, sketch, sketch, this scratching on the car. And they both about jumped out of their seats, and so they kinda tried to ignore it because they didn't really want to find out what it was. And then all of a sudden, they heard this sketch, sketch, sketch on the car. So the guy decided that he better get out and check and see what it was. Make sure it wasn't anything that was going to bother them. So he told the girl, "Now look. When I get out of the car, you lock all the doors, and don't you open them for anybody and don't you get out for anything, because I don't want anything to happen to you, and I'll be back in a little while."

So he got out of the car, and she locked all the doors, and he was gone for a little while, and she kinda got worried, but she tried not to think about it. So she decided that she was going to just close her eyes and think about good things so she wouldn't get scared. And he was gone, and he was gone, and he was still gone. And she started hearing that sketch, sketch, sketch, sketch, sketch. She tried not to think about it. And he was gone, and he was gone, and finally about this time, she fell asleep, she was so worn out waiting for him. And the next thing she knew since she woke up and it was daylight, and so she got out of the car. She decided that it was okay then to unlock the door. So she got out of the car to look for her boyfriend or go get help or something because she was really worried about him. And she looked up over the car, and there was hanging her boyfriend from the tree branch over the car, and his feet was hitting the top of the roof going sketch, sketch, sketch.

66. LIVER FOR SUPPER

One day, there was this little boy, and his mother sent him to the store to get some liver for dinner. She gave him $5, and he went to the store, and instead of getting the liver, he saw a roll of penny candy that he wanted. So he spent the money on the candy. So he knew that he had to have some liver, so he went by the graveyard, and on the way back, and he dug up his aunt's liver. He took it home, and his mother cooked it for dinner, and she told the little boy, "My, this is very good liver. We'll have to send you to the store again some time."

So a couple of day's later, she sent him back, and he again wanted the candy, so he spent the $5 on the candy, and he went by the graveyard again and got his uncle's liver this time. So he took it home, and his mother said, "Mmm! This is absolutely delicious. I am really proud of you, son!"

So she sent him to the store a few days later again to get some more liver, and he again spent it on candy, and he went by the graveyard and got his grandfather's liver this time. A few day's later, it was about midnight, and he was up in bed asleep, and all of a sudden heard this voice: "Billy, I'm on the first step. I'm on the second step. I'm on the third step. I'm climbing up towards you. I'm on the sixth step. I'm on the seventh step. I'm coming to you, Billy. I'm on the ninth step. I'm on the top step. I'm on the top. I'm right outside your door. I'm right next to your bed, Billy. Gotcha!"

67. THE GHOST OF IROQUOIS PARK

Well, it all happened about a year ago. Now a few of you might not believe this, but it's true. One night about four, oh, about twelve or one o'clock in the morning, I was walking down this dark road up near Iroquois Park. Now I was in a cemetery, so this is what makes this kind of a scary story. As I was walking, I heard somebody else walking, or so I thought, in the leaves, and I knew I was on an asphalt road. And I kept looking down, and I kept hearing these footsteps, and I looked down once or twice more to check to see if it was just me and whatever it was, the footsteps in the leaves kept going faster and faster, keeping my pace. So then I started trotting, and it trotted. And I started to run a little bit hard, and it ran. And I ran harder, and it ran, and so I said, "I'm going to figure out one way or the other if it's just me or not." So I ran as fast as I could and came to a complete stop. And whatever it was didn't stop; it ran on a few feet.

And so there I was, in the middle of this dark road all alone with something over in the road, and I couldn't figure out what it was. So being kind of foolish, I went over to the woods to investigate. At first, I didn't hear nothing, and then I heard footsteps again coming out of a circle. And they came closer, and closer, and closer, and still I didn't see anything. And then I felt some cold chills going down my backbone, and I turned around, and I looked, and there she stood: the famous headless lady of Iroquois Park. And I didn't know what to do at first, because all I could see was a woman holding her head in her hand with blood dripping out. I guess I was terrified. I don't know, but I ran like a mad man until I finally got away from there. I think I ran for a long time.

68. THE GHOST OF POTTER HALL

A girl killed herself in Potter—I think it's about twelve years ago—in the basement. And everybody says that the basement's haunted. And you go down there, and you do hear noises, but it could be the building itself. There's this one room. It's just real eerie down there. Nobody's been down there, and it's just storage. I know that a friend of mine took some people downstairs to show them the room where Allison lived and killed herself. She hung herself from the pipes. This guy with her friend went to the door and shook it as a joke. He shook it real hard, and they all ran because they were scared. Her friend turned around when they got to the stairwell, and they looked back: the door was still shaking. It happened last spring.

My roommate and I would play with the Ouija board upstairs and stuff. Our room was directly above Allison's room. And he didn't know that had anything to do with anything. But like one month, he talked to this ghost, and he asked it to give us a sign at night. It said it would but not what it would do. But it said it would happen that night, and it would scare us. So we fell asleep finally, and in the middle of the night, we both wake up, and I heard it, and she [my roommate] felt it. Her desk—it just slid and hit the wall. I heard it hit, and she felt it hit because it moved her bed. The windows were shut, and the door was shut and locked. We were both asleep. I know I didn't do it, and she didn't do it. It happened about 3:00 A.M.

69. THE UNSEEN FEELING

During the time of the slaves, slaves were looked upon as being no more than a possession. And more often than not, the owners thought much more of other possessions such as horses and prize dogs than their Negro slaves. Many times, slaves would receive severe punishment, such as whippings, if one was caught "out of his place."

Although the slave owner was not such a unkind man on this particular property, the very nature of trading, buying, and selling slaves kept all slaves leery of their masters. The master's house sits on a high grade with the family graveyard being to the lower right of the house.

The slaves lived on the other side of the master's house about a quarter mile away. The slave family often was broken up at auction, but the master on this farm bought only families as he believed it wrong to split the families up.

Around 1830, the master bought a family of slaves who had two small boys. The boys were, as all boys are, curious and wanting to see everything. The father decided to keep the boys away from the master's house out of fear that the master would punish the boys. He decided the best way was to scare the boys with a tale about the graveyard. He told the boys that every night about dark, a strange noise was heard and figures were seen rushing across the cemetery.

The boys told their father they were sorry and that he was right. The father was surprised and a bit disturbed, so he decided to check out the situation. When he saw the graveyard, he heard the noise and saw the movement. From that moment on, the legend that the original settler had haunted his family grave was heard. Superstition was high, and the legend remained with no one disproving the story.

70. DOG GHOST

Ah, you take our old family doctor at home. Back in them days, they rode a horse all the time going to see his patients, and he passed a cemetery. We knew all about the cemetery, well, acquainted with it, and it, it was at Highpoint, Kentucky. And, ah, this doctor's name, Simmons, Doctor Simmons. And, ah, he said a little white dog would run out and follow him along the highway for a little ways, then just disappear. And said he didn't pay not much mind to it to start with but just kept on and kept on. He said it would come out and run along after his horse and just disappear in mid-air right in front of his eyes. That's the end of that one.

71. THE HAUNTED ROCK

There is a big rock around home where everyone says a ghost or some type of spirit lives. Before there were many cars in Leslie County, everybody rode mules and horses.

About ten miles above this rock, a young girl and her husband lived. The girl was pregnant, and in those days, there wasn't many doctors, and they usually were so busy they didn't have time to deliver babies, so there was an old woman who lived in Hyden who was a midwife, and she did most of the birthing around there. So when it came time for the young girl to have her baby, her husband was away from home and her neighbor had to ride her mule into town and bring back the midwife.

When the woman got to the rock, she felt something get on behind her, and when she turned around, she couldn't see a thing. The mule had slowed down, and it seemed whatever it was, was so heavy the mule could hardly carry it. The woman became terribly frightened, but there was nothing she could do. As she came into the town, she felt whatever it was get off, and the mule began to pick up speed. She went to the midwife's house, but she didn't tell her what had happened because she was afraid she wouldn't go back. They started on their way, and when the women passed the spot where the creature had gotten off, it got back on the mule with them again. The mule began to slow down again; it seemed to be so tired it couldn't make another step. The midwife asked the woman what was wrong with the mule, but the woman wouldn't answer her. When finally they got back to the rock, they felt the creature get down.

This same thing happened to many people in the community, but no one ever solved the mystery of the big rock.

72. The Face on the Window

One night several girls were at the home of [the victim] getting ready to go to a ball. It started thundering and lightning. She knew her parents wouldn't permit her to go to the ball in the storm. She was very angry. She went to an upstairs window and started cursing the Lord. While she was still standing there, the lightning struck her.

She said that her father told her that the image of a girl was left as a shadow on the window. She said that they had painted the window all different colors trying to cover the shadow up, but at times during thunderstorms, the image can still be seen.

73. Butcher-Knife Jane

Once there was a married couple named Jane an' Bill. They lived very happy, till one day Bill's mudder come to live with them. Now Bill's mudder was a persnikkety old woman that had to be toted [waited] on most of the time. Jane didn't like this a-tall.

One day, Bill had to go to the next village to buy somethin' an' would be gone for the day. While Bill was gone, Jane got to thinkin' about how she was goin' ter git rid of Bill's mother. Jes then, one of the hogs came snortin' through the cabbage patch, an' this gave Jane an idea. Jane first wen' to the kitchen an' got a butcher knife. She then killed Bill's mudder an' dragged her to a side shed where they did mos' of the slaughterin'. She cut the body up in little pieces an' fed most of the parts to the hogs. Some of it, though, she took back to the house with an' started it a'cookin'.

Later that night, Bill come home, an' he asked whar his mama was. Jane said they'd had a fight, an' his mama packed her grips an' gone to live with

Bill's brudder. Bill didn' like it, but he didn' say much. Jane then started to give Bill some of his cooked mudder. Bill ate some, but hit made him a little sick 'cause hit was so stringy. That night, Bill's mudder came back an' started hootin' in the hog pen. Bill got up an' heard the hootin'. Then Jane heard the hootin' an' got scared. Bill's mudder done come near the house now, an' she started callin' fer Bill. Bill was scared too, but he wen' out, an' his mudder tol' him what his wife had done. Then Bill wen' to the hog pen and foun' some of the bones. Jane was carted off by the sheriff the next day. But even now, Bill's mudder comes hootin' a roun' lookin' fer a bone that one of the hogs musta ate or rooted under the ground.

74. The Screaming Woman

During the Civil War, the daughter of a land owner who resided on the Levisa Fork of the Big Sandy River became pregnant. This was embarrassing enough for her, but to make the problem worse, all the respectable young men of the area were away. This left only the slaves as possible fathers, which one turned out to be. The girl, afraid of the shame for herself and her family, decided the only solution was to kill herself. She didn't know how to do it, but she had a little time to figure a way.

Because of the lack of men and the work that had to be done, she sometimes had to help the slaves do chores. One day, they were carrying water from a rock at the river, where the boats tied up to the steeple. She was said to have made a couple of trips for water and was the last one let on the rock filling up her bucket. After a time, she didn't come up from the river, so they decided she must have went swimming. However, after she didn't come back within a couple of hours, they went to check and couldn't find her. They even checked the bottom of the river to see if they could find her, but she wasn't there. Her body was never found, and she was never heard of again.

But it is said that every night at twelve o'clock, she can be seen climbing out of the river and onto the rock. She will then scream and jump back in the river.

75. The Legend of Doc Wright

There once was a man named Doc Wright who owned a very large farm. On this farm, Doc raised horses, but he would hardly ever sell a horse because he dearly loved them. Well, Doc being like he was got into some financial difficulty and went bankrupt.

One night, Doc said he wasn't feeling well and told his wife who was sitting in a chair reading a book that he was going to bed. About fifteen minutes later, she heard two shots, and she rushed into the bedroom and found Doc covered with blood. Well, the police said it was a case of suicide, and Doc was buried.

About three months later, a hired hand who had worked on the farm was walking through a field when he saw Doc or what looked like Doc riding his favorite mare. He shouted to Doc, and when Doc looked around and saw him, he kicked the horse and took off running. The hired hand caught up with the horse in the next field; he was just standing there grazing without a bridle or saddle.

About a year later, Doc's wife moved away to Lexington, but the hired hand remained in the county in which he lived. One night, the hired hand walked by the old house which was boarded up and unlived in. He heard a noise inside the house, took a board off of the door and walked in the house. He opened the bedroom door, and there in a chair sat Doc reading by an old lantern. When he saw the man come through the door, he ran out the back door. Since that time, the ghost of Doc Wright has not been heard of or seen again.

76. THE LIGHT ON THE ROAD

Walter Groce an,' uh, Homer Butler and Delmer an' all of 'em were down over here to Herschel Groce's over here playin Rook one night, an' they played till about midnight. Long about midnight, they had to go home. So they lived over yonder in the holler, way down below there. So they got out of the path an' started, why, there was a light just started follerin' 'em jist right off the ground 'bout two or three foot high. There's an old man that, uh, bootlegged all the time an' sold whiskey, an' so he'd been a-comin' through there with barrels of whiskey ever once in a while an' so along about where this light was, why, uh, he'd seen the light two or three times comin' along that road right behind his wagon. So these boys that night had been a-listenin' to haint tales an' stories, ya know, an' they got out there an' started down this same road that this here old man been seein' these lights. An' this light come right up behind 'em, ya know, an' started right on jist followin' 'em, an' when they'd stop, hit'd stop.

So they got on way on over the hill, an' one of 'em's small, an' the others run off and left him. An' hit, this light ud jist go right up to this little boy, an' then it'd stop. Well, he fell two or three times, and it'd stop, an' they couldn't git it away from him. So they run on to the house, an' when they went into the door, why hit followed 'em right in the porch. The light come right in on the porch. An one of 'em run in there, knocked the door down, jest run again the door an' knocked the door plum down an' fell in the floor, an' that light jist turned an' went right back up the hill after he got them run in the house, why it went back up the hill.

That's a true story. Walter Groce, he's one 'em that seen it.

77. THE PEDDLER'S GHOST

What it was—an old pack peddler came to the house, and this old farmer seen all his stuff in the pack—jewelry and everything. His wife seen it, and I guess they wanted it. They caught this old man asleep in that room, took a saw and cut his head off. They took his head and his horse and throwed [them] in the damn cistern, and they took his body without any head on it and put it out there in the road under a tree. Anybody that come along where it was at—sometimes it'd be a headless dog and sometime it'd be a headless man—it'd come up and try to hug you.

So, two old guys thought they'd play a joke on a preacher. They told this preacher about it and asked him if he'd be scared to go down there, and he said no. "I'll go down there and find out what it is." So this preacher's gone down right far, and this thing started hugging him. The preacher says, "In the name of Jesus Christ, what are you doing here in this shape?" When he said that, this thing wanted to tell him what this farmer had done, see? He said that they never did do nothing with all that stuff they stole. He told him to tell his kin folks about it, you know, and to get his head and put it back with his body. When he'd done that, the haunt went away.

78. THE THING ON THE ROAD

Back about twenty-five or thirty-five years ago, they used to warren people on the roads, country roads, work roads. They wanted me to work roads down here by Poplar Springs, and [we] went out that morning and were working along dinner. We all sat down to eat our dinner. We got to telling jokes, like, and Brother Booker was there, and he told one [and] said it was the God's truth.

[He] said back when he was young, he was mean as the very old devil hisself. He said he didn't care what he said or done hardly. Said he went to take his girl home one night and said on his way back, he heard something in the air. [It] went like wings of something fanning through the air and said he looked back, and there was something big and white about as tall as he was settled down right behind him. He said hit commenced walking up pretty fast. He thought to hisself, "You're in a bigger hurry than I am. I'll just give you the road." And he said, "I just walked over to the side of the road and it just fell right in behind me."

He said he got scared, and he started to run and he happened to think of a big straw stack out up on the hill and said he run until he was just about out of breath. He got on top of the hill, and he went for the straw stack—went up on top of it and said he felt safe then, and he give it a cussin'. He said it screamed out big 'n loud, and at that time, it changed. He said it looked like it was on a big white horse and said it looked like somethin' white on that horse. It looked like somebody with their head off. He said it had a big dagger it drawed on him. He said he went to screaming and hollering. He said they was a man lived about a mile down the road, and it woke him up. He said he told him to come there just as quick as he could and bring his gun. In just a few minutes, he was there, and he asked him what was the matter. He said, "Somethin' has got me up this straw stack and won't let me down." And he said, "Where's it at? I don't see it." He said he told him, "It's right over behind that man." And when he got out there, that thing come from around that straw stack, and he said he lit out and ran just as hard as he could and beat him down to his house. He said he stayed all night there at that man's house. The next morning, they got up and went up there to see if they could see any sign of anything, and they couldn't see any sign of nothing at all.

79. THE VISITOR IN THE KITCHEN

The strangest thing I saw here, I was doin' dishes and had this feeling there was someone watching. I turned around, and there was this little girl. She was standing in the door. I said, "Who do you belong to?" I thought it was this lady down here's friend's [little girl]. She didn't say anything. She just turned around, and she come straight through here. I followed her in straight through here. I followed her in here straight through to the door, and by the time I got here, she was gone. And I thought, "My goodness! That little girl must've been really movin' on!"

Well, I didn't think anything about it the first time. That didn't bother me too bad. But a few days later, I had that same feeling and turned around, and this time, she was standing back towards the hallway. I turned around. I said, "What are you doing?" Never opened her mouth, but this time she looked straight at me, and the only thing different about her that she didn't even look real or anything was her eyes, and they were just as blue! You know how it looks after a rain? That's the way her eyes looked. They were just as blue as could be. So she come this way, and I went that way [and] said, "I'll head you off, little girl. See who you belong to. You ain't scaring me!" By the time I got around, nothing!

CHAPTER SIX

Louisiana

✝

80. T-Frere

Throughout my life, I have heard of supposedly true stories of how different ghosts, goblins, and phantoms have disturbed people's lives. I have always thought of the people who told these stories as a little crazy or who just wanted to show off in front of friends. My feelings changed one dark night when three friends and I visited T-Frere's cemetery. It was a fall Friday night in Lafayette, Louisiana, and my friend Don and I had just finished playing a football game. We were meeting two other friends, Lindsay and Alexis, at the field house. After congratulating us for our win, Alexis asked, "So what do you guys want to do?" Don and I were pretty tired and really didn't care one way or the other, so I simply said, "Whatever y'all want, it really doesn't matter." Lindsay asked, "Well, how about going out to T-Frere's cemetery? If you aren't scared." Don and I didn't get too excited by this idea because we had all been there two or three other times, but since we didn't have any better ideas, we agreed to go.

Lindsay, Alexis, Don, and I all piled into one car. As we stepped out of the car, a cool October breeze sent shivers up our spines. We started walking up the dirt trail that led to the cemetery. A quarter moon that was barely shining in the sky made the trail almost completely hidden. A cold drizzling rain was falling, and the freezing drops almost made us turn back, but we had come too far to turn around now, so we entered the cemetery.

No farther than ten yards from the entrance were the tombstones of the Boudreaux family. Lindsay, said, "You all know the story behind these tombstones, don't you?" We all knew, but she proceeded to tell us anyway. "The large tombstone is for the mother, and the little one is for her little girl. Look how young the child was when she died." The girl was five when she died. Lindsay went on: "Yeah, the dad had left the two, and the mother went crazy and blamed it on the daughter. The mother ended up killing the girl and herself. Now the two are dead right in front of us." Suddenly, Don yelled, "Look over there!" We all looked and were staggered by what we saw across the cemetery. A large, gloomy, manlike object was standing in the middle of the cemetery. The ghost seemed to be preoccupied with something, and luckily, it didn't seem to notice us. I asked, "Do you all see that?" Everyone said, "Yes!" Fear ran wild in all of us, but I still wanted to be positive that the object was truly a ghost. I said, "Let's get closer and make sure it's not a shadow or something." Don replied, "Man, it's glowing, ain't it! It sure ain't no shadow!"

We all crept slowly behind the ghost. No one said a word, and the only sounds were of the wind blowing against the trees and the leaves rolling along the grass. After walking twenty yards, we all stopped and stooped down. The image was clear now. It was the ghost of a woman, probably that of Mrs. Boudreaux. Maybe she was guarding the cemetery. Whatever she was doing, she was very scary. Don whispered, "I've gone far enough. See ya!" He sprinted toward the trail that led back to our car. Alexis and Lindsay ran with him. Before I could even get the words "Wait up!" out of my mouth, They were almost out of sight, so I tried to catch up. We all got in the car and raced home, trying to get as far away as possible.

Later, we all agreed that ghost wasn't a figment of our imagination because we all saw it. We will never visit T-Frere cemetery again!

81. THE RUGA-RUE

On the bayou, my grandmother and her eleven brothers and sisters grew up. They would play and have fun but came in at dark. Her mother would say that when it got dark and the bats would fly, the dogs would howl that the Ruga-Rue was hunting.

She [my grandmother] told us that one year, people's dogs all over town were being ripped apart and eaten. The men of the town got together in search of the animal causing the destruction. They found no traces except huge claw marks on a cypress tree. The men didn't know what it could be because they didn't have an animal around that could do this. Not long after the discovery, a man in town heard something in his barn disturbing his animals. With a lantern in one hand and a gun in the other, he went to investigate. When he entered the barn, he was attacked by a huge animal with big claws. He managed to fire a shot and hit the monster. The man's neighbors came to see what had happened. When they arrived, they said you could smell something real musky. The guy bleeding to death was bandaged up and brought to the town doctor.

The next morning, a few local town people went to investigate. The man's cow was half-eaten by something with huge feet that had long claws. The men noticed where it had run into the barn and followed the trail. About 100 yards from the barn, they found a naked man lying there who had been shot. They said that the footprints changed from animal to human where the guy was lying. The man turned out to be a local farmer who had gone hunting and disappeared three years back. From then on, my grandmother said she knows the Ruga-Rue is a man trapped in an animal's body.

82. THE FIFOLET

It's a story that my grandparents and daddy told me from south Louisiana in the bayou country. It's about the Fifolet. It's a French name. It's supposed to be babies that died before they got baptized. I reckon it's they're in-between [heaven and hell], or they never got saved. It's in the woods and the swamps, and these little fire balls float around. The story is that they'll fly around and get you lost in the woods. They'll try to get you to follow 'em and get you lost in the woods or in the swamp. My daddy said that what he was told and what everybody was told and people would say that's seen 'em is the best thing to do is to sit down, and if you could find a tree stump or something that's flat and put a knife in it that the fireballs would fly around it, and in the morning you would find blood on the knife where the little kids cut themselves.

I don't know how true it is, but there' been several people in my family who's heard about it. My uncle said he's seen it. So that's the story of the Filles Follies.

They say, though, that the red balls are really methane gas. People have told me about the blood on the knife.

83. THE SPECTRAL CARD GAME

This happened in '86 or '87. I was somewhere between eight or ten [years old]. It was either Rose Land or Roseland. I can't remember. It was just outside Bungaloosa. It was back in the woods in an old plantation house. I didn't live down there. We went down there for a karate tournament. And my dad had a friend, and it was his house, and we stayed down there.

I'd been asleep. Somethin' woke me up. I don't know what it was. And I heard voices in the hall, and I figured the guy who was in the house was up or somethin'. So I walked down the hall, and when I did, that's when I saw the two legs hangin' out of a hole in the ceiling. And at first I thought I was asleep. Still dreamin' or somethin'. And then I heard him laughin,' and I saw the card fall. It was either the Ace of Hearts or the Ace of Spades. I don't know. But it was an ace, and when it hit the floor, the legs and the card disappeared, but I could still hear the laughing.

And that kind of freaked me out, but I heard a noise downstairs—noise and music—so I figured they were eatin' or somethin'. And I started to go down the stairs. They had real steep stairs. And I felt real cold air. But it wasn't cold. It was hot. The rest of the house was hot except for the stairway. It was really cold. And I walked down the stairs, and I went over to the jukebox which was right outside the kitchen to see if it was on or somethin', and it wasn't. And then I walked past the kitchen door, and I saw somethin'. I wasn't sure what it was, so I went back and looked, and that's when I saw the Confederate soldiers sittin' around the table. One was playin' the banjo. Four or five were playin' cards and drinkin'. And then one of them stood up and threw his hat at me. His hat hit me, and they all disappeared, but I could still hear the music. And it was like a cold wind coming from the kitchen.

And after that, I went and woke everybody up, and nobody believed me except the guy that owned the house. He told me that he had neard noises in there before, but he had never seen anything. And that there had been some Confederate soldiers that were either killed there or were buried out there. It was a plantation that the northerners had taken over.

84. GHOST IN THE BLACK ROBE

There's this road that we call Cooper Lake Road. It's just kind of a real winding-like road. And it's a lot to go around town—to come out at this subdivision called Log Cabin. There've been many, many accidents on it because it's just one of those roads that kind of provokes accidents. But, uh, at any rate, this girl and her boyfriend were driving on it one night, and he lost control of his truck, and they drove off into a ditch and hit a tree. The boy was killed; the girl—she was not really hurt.

Well, six months to a year later, she got her life back together and got pretty much over and started seein' someone else. Then she stared havin' these nightmares that—you know—that she was goin' to be haunted. Somethin' like that. She thought it was just—you know—from bein' in another intense relationship after her boyfriend had died.

One night, she and her boyfriend were goin' down the road, and they had a wreck, and no one really knows what happened, but when they found the bodies, both the heads were chopped off. And they say the way that happened was that it could have happened in the wreck. And that the boy she had been dating who had died, that you can see his likelihood [likeness] if you're lookin'. [He's] dressed in a long black robe carrying a knife. And they say that's what killed 'em. It's just a solid black robe with a black veil. You can't see his face. But you've got to know he's there because you won't never see him because you're not lookin' for him.

85. GHOSTLY FOOTSTEPS

I have one [story]. I'm not sure exactly what it was. If it was a ghost or not. I lived in a trailer park about ten miles outside of town. And it was two miles down this road called Old Bonita Road. Well, my Mom worked graveyard—she was gone all night, and I was there all by myself because I'm not used to bein' alone. I had a friend that lived a mile-and-a-half, maybe, from my house. I called him up that night, and we were talkin'. I asked him if he'd come over and stay with me for a while 'cause I was scared. He said, "Sure," but he had to walk because his car wouldn't start. And so he walked up there.

I talked to him when he got home, and he asked if it'd be okay if I loaned him a flashlight, and I said, "Sure." This went on for about a week, and finally, I asked him why he wanted a flashlight. Couldn't he see at night? He said, "Yeah," but when he was walkin' down this road, he could hear somethin' followin' him, kinda-like out in the woods. He had to walk right by a woods the whole time. I said, "It was probably, you know, an animal or somethin'." He said he shined his light out in the woods, and he could never see anything, but he could hear these little footsteps echoing through the sticks and the leaves and stuff. He never saw anything. He never heard anything. But whenever he stopped, it stopped too. He never heard any animal growling or yowling or whatever. Never heard that.

86. SCREAMS IN THE WOODS

I'm not originally from Louisiana. I was born and raised in Montgomery until I was sixteen. My mother and I moved back to Louisiana two years ago, so I haven't lived there very long, but long enough to get the general idea of how things are done there.

I'm from Bastrop, Louisiana. Most of the ones [stories] I know are completely centered around my small town because I've never really been anywhere else in Louisiana.

Several years ago—I guess ten or fifteen years ago—there were these four kids—four teenagers, a girl and her boyfriend and two of their friends. I'm assuming it was another boy and girl. Well, they were going down the dirt road to what we called "the hangout," which was right down by the river. A lot of teenagers go out there on the weekends because we can get away and kind of be by ourselves. The dirt road is really, really bumpy. To say the least, it's not a good road, even in the best of conditions. But coming back out, you have to come to a "T," and you have to take a left to come back to town. Well, if you don't stop, you go across the road, and there's a bayou. It's about a two-hundred-foot drop from the road to the water.

Well, they [the kids] had been drinking, and whoever was drivin'—I think it was the girl's boyfriend—they didn't stop. They went on through; they sailed through the trees. And it killed all four of them.

Well, it took two weeks to find the girlfriend's and the boyfriend's bodies. They found the other two very quickly, and if you're out there by yourself, if you're not—like—in a vehicle, you're just sittin' there listenin,' you can still hear them screamin' as they crash through the trees.

87. THE LALAURIE HOUSE

I'll have to refresh my memory. That's the one where the wife of the doctor had been dismissing herself from the parties that her husband would throw. She'd make some kind of eye contact that only the two of them understood. She'd disappear and reappear one or two hours later in an entirely different outfit.

[One night] a fire began in the kitchen. It was started by one of the slaves who had been chained to a stove. It was my understanding that she was trying to kill herself, but it may have been an attempt to bring this whole thing to light. Of course, it was only after the fire that they discovered that she had been going upstairs all this time to a secret chamber and torturing people—slaves. Another lady, [they] had cut off her arms and legs and basically just left the head and torso. Another woman, she [Delphine Lalaurie] had bent her limbs around—broken the bones where necessary—in order to fit her in this tiny cage. This left the woman crippled—she walked like a crab.

As I recall, they [Delphine and her husband] both got away. There are two theories about what had happened. One is that they managed to slip back to France. The other is that they continued living across the lake [Pontchartrain] somewhere in dire poverty.

They say that different types of people lived in the Lalaurie house down through the years. It became a boardinghouse for Italians and a saloon. People said that they would wake up hearing the screams of the slaves being tortured. Some also said they saw a lady with a whip chase a girl across the roof of the house until she fell off and disappeared.

88. THE OCTOROON GIRL

There was this girl who was an octoroon. She was very beautiful. She was selected by this fellow to be his mistress, which, by the mores of the times, should have been honor enough for her, but she wanted to marry him, which was pretty much *verboten*. And he tried to reason with her and told her, "Look, this wouldn't be good for either of us because it would ruin my reputation. I wouldn't have any money." Apparently, that was a good enough explanation at the time, but she wanted to marry him, and that was it. So she came back with the same request, and he said, "Okay. But I want you to prove your love for me. Go up on the roof. Take off your clothes, and wait for me." Thinking, of course, "It's winter time. She's not going to do that." This way, he could forestall her.

So she actually went up [on the roof] and did that. He lost track of the time. He didn't realize until morning that she was up there, and he got all worried because it was very cold and raining. When he got up to the roof, he discovered that water had frozen [and] ice had formed on the roof. He immediately thought that she had fallen to her death, but she had worked her way over to the shelter of the chimney and frozen to death there. He then slipped off the roof, and nobody knows whether he did it on purpose or not.

They say that you can see her naked body on the roof of the house on very cold or stormy nights in December. She walks across the roof all night and then, when the sun comes up, she disappears. Some people have also said that they have seen her lover playing chess all alone in the house. It's a pretty sad story, really.

89. THE BEAUREGARD-KEYES HOUSE

I do remember one thing about the Beauregard-Keyes House. They changed the house—tore down part of it. The thing I remember is the idea that ghosts don't walk through walls. But if you tear down the structure they had lived in and put up a new one, they will walk through where the door was, even though there might be a wall there now.

The Mafia tried to get protection money from this guy. And the guy went ahead and armed himself and his relatives and even some of the women. I think they [the family] heard them [the Mafiosos] coming, and there was a big gun battle, and miraculously, [the family] killed all of them. Supposedly, you can still hear the gunshots, so that whenever people call the precinct, or whatever, the police will ask for the address, and if it's the address of that house, they don't respond. They won't even come. So you don't want to get a house in that area because you might get that house number.

90. THE SULTAN'S HOUSE

This sultan showed up one day looking for a house to rent. He was interested in renting a house. He had made huge deposits of money at $100,000 a crack at different banks in town which he used to establish credit. And the fellow who owned the house had fallen on hard times during Reconstruction, so he was perfectly happy to lease this house to this guy. And he moved in. He had his harem on the top floor. He also had his eunuchs. The house had elaborate galleries. And he started to do some unauthorized renovations. He secured the doors and was always entertaining. The folks down the block would hear the sound of him entertaining.

Then one night, somebody walked by. She didn't hear the usual revelry, and she thought that was strange. She looks up and sees a drop of blood—

drip, drip. The next thing she knows, there's blood everywhere. The police had a terrible time breaking in because the doors were reinforced. But finally they beat down the door and find basically a slaughterhouse inside. Somebody had come in and just done everybody in.

There are a couple of theories. Some people thought that it was the sultan's brother [who was killed]. In other words, the fellow who had rented the house was an impostor. His brother—the real sultan—exacted revenge by slaughtering everybody in the house.

People have said that they have seen a man dressed up in Oriental garb walking around the house late at night. They've also heard soft footsteps and horrible screams which sound like they're coming from people being killed.

91. ST. LOUIS CATHEDRAL

The Spanish had just taken over [New Orleans] in 1764. Five years later, there were six aristocratic Frenchmen who opposed the Spanish, and they were executed. Five were shot by a firing squad, and one was stabbed to death with a bayonet. The Spanish weren't going to bury them. They were just going to let the bodies rot outside, but the priest of St. Louis Cathedral, who was French, said, "French, Spanish. We're all the same." He thought that the men should have a good Catholic burial, even if they were convicted criminals, so he arranged to have the six bodies taken to the church. He celebrated a Mass for the men and had them taken in a funeral procession to St. Louis Cemetery No. 1, where they were given a proper burial. The priest who conducted the funeral had a beautiful voice, and if you go out there at the right time, you can hear him sing the "Kyrie." It goes without saying that this man became a hero to the French because he had the guts to defy the orders of the Spanish.

92. THE GLOWING TOMBSTONE

(WPA)

Years ago in New Orleans, there was a prostitute who made large sums of money. Not being able to spend so much money, she decided to buy a fine monument for herself and have it ready when she should pass on. She bought a lot in Metairie Cemetery and had a monument erected. At the front of the monument stood a life-sized statue of a saint. Years passed by, and this woman died and was buried there. Soon after, it was noticed that each night at a certain hour, a red light would appear over the head of the statue and stay there for several minutes. Many believed that it was haunted, but it was finally discovered that a switch engine on the railroad nearby would stop at a certain place each night for a few minutes, and the light from the engine was reflected above the statue's head.

93. GRAVEYARD DARE (WPA)

Down in Alexandria, Louisiana, a man had been buried. After the ceremony, a number of his friends were talking about the events of the day. Then the conversation turned to spirits, ghosts, and the like. One man in the crowd said that he did not believe in such things and for $5, he would dig down to the casket and stick his knife in the box and that he would do this at midnight and leave his knife there for proof. The crowd called his hand at once.

When midnight came, the man who had made the boast went to the cemetery armed with a shovel and his pocket knife. He dug until the box was exposed. Then he took his knife from his pocket and opened it. When he leaned over to stick it in the box, his overcoat got in the way, and he pinned it to the box. It was such a dark night that he could not see what had happened, and the man evidently thought that the spirits had him because he died of fright, and his friends found him there the next morning with his coat pinned to the box by his pocket knife.

CHAPTER SEVEN

Mississippi

✝

94. Stuckey Bridge

Stuckey Bridge is in the southwest corner of Lauderdale County. You go down Interstate 59, and you take the Savoy exit. And when you take off the exit, you go to the right. There's a road to the left real quick, and it'll have signs, I think, that say Dunns Falls. You keep going down that road. You don't turn on the Dunns Falls Road. You just keep going, and you drive a good ways, and you come to a deep curve where there's a dirt road that—there's like a fork, like a triangle. And there's two dirt roads. The one dirt road forks back onto the asphalt. And you would turn left and go off onto that dirt road, and that road takes you to the Stuckey Bridge.

Now as far as it's really haunted, I don't know. That one, as I said in the story [on T.V.], is probably folklore. I know my grandmother grew up in that area. My grandparents' farm is not far from there. My grandmother grew up in that area, and they did not like to go down into the swamp during the night. Now my mom laughed about my stories because she said that when she was a teenager growing up, that was their hangout place. But it was a lot of folklore. Mr. [Jim] Dawson has done some research on the bridge.

Now as far as Mr. Stuckey [is concerned], he was part of the Dalton Gang, and it is said that he committed the murders. The bridge was called "the hanging bridge," and supposedly, Stuckey was hung on the bridge for his crimes. It's said that if you go down there at night, you'll see someone walking across the bridge with a lantern. You'll see people moving around.

And supposedly, what it was, Stuckey had an inn there. This road brought you out of Enterprise. Also, the river—people would go down the Chickasahay and up the Chunky to do their business and sell their cattle or whatever. And he [Stuckey] had an inn there. The story goes that on the way back when you had your pockets full of money from selling your wares and all, he would kill [you], and the bodies are buried in the ground around the bridge. Supposedly, he killed around twenty people before he was caught. And that's where the sensation was—that you can see, like, a lantern light moving across the bridge. But like I said, I've never found any documentation for that story. This is a folklore story that was handed down from my grandmother to me.

95. Missouri Larkin

The story goes that Missouri Larkin and her husband were working in a field out around Okatibbee Creek, and all of a sudden, Missouri comes up missing, and her husband said that she just "disappeared." Wasn't any chariots that came out of the sky and got her; she just disappeared.

And she began to be seen in what they call the "Red Line" area, and she was seen around town, you know, mostly in the black section. And she'd been seen trying to convince people to come with her. This went on several times, and then there were three other ladies who went into a field close by the field where Missouri disappeared. One of the ladies mentioned that all of a sudden, Missouri appeared to her and motioned for her to follow, so she followed her, and all of a sudden, Missouri laid down on the banks of the Okatibbee and rolled off into it, and she was apparently trying to [show how she died].

The story goes on that they went and searched the banks and drug the lake and searched for her body but never did find it. That one [story] is supposed to be true.

96. Ghost Possum

This was told to me by Robert McClelland, a black man from Canaan, Mississippi, in northern Mississippi. He declared that he had the most outstanding possum dog in the state of Mississippi. This dog would never fail to find the possum. He [the dog] never lied. If he ran to a tree and barked, the possum was up it.

They were out hunting this time. The dog started training a possum, and it carried them in the vicinity of a cemetery, and by the cemetery, it seems that the trail got hotter and hotter. They came next to a cornfield. The corn had been harvested. There was one stalk left standing, and this dog—Old Lige—carried this trail to that cornstalk, sat down, and started barking, and by the time they got there, that dog was having a fit. It was like that possum was only two feet from him. And all of a sudden, this white thing rose from the cornstalk and floated off into the night.

97. THE CRITTER ON THE CHURCH

[This story] is a joke. There's no truth to this one. My grandfather told me this one originally. That's where I got most of my stories from—either from him or my great-uncles on my mother's side of the family.

According to my grandfather, there was this black man who was visiting a woman who was not his wife in the community. To get to this lady's house, he had to pass right by the Methodist church, and the Methodist preacher would see him headin' out to go see his lady-friend in the evenings. He was going to inquire after him and remind him that this wasn't somethin' nice to do. A few days later, he stopped him and asked him, and he said, "Yes, sir. And you know, it's the funniest thing. Last night, I was passing by the church, and there was this critter sittin' up on the steeple." The preacher told him, "It's your conscience warnin' you because it knows that you've been sinnin' and that the devil's goin' to get you."

Well, the next week, he saw the old man goin' by, and he stopped him, and he asked him if he was goin' to see the lady, and he said, "Yes, sir. And that critter was up there again." And the preacher reminded him again that it was his conscience warnin' him against sin.

This happened two or three more times, and finally, the preacher decided he was goin' to scare him. So he waited til that night that he was goin to see his girlfriend, and he got decked up in sheets and stuff and climbed up on the roof of the church up near the steeple and sat and waited for the old man to come by. Well, the old man comes by, looks up at the roof, and his eyes get real big, and he takes off down the road.

Preacher sees him the next day, and he asks him, "Did you see your girlfriend last night?" And he says, "Yes, sir." And he says, "Did you see that critter up on the church?" He said, "You know, preacher, it just about scared me to death. I came by the church, and I looked up on the steeple, and, Lord help me, there was two of them this time!"

98. THE WHITE WOLF

I asked my Mom about this story, and she ate lunch with me this afternoon so that I would get it straight. John Garrett lived at this house. This is my great-grandfather, and his daughter, my grandmother, lived and still lives there. It's on this hill, and there's a valley in between where they farmed. There's a road that goes around the farm that connects the two houses.

Well, when John Garrett was dying, they didn't know he would recover—well, they didn't know he was dying. Well, my great-grandmother saw a white wolf run through the house, and she immediately told one of the children to run across the field and tell my grandmother. Well, when the child got there, my grandmother already knew that the white wolf had taken his soul to where he had grown up. She knew that he was already dead when the messenger got there; she already knew it because she had seen the white wolf, but he never appeared again. The white wolf took the soul to where it had originally been given birth. John Garrett's soul had originally begun in the house where my grandmother lives now. The wolf just took the soul under the house, and it never reappeared again.

This house is in Lauderdale County out toward Dalewood. This probably happened in the 1920s. My grandmother is a full-blooded Indian.

99. THE HAUNTED NURSING HOME

This happened at Queen City Nursing home [in Meridian, Mississippi]. It used to be St. Joe's Hospital. It's by the Chevron Station on Eighth Street and two blocks over. I worked there for two years, but I don't work there any more.

This took place in Mr. Holland's room. He only stayed there a little while. Reverend Strong was in there. He died. Mr. Holland talked about some little boy. And I had heard about the child before talking to him. When the patient is deathbed delirious and is yellin,' "Get him out! Get him out!" [we know that the boy has been there]. That's how this other guy was. He [Mr. Holland] was a new patient here—he had only been here a while. He started callin' to the nurse's station, sayin,' "Get the little boy out! Get the little boy out! And close the door!" I said, "What are you talkin' about?" 'cause I had heard other people talkin' about it [the ghost] but had never had a patient lucid enough to talk back about it other than to say, "It's kids in the hallway." And he told me that there was a little boy standin,' peekin' from behind the door at him, and even as we spoke, the child was just, like, in the corner, watchin' him, sort of wavin' at him. He said it was a dark-haired little white boy standin' up behind the door, and he said, "Tell the kid to get out and close the door!" Well, tellin' the kid to get out was not goin' to help. But anyway, I just, you know, said something and closed the door so he would be comfortable, and that was the first patient.

And then when Reverend Strong got bad, he was sayin' the same thing. He had gone to the hospital and come back, and his first night that I was there with him, the first thing he said was about the little boy. And I said, "Oh, yeah, better watch him!" The other nurses said, "You're being morbid." And we got to talkin,' and I said, "Remember last time?" And we started talkin' about the other patient, Mr. Holland. And it was the same thing. We started talkin' about the little white boy behind the door. And sure enough, he did go on and die two days later. He kept on the button and tried to get out of the bed—stuff like that. "Tell the kid to get out!" It was real spooky.

It kind of has to be [the truth] because nobody told the new guy the old story, and nobody definitely told Mr. Strong. He was unbalanced when he came. So when they had the same manifestations, you've got to feel there's somethin' to it.

100. THE OLD SHELTON HOUSE

It's the year 1937 when—as far as I know to my knowledge—when the old Shelton House was built, single-story, but rather huge. And the last time it was lived in was '76. It is located on Shelby Road, half a mile from the main house. And, uh, it's down a lonely dirt road, and we used to go there and play and everything. And as the legend goes, the last people that had lived there had murdered their kid. I'm not exactly sure how [the child] was related to me. He was a cousin, second or third, on my Dad's side of the family. The man had gone inside and killed his three-year-old son and buried him under the back doorstep.

When they would go to bed at night, they would lock the door of the house, and the next morning when they would get up, the doors would be open. And it continued that-a-way with strange sightings and stuff. I'm not exactly sure what they saw. But it continued that-a-way, and when the house was deserted, at night you could see a red light coming out of one of the rooms. I'm standing here trying to picture it, facing the house, and the bedroom in the front of the house would be on my right. And every night, there would be a red light in the room, a faint red glow, even though the electricity had been turned off for years after the last family had moved out. The last of the Sheltons had lived in the house in the 1950s, so there had been tenants and stuff moving in and out for years, but it was still highly unexplainable, except that it was credited to the kid being buried under the back doorstep. No one has ever dug anything up. The house is gone now. We tore it down, but the steps are still there.

About five years ago, me and my cousin was going hunting late one evening. It was cold then like it is now. And I noticed that my cousin had a blank look on his face, and I walked around and looked, and floating right above the chimney of the house was a—a ghost. It's hard to describe the thing. It—looked—female, I would say. But other than that, it had an indescribable, decayed look. But I don't think I ever went back down there ever since then.

101. Phantom Hitchhiker

On Highway 45 South, I was about four miles outside of Scooba. It was, like, about 9:00 at night. I can give you the year—'85, '84—'84. And now there's a lot of construction going on, and that place is pretty [cleared off now]. There's a little bridge, and they have a bunch of trees near there. As soon as I went over the bridge, I felt—you know—I felt like there was a coldness in the car—you know. It wasn't air-conditioned. And I started sweating. I didn't notice anything at that point. Something told me to look back. As I was driving this way, I turned around and looked over my shoulder. And I saw in the extreme right-hand corner of the back-seat [that] there was a lady sitting. She had gray clothing on, and I couldn't see her face [because of] a shawl or something else of that nature which covered it up. And I said, "Who is it"—you know—several times, and there was no response. But that time, I felt a little more the sense of something unnatural being there. And literally, this happened: the hair on top of my head stood up. I looked back several times to make sure that I was not seeing shadows or a figment of my imagination

At that point, I was looking for some light or farmhouse or something where I could pull over and see what was going on, and finally after about four miles, I came down to Scooba and stopped, and then at the point, I didn't see anything. But [before she disappeared] I looked over my shoulder for at least four or five times. But I could not see—there was no face to that woman, and she was sitting like this [informant crosses his arms] and didn't say anything.

102. Midnight Visitor

I have a personal experience that I've never really told a lot of people about because they think you're crazy. I woke up one night—now, I was not asleep—I woke up, and I saw this figure standing in the hallway. I can tell you what they had on and everything. It was somebody that I had known—a child that had been killed in a car wreck years before. She was standin' in the hall, sayin' somethin' to me. I got up out of the bed, and when I headed that way, it was like it faded out. But the strange thing [was] the night before I went to bed, I looked all over my house for my car keys and couldn't find them. I had a pool table sitting in the middle of my dining room. I looked on that. I could not find them anywhere. The next morning, my keys were layin' in the middle of the pool table.

I'm tellin' you now, it was scary. I never told anybody because, you know, they'd think you were havin' a dream or somethin'. But I was awake, and I got up out of bed, so I know that I was not dreamin'.

I was teachin' school, [and she] was a teenager that I had at camp, and she'd been killed quite a few years before. I had worked with her quite a few years at Girl Scout Camp, about three or four summers. We had a pretty good relationship. And it looked just like her face. I can tell you the clothes she had on and everything. When I woke up the next day and those keys were on the middle of the table, that—that makes you think about it!

103. Old Mossback

There was a real interesting story that they told just for fun, I think. They told it at Boy Scout Camp. There used to be an old Boy Scout Camp just south of Meridian—Camp Binacci. And you know how Boy Scouts are. They'd get around the campfire and tell these stories, you know.

This one's about Mossback. You heard about Mossback. He was an Indian that apparently the white men killed, and they kept his head. They threw his body in the lake down there and took his head back to show that they'd killed him. And the story went that Mossback on certain nights would get up and go looking for his head. And if you felt somebody feeling around your head, it was probably Mossback looking for his head. And of course sometimes, one of the counselors would slip in and touch the boys' heads at night. And that was a pretty scary thing, you know. They told it like it was true, but I'm sure that it wasn't. It caught your attention, though, with the shadows and all.

104. The Golden Arm

I first heard this story when I was a young boy about eight or ten years old. I was in the Bienville Elementary School, and the principal was an old bachelor, and he liked to tell ghost stories. So it was on Halloween Eve. Mr. Tom Tetter was the principal of the school. And he had all the little children gathered out front, and he started this fascinatin' story by sayin,' "There once was a man in a small county village who was such an unusual person—the main thing that was unusual about him was he had a gold arm. His right arm, as a matter of fact. And when he shook hands with people, they took this golden arm in their hands, and they were so fascinated by it.

"So finally, after some years, this man with the golden arm died. And they gave a big funeral and carried the casket out to the graveyard and buried it. But there was one man in this town who went home and kept thinkin' about it: 'That man out there with that golden arm is buried in that grave. And the thing is solid gold. I want that golden arm!' So he went out in the darkness, dug down in the ground, and opened the casket. Cut it [the arm] off and brought it back home. Put it on his bed. Tried to go to bed and go to sleep.

"But after a while, he heard a noise come up on the front porch of his house. Heard the door open. And as the door opened, he heard a voice saying, 'Zzzzzzzzzz! Who got my golden arm? Zzzzzzzzzz! Who got my golden arm? Zzzzzzzzzz! Who got my golden arm?' He just got closer and closer. Well, the man, he covered up his head and did everything he could to get away from it. But the voice kept comin'. Didn't see anybody, but he heard its voice, 'Zzzzzzzzz! Who got my golden arm? Zzzzzzzzzz!' Got closer and closer. Finally, he couldn't take it any longer. He raised up in the bed to see, hopin' to see [what it was]. Then he heard one last time: 'Zzzzzzzzzz! Who got my golden arm? Zzzzzzzzzz! You got it!' "

He [the principal] jumped in our faces. And all of us sat in the front row, and the little girls almost fainted because it was a frightenin' thing. That's the most interestin' Halloween story I've ever heard. I live in a community where there were two big slaveholders, and there were many stories that were handed down. I made contact with folks when I was a boy who were children of those slaves. And the community was full of those people. And they had lots of stories like that. I'm not even sure what they call the thing. "The golden arm" or somethin' like that.

105. THE GRAND OPERA HOUSE

The only experience that I've ever had in the Opera House was right after we began the restoration. The Opera House, as you know, was sealed up from 1927 until 1988. And very few people went in unless you knew a connection or worked at Mark Rothenburg and knew how to get in from there. In 1989, I worked over there as an assistant to Eliott Street, who was the director. And the only experience that I have ever had—I was on a tour with a group of ladies, and it was in February on a cold, rainy day. We were in the Opera House, and all of a sudden, we heard this crashing sound, like breaking glass. And it sounded like it was down in front—we were in the actual theater part—it sounded like it was down in front where there are some old offices on the front of the building on the second floor. We walked up that-a-way, and we couldn't find anything that had happened. We thought that maybe the wind—because it was getting very stormy outside, a window had fallen.

Well, we finished the tour and left, and I went and told Eliott Street about it, and he and I went back. We went all over the Opera House and checked all the windows and never could find broken glass.

And after that, we had some young students who volunteered time too—they were two sisters—and one day, they came across the street and said they weren't going back there unless somebody was in the building with them on the stage. And that happened several times. Then my children—my daughter and my youngest son—were over there with me one time, and they heard it. Now this ghost supposedly is a woman too, and she can be heard singing on the stage. And Eliott had never had any sensations for a long time, but after a while, he began to sense the people. You can sense sometimes when you're on the stage that somebody's in the building with you. That they're on the stage with you. But she's never actually been seen. She's never visualized to anybody, but her singing has been heard, movement, noises, that kind of thing. We don't know anything about her. We don't know her connection to the Opera House—who she was, why she would stay. And with all the research that has been done, no one has finally come up with an explanation as to why this person would be there.

There is a painting above the stage of a woman who is called "the Lady." Nobody knows who she is. During the time the Opera House was built, Sarah Bernhardt was a very popular actress. As a matter of fact, she performed there. The portrait of "the Lady" is very similar to portraits that have been done of her. And that was very popular for theaters to put up pictures of her and Lillian Russell. One theory is that it could be the mistress of Mr. Lee Rothenberg, or his daughter. It's a beautiful portrait, but it's not enough detail to match it to anybody. And that's how the Opera house got its name of "the Lady." And who knows? Maybe the ghost does have a connection to the portrait. I don't know.

106. THE HEADLESS HAINT

There's a small, unnamed creek that passes through the property that belongs to my father now. It belonged to my grandfather. It passes through several "homesites," as they call it, in Kemper County. And, of course, during the time of the Civil War and before, it was used for watering cows and washing clothes and things like that. According to the story, right after the Civil War during some of the more turbulent times when there were skirmishes between the Negro settlers and the white people, a young black man was decapitated, and his head was carried along the creek bank, through the several properties, displayed in a cotton basket. Okay.

Now, according to the legend, on the anniversary of his death, the cotton basket and the whole procession appears and follows the course of the creek bank. I've heard my daddy and my granddaddy talk about it. I've never heard them claiming to have seen it, and I know that I've never seen it. I do know that what I believe is part of that story is what they call "foxfire." We have several cases of that, usually in the late spring, where you can see a bluish glow. That's real common along that creek bank in the late spring and sometimes in the late fall.

107. THE HAUNTED APARTMENT

When I was a student at Hattiesburg, I lived in this apartment, a ground-floor apartment, and the door used to be always open because he [my roommate] and I had friends who used to come in while we were in the library or working in the lab or something. They would come in and sit down in our living room.

One evening, I had gone to New Orleans and came back pretty late at night. I wanted to get in through the front door, but the door was locked, and I thought, "That's strange. Who would lock the door?" But anyway, I went around the back. The back was really dark, and as I entered the apartment, I heard something fall from the roof. It was not like a cat or a dog. It was a much heavier sound than that. But I didn't see anything.

Ah, but later on, people would tell us that when they came in at night and flicked the lights on in the living room, they could smell perfume and stuff of that kind.

But one night, what happened was that I was asleep, and my studying desk was behind my bed. And I hear, like, one of those plastic grocery bags, you know. I heard some crumbling noise. I thought it was just my roommate getting up to get some aspirin, you know, so I didn't even open my eyes and went back to sleep.

Next morning, you know, my roommate came by and said, "Did you come into my room?" And I said, "No." And I said, "Did you come into my room?" And he said, "No." Then he said, "Come look at something." Somebody had bent his closet door all the way, like this. And, you know, it was just bent in a round shape.

And another night, what had happened was—and this is truly amazing—you can ask my sister, you know, or my wife. We had gone to sleep, my roommate and I, and at that point, we'd lock the door up tight when we'd go to sleep. I went to the bathroom, right? And into the kitchen, right? And in the kitchen were two sacks of groceries, and in the sacks were chicken, salt, bread, peanut butter. But again, there was no connection. I don't know if it was a ghost or what it was.

Another night, I was in the kitchen doing something, and my roommate was in the bathroom. It was about 7:30 in the winter time, and somebody was calling his name. It was a nasal tone. So I said, "Who is it?" And I went out the back door, and he came out, and he said, "Did somebody call me?" We looked, and there was nobody.

And then another time, he and I had eaten lunch on Saturday, and then

I went to the library. I don't know where he went and I came back from the library at 11:00 or 12:00. The next morning, he said, "Do you want to eat something?" I said, "What do we have? I don't think we have anything because what we had yesterday, we left it out, and it's not good for eating anymore." He says, "Well, those are on the stove." He left them on the stove. The stove was on, and the food was warm, and neither of us had turned it on.

108. THE GHOSTS OF MERREHOPE

This was in 1973, and I was just coming out of college, and this boy I was dating—he was not from around here; he was from the Navy—and I had told him about Merrehope. So we drove over there, and we came up on opposite sides of the house. But I came around the corner on the porch, and he went around the front of the house. He mentioned he had seen my shadow, but the way the light was, it couldn't have been my shadow. About that time, Merrehope was being restored, and they didn't have the lace curtains on the windows yet, and you could look in, and there she [a female figure] stood, in the center of the room, looking at us.

A few days after that, I came to Merrehope to work as a tour hostess, and one of the ladies that was on the board at the time and was very active in restoring the house told us that she wanted me to see these portraits. These portraits had just been given to the Merrehope Foundation, and they are of Pristina and Eugenia Garry. John Garry moved here from Livingston, Alabama, around 1867–1868. They bought Merrehope—what was then Merrehope—in 1868. But Eugenia and Pristina never lived in Merrehope. They died at the end of the Civil War of consumption. And they are actually buried over in Alabama. And it was the first time that Eugenia had started being seen and also the first time in dealing with Merrehope that I had been really conscious of spiritual activity, I guess you'd call it.

But that summer, odd little things would happen. You'd start feeling like someone was in the room, or you'd see a shadow move by you. You'd hear, like, footsteps walking around the house. She likes to move things around, you know, little pieces of what-not. Sometimes, pieces of furniture—just a chair—would be moved from one room to the next. I'd leave work, and when I'd come back, there'd be a chair sitting in the middle of a hallway for no reason. And I'd call everyone I knew who had keys, and no one had been over there. And, just odd things through the years.

And other people have seen them. The people that live across the street from Merrehope in a corner house also have seen her. Eugenia's portrait is in what we call the "museum room." It's in the northeast corner of the house, and that's where a lot of the neighbors have seen her standing. There or downstairs. Through the years, different tourists have come in, and they'd comment about feeling funny. Last fall, I was doing a tour for a group of women who were having a dinner party. When we have parties, I come in. I just do the history and talk about the architecture and all. And it depends on who's on tour whether we make comments about the ghost stories. You can sort of sense which groups would enjoy it and which groups wouldn't. And this group—it was a large, large group, so I really wasn't going into ghost stories that night. And we were touring both Merrehope and the F. W. Williams house, and when we left Merrehope and started over to the F. W. Williams house, two ladies came up to me, and two more behind them, and said, "You have a ghost in Merrehope, don't you?" And I said, "What makes you say that?" And they said, "She was singing in the bathroom." Off to what we call the "bride's room," there's a little bathroom. And the bathroom section of the house—you have to understand the architecture of the house. It may have some connection to Eugenia. Everyone wants to know why she's in the bathroom. The bathroom's in the back-L of the house, the older section of the house. And the Garrys added onto the house when they bought it in 1868. In 1904, the F. H. Floyds bought the house, And from the first section that the Garrys built and the original back-L of the house, which was the cottage built in 1858, they moved the back-cottage part—the L part—back and built in a big section where the dining room and several bedrooms now are. For some reason, Eugenia likes the bathroom too, and she's played tricks on us with the lights. You'll think at night that you're leaving, and all the lights are out, and when you come back in or go to get in your car, the light in the bathroom's on. People that have lived in the apartment in the back section of the oldest part of the house have made comments about hearing pianos played at night in the house, people walking around and talking. One man I remember lived there; he got sick. And also at one time, my sister lived in the house. She talked about when she was sick, she felt comforted, like someone was sitting there trying to comfort her, and this man had also made this comment.

She's a very living ghost, a very protective ghost. Merrehope in all the years that it's been there—the foundation bought it in 1968—had never been bothered. It's never been vandalized until this year. I was president in 1991. We had a robbery one Sunday morning. They broke into the back part of the house and went into the apartment. The police in their investigation said that for some reason, they [the robbers] stopped; they left. My sister was living there at the time, and we both looked at each other and said, "Eugenia!" She must have appeared or something to them because the police said that it was like they had just walked out during the robbery. Of course, it might not have been Eugenia.

Then later, my daughter about three years ago had Eugenia appear to her twice. She was over there—we were having another party. Eugenia likes parties. And we were having a Halloween party. One of the big corporations in Meridian was having a national managers meeting here in Meridian, and they had rented Merrehope on Halloween night for a reception and party. We had different people, like my daughter and her friends and myself, who were dressed in period clothing to tell the stories and to be in the rooms when people walked in. And my daughter was standing in the balcony outside the room where Eugenia's portrait is. She felt like somebody was watching her. She turned around, and Eugenia was standing in the window. This was the first time; she [Eugenia] appeared to her later that night. That night, one of the young black men in the neighborhood was walking home—he and a friend—and she was standing in a window again, watching out. And that's what the neighborhood talks about. They talk about seeing the lady in the long dress. And if you've ever seen her, you know that it's Eugenia. She looks just like her portrait.

And the reason I believe she goes with the portrait is that when Mr. Garry died—he died in the 1880s—after that, most of his family moved to the Mississippi Gulf Coast. In 1969 when Hurricane Camille hit, the portraits were damaged by the hurricane. And we had them sent off to the Mississippi University for Women to have one of their professors look at restoring the portraits. While they were up there, nothing happened. Eugenia wasn't sensed. All activities stopped. And the portrait was gone for several months. And then when it came back, everything started all over again, so I think that she goes with the portrait. She may have a connection to the house because when they moved here, Mr. Garry's father was still living. He passed away there at the home. Not surprisingly, her sister Pristina has never been seen there. She's not as sociable.

The thing that is odd, that makes me feel a little more credible, is that there have been—Merrehope is not air-conditioned on the upper floor. And in the summer, it can get extremely hot up there because we keep the window sealed for security reasons. And we usually just have the hall doors open to get some air circulation. And a lot of times, tourists will walk in that room, and when they get close to the portrait, they will say, "I thought you said it wasn't air-conditioned up here. You can feel the coldness."

But like I said, there are really two ghosts at Merrehope. There's one that we really don't talk much about quite as much because it's a more recent ghost. When Merrehope was being rented out as apartments, the last man that lived there committed suicide, and when the Foundation bought the house and went in to restore it, his room was left just like it was the night he committed suicide. And in his room, you have sensations sometimes. It's not quite the same feeling as with Eugenia. You get that tingling like when you're up there, and we're talking about her, and you feel like she's there. Or you may not be talking about her, but you can tell when others that are sensitive to her can sense when she's around. In his room, sometimes you can smell cigar-cigarette smoke. He was known for throwing poker parties. His room also can be extremely cold sometimes. And his footsteps—you can hear him moving, but his footsteps are heavier. But he never seems to leave that room. Eugenia seems to move around. And for some reason, he's scarier to me, so I stay away from him. I don't know what it is; I don't know why. It's just a different feeling. We don't really tell his name because his family's still here. We don't talk as much about him. Eugenia's a more popular ghost.

About a year ago, we got a new security system at Merrehope. I think it was a year ago last Christmas. And all of a sudden, the security system would go off in the middle of the night, and the police would go running over there, and nothing was there. They couldn't figure it out. So one day, I was over there when a man was trying to fool with the alarm system, and he said there was nothing wrong with it. He said he couldn't even see why a big storm would set it off. There wasn't enough vibration. They have motion detectors in the security system at Merrehope. It wasn't vibrations or the wind that set it off. I just looked at him and said, "It's the ghost."

Oh, the most recent time was this summer that the ghost was seen. You know, ghosts like to move a lot, or at least that's what I've been told. During restoration work, ghosts are often seen. It's like if there's some kind of activity going on in the house like that, ghosts will be seen a lot. Back in the summer, we were having Merrehope painted. And also we were having masonry and carpentry work done on the house. And this paint contractor's wife drove up around the back of the house where there is a set of windows in the kitchen. And it was late afternoon when she went over there to see if she could find her husband. When she drove up, she saw this young woman with dark hair standing in the window looking out the window. But she [the wife] didn't come in the house. She [the wife] said the woman stood there for a long time. Then the woman turned and walked away. She asked her husband later on who that might be. And her husband said, "I don't' know. I haven't met a woman that looked like that." And so the next day, he told the hostess at Merrehope, and she said, "Well, you need to talk to Fonda Rush." So I went over there later on to take care of some business, and the hostess said that I needed to talk to him. So I went out there and I asked him. I didn't say anything about the ghost. I said, "Who was it your wife saw?" He described her, and that's when I told him the story about Eugenia.

109. THE GHOST OF CITY HALL

And then we have ghosts here at city hall. I call him old Mayor Parker. When this building was built in 1914, John Parker was mayor of Meridian. He served two terms as mayor, but not consecutive terms. And in his second term, he died of a heart attack right here in city hall. It was actually on a train trip to Hattiesburg. But there are things that happen at night when you are in the building and that the custodian is always talking about. They'll come in and find lights cut off or lights on, or they'll come in and hear voices. There's also a lady that died here in that building. The old jail was in the first floor.

The reason I call it Mayor Parker is when Mayor Kemp was mayor of Meridian, I was in his office one day discussing something, and he got to asking 'em about Mayor Parker. His grandson was a friend of Mayor Kemp's. He was asking me what he was like as a mayor and what kind of information I had on him. I was turned just like I am now. Mayor Kemp was sitting across the desk from me, and my back was to the light. As you go into the mayor's office, there's a light—it's not a spotlight—on the wall. And all of a sudden, he said, "Did you see that?" I said, "No. What are you talking about?" "I've noticed that every time we start talking about Mayor Parker, that light comes on. And when we quit discussing him, the light goes off." So we did a little experiment. We'd talk, and then we'd quit. And sure enough, the lights went on and went off. It could have been a short or something.

But anyway, that's why I say it's Mayor Parker. The custodian won't talk to just anybody about ghost stories. There are just a few of us around now who had had things happen to them. We have a new security system now. Our old security system used to go off and on at odd times during the night. I always teased him [the custodian] that it was the ghost fooling with the security system.

110. THE F. W. WILLIAMS HOUSE

The F. W. Williams house does have a ghost story too, but it's a little odd. It was moved behind Merrehope in 1979, November 1979. That house was built in 1885 by Mr. Frank W. Williams, who was one of the founders of the United States Fidelity and Guarantee Insurance Company. He built it as a wedding gift for his wife. Miss Mamie's sister, Miss Daisy, became a secretary in Mr. Frank Williams's insurance company. He had the Frank's State Agency here in Meridian, which was a division of USF&G, and she later became a partner. She was the first woman in the state to become a partner in an insurance company. Miss. Daisy never married, and Miss Mamie deeded the house to Miss Daisy because Mr. Frank gave Mamie the house. Mamie went to get on the elevator one day, and for some reason, she wasn't paying attention, and the elevator did not come up, and I guess her thinking it had, she stepped off into the shaft. She died several days later of her injuries. Well, the house reverted to Miss Daisy.

Mr. Frank moved out and went to live in his parents' house because he didn't think that it was proper for him to live with his unmarried sister-in-law, and they were in their sixties when this happened. But Miss Daisy outlived everybody. She lived to be 104.

But I've never had any sensations or feelings in the F. W. Williams house. But last Christmas, we got a call from the Mississippi Department of Health. They have offices over in the Office Plaza. It's a building next to the Sonic Drive-in. The F. W. Williams House was next to the Sonic Drive-in, and it was moved back behind Merrehope to preserve it. And where the Sonic is is where Mr. Frank's father's home was called the Towers. And they [the Mississippi Department of Health] called us and said they wanted to have their Christmas party in their ghost's home, and I said, "What are you talking about?" They said that their offices are haunted, and they believe that—they're not sure who it is, but they think that it has a connection to the Williams house. And they came and had their Christmas party there [at the F. W. Williams home]. It's a late Victorian-Queen Anne house—and a lot of gingerbread. Maybe if there is a ghost, it went right back where the house was originally.

CHAPTER EIGHT

NORTH CAROLINA

✝

III. UNCLE ISUM'S TREASURE

This story is from my mother, Mary Lancaster Bradley. This is the way it was told to her by her grandmother, Mary Hines Lancaster. During the Civil War, sometime between 1861 and 1865, my Uncle Isum Hines lived in the foothills of the Appalachian Mountain range, on the edge of Polk County, North Carolina. He and his wife and two daughters had a nice southern home there. It was a common occurrence during the Civil War for the northern soldiers to stop at these kinds of homes and demand food and help themselves to any money or any valuables that they could find.

On a cold October evening after hearing that the Yankees were nearby, Uncle Isum gathered all of the money, silver, and jewelry and many other valuable items in their home and packed them in a strong metal box. Then he took the box and shovel and went off alone down the block into the road and then in a nearby wooded area. Much later that evening, he returned.

Sure enough, that very next evening, true to rumor, the Yankees came forcing their way into the Hines house, demanding food and money and attention. At the same time, my aunt was being imposed upon to prepare a meal for the northern troops, and Uncle Isum was being tortured in an attempt to get money or anything of value that they could rob. But needless to say, they received no money or information from him, but because of his silence, he was beaten severely, and his bare feet were even placed on hot coals on the hearth in front of the open fireplace. And in spite of all of this, the soldiers still went away empty-handed.

Uncle Isum had been so cruelly treated by the enemy intruders that day that soon after their unwelcome visit, he died, unable to tell his family where he had hidden their valuables. And not long after, my aunt and the girls began to experience great financial need. That's when strange things began to happen. Late each evening, the front floor of the Hines home would open, and noises as if voices could be heard, but they couldn't quite be understood. Uncle Isum's chair by the hearth would rock with nobody in it while the babbling voices would swell underneath the chair.

These strange things continued to happen for quite a while and at the same time each evening. The women, however, were rather hesitant to tell anyone because they were afraid that they wouldn't be believed. Then one evening, a neighbor who happened to be passing the Hines home heard the strange babbling sound coming from a rock. So he followed the noise and went on the porch. The front door was opened for him, without his even knocking. Because he saw no one around, he called out to make his presence known, and my aunt came from the back of the house and invited her neighbor inside. In answer to his question, my aunt told my neighbor of the strange recurring happenings. Although the neighbor was a physically strong gentleman, he couldn't shut the door when he tried. There seemed to be an even stronger force that couldn't be seen pushing against it. As he pushed, the babbling continued, and some of the noises became louder and more distinct. From time to time, Uncle Isum's voice became recognizable, but it was still difficult to recognize what he was trying to say,

The neighbor said that he must go, and he started preparing to leave. As he went out the door down the steps and out the walk, the babbling noise seemed to be right behind him, and then under his feet, and then just a step ahead of him, as if it were trying to lead his way. When he reached the tool shed, which stood on the corner at the end of the walk, the sound seemed to rush in where a shovel was hanging, and then back at the neighbor's feet. Finally, in desperation, the neighbor entered the shed, picked up the shovel, and followed the eerie choir, which suddenly took on a happy note, as if they were pleased with his actions.

The man trailed the voices into a wooded area where an old chimney stood, decaying. The babbling went hastily into the fireplace of the old chimney, become louder and even more excited. The man began to dig and soon stuck upon a hard object. When the object was lifted from its hiding place and handed to my aunt, who had followed with excitement, the noises stopped and were never heard again.

112. HELEN MOUNTAIN

I do know of a mountain called Helen Mountain. And I was up there, and you go up there, and you're supposed to say, "Helen" three times. You know, "Helen! Helen! Helen!" And there's a rumor that if you yell, "Helen, I'm the father of your baby," that you'll die in three days because her son or somethin,' when she was pregnant, she was killed or something' happened before the baby [was born]—I don't know.

But on the way back down the mountain, the window started goin' down. We were in an old Buick Skylark—probably an '85 model—so the only place is right in the middle to turn the windows up and down, you know. So I said to my friend Adam, "Adam, stop doin' this, man." And my friend in the back, Sean, he's freakin' out. So I push it back up, and it's pretty hard to push up. It wasn't like—you know, you just barely push an automatic window, and it'll go up. I was pushin' hard. It went up. We sat there for a minute. I said, "Stop it, Adam. Man, you're scarin' me!" So I pushed it back up, and this time, it was even harder. So I put my hand over it. And that's the only place. There wasn't even a place over the door. Just right there in the middle, it went down again. My friend Sean starts screamin' and yellin' and kickin,' "Let me out of the car! Let me out of the car!" So we get down to the bottom of the mountain, and we look at the odometer, and it went to zero. So we drove as fast as we could.

It's in Fletcher, North Carolina, where Fletcher Mountain is. It's pretty eerie. But they've built a big housing development up on the mountain now, and they've blocked it up. So that was pretty spooky.

113. CHANTELOUPE

It's [Chanteloupe's] just an old mansion that's supposedly haunted. It's in Flat Rock, North Carolina. It's like a plantation. I've had a couple of friends who have gone down around there. We rode down there one night. We drove up, and it wasn't any lights on, and when we were leavin,' the lights came on. And we went down, and there was a guy there, and we thought he was the one cuttin' it off. So the light went back off, and he went downstairs, and he said he was the only one there. Then when we came back up, the light in the top floor—it [the house] had three stories—came back on, and he was still at the door. It's kind of eerie. I don't know the full details [behind the history of the house].

114. The Brown Mountain Lights

I've had students who've said they've seen this one. In North Carolina in the mountains, there's a place called Brown Mountain. It's in the Great Smoky Mountain National Forest right on the Blue Ridge Parkway.

I have heard this sort of story from other parts of the country as well. There's this phenomenon called "The Brown Mountain Lights." At certain times of the year, apparently, there will be these lights, in the shape of balls, I assume, and if you're on the next mountain over looking at the panorama in front of you, the lights will kind of come up the side of the mountain and rise up in the air and disappear.

Of course, there are various spiritual accounts of what they are. They are Cherokees who were left behind on the Trail of Tears, and they are looking for their comrades. They are Cherokee women whose husbands were killed in battle, or they are Confederate soldiers who were lost, or whatever. It's [the phenomenon's] taken on ghostly associations.

115. The Paul Green Theater

There is in Chapel Hill an outdoor theater that Paul Green developed. He was a teacher there for years and years. The Paul Green Theater is on the edge of the campus in a very wooded area, and it is said to be haunted by the ghosts of Confederate soldiers from the War between the States, and we had a lodger—a woman who was a devout Roman Catholic—and she told us that she knew a woman, a friend of hers, who was also a devout Roman Catholic who was studying for final exams there at the Paul Green Theater—I don't know if this would have been the fall or spring term— and this was during the day, and she said she looked up from her books, and there was this shade of a person. In appearance, it was insubstantial. It didn't look like you or I, and she knew all of a sudden that this person was a spirit. She looked at him for a while, and he didn't say anything.

Then she asked him, devout as she was, if he was in purgatory and needed her prayers. Then she said this visitation disappeared.

116. THE DEVIL'S TRAMPING GROUND

I've had students who I can't say take it [this story] very seriously, but I have had students from Siler City, North Carolina, say that this story still has currency. My recollection is that it's some sort of municipal park in Siler City, North Carolina, about thirty miles southwest of Chapel Hill. I guess that it's not a whole lot bigger than Livingston, Alabama, really. In this park is what I gather to be a clearing in the shape of a circle. And the devil is said to haunt this place, and people are said to have spent the night there to test it [this story]. They will come away horrified and refuse to talk about what they have seen. And these are legends that have grown up around [the park]. People still talk about this place.

117. THE DEVIL'S CHAINS (WPA)

Dar was a big ole two story house in Scotland County dat I 'members as being hainted. Dey says dat 'fore I was borned, a long time 'fore I was borned, dat a man what was a evil man died dar.

He cussed, dey said, an' he says dat dere ain't no God, ner nothin'. He stole, and dey say dat he murdered too; I don' know 'bout dat.

Anyway, dis man dreamt one night dat de debil tol' him dat he was gwine ter chain him atter he died an' make him walk through de world wid dem chains rattlin' as a warnin' ter de rest o' de evil folks.

Well, shortly atter dis, on de night he was a corpse, his wife hyard footsteps in de room whar he was lyin,' and' she goes tiptoein' inter de room, an' dar she sees de ole debil puttin' little chains on her dead husband's ankles. She screams, an' de folks comes a-runnin,' but de debil am done gone, an' de chains am invisible ter all of dem but her.

De night atter he am buried, she hyard footsteps an' chains goin' clank, clank, clank. She hyars de do open, an' she sees her husband when he comes in. As he comes a-clankin' ater de bed, she 'low, "Git in de bed, honey." De man ain't hyard a word, least ways he ain't answered her a word, but he keeps a-walking' roun' an' roun' de bed. De next morning,' dat woman moves from dar.

De tale got out, an' other folkses tried ter stay dar, but de noise o' de clankin' chains was so loud dat dey can't sleep a wink. Dey'd git scared atter a while an' leave, but as dey'd run 'cross de yards, de clankin' chains an' de footsteps 'ud foller 'em. Folkses had quit trying ter stay dar 'fore I can 'member, but dem what pas dar at night claimed dat dey could still hyar de chains.

118. The Ghost from the Revolution (WPA)

In Green County, near Snow Hill, sets a big old house, that dates back before the Revolutionary War. Nobody has lived in it for a long, long time because of the ghosts of a woman and two British officers' "haints" the place.

The man who owned the house was a Whig, but his pretty young wife was a Tory. She didn't let her husband know this, however, and all of the time she was helping England, she played that she was helping the Colonies.

The man suspected nothing at all until he came home one night during the war. He saw a light in the kitchen, so he sneaked up in the chimney jam and listened. He soon found that two British officers were in his house drinking his cider. He was mad then, but as he listened, he heard his wife tell them something about the Rebels, and he heard them laughing and calling him an old fool. He waited as long as he could, then he walked in at the door, and with his old musket loaded, he killed all three of them.

Since that time, they say, the gun can be heard firing three times, a woman screams, and a man groans. Looks like if they were that old, they'd be too tired to groan anymore, don't it?

119. Ghost of Black Beard (WPA)

You know that Edward Teach or Black Beard as he is mostly called owned a mansion in Elizabeth City. It was built on a little elevation, an' an underground passage led to the Pasquotank River.

The house was surrounded by a high wall with barb-wire. The place had long been deserted by human beings, but rumor had it that it was frequented by horrible beings which were the spirits of Black Beard and his pirate companions.

The neighborhood tales said that the garden adjoining the old mansion was the burial place of the pirate's gold. It was also said that there was a great chest of diamonds and other booty found on the high seas. Even the tunnel was said to be lined with gold. Black Beard had used this tunnel as a means of getting to the ship quickly when danger threatened.

It was in July 1931 when a German by the name of Al Shueler, a Negro by the name of Charlie Mitchell, and I decided to invade the haunted castle in search of treasure. We drove the car near the fence and using burlap bags to cover the barbwire, we climbed over carrying a money rod which had broke all three of us.

We started the search, and the needle on the money rod turned down, and we grabbed our spades and fell to. We dug in silence for a second, but a whirring noise caused us to look up. Coming swiftly in the air from toward the river, we saw a swarm of white birds which at first appeared graceful, but on nearer view became suddenly repulsive. The birds screamed as they flew toward us, and we saw that they were indeed white vultures with human haids. Their screams grew more horrible, and as I stared at them, I noticed one with a long black beard and wicked glaring eyes. The spade dropped from my hand, and I turned to look at my companions, but they was flying across the garden. I screamed and followed 'em.

Charlie climbed on top of the fence, but the barbwire caught and held him fast. In front of my eyes, he slowly turned white, hair, face and hands. The German fell on his knees praying to all of the saints, and I said nothing until he asked God to bless the Kaiser. I said, "Damn the Kaiser! You need help worse than he does!"

After a minute, we found where we left the burlap on the wire, and the German and I climbed safely out. Then we went back to help Charlie. He was still on the fence, really whiter than I am, and his eyes were bulging and shining lights. I got him down at last, and I said, "Charlie, is it really you?"

"Yassir, Mr. John, hit's me dat is, iffen hit ain't another haint." When I turned back, the big German was on his knees. I heard him thank the Lord for our delivery, and then I heard him [the German] call the Kaiser's name.

120. A True Ghost Story

(WPA)

I was an overseer for an old woman, a widow, Mrs. Katy Barnes, in 1859. She had plantation and many slaves, but she was considered stingy. There were two houses, beside the slave quarters, the great house and the kitchen. Miss Katy lived alone in the great house, and she died as she lived.

Every morning, she was accustomed to rise early and go to the smoke house to give out the day's rations, but one morning, she did not appear. After waiting for several hours, her son who lived nearby forced his way into the house and found her dead in bed.

After her death, his wife and child, distant relatives of Miss Katy's, moved into the big house. The first night, just as soon as the lights were out and they were in bed, something began slowly to pull the bed clothes off of the bed. The man struck a light but could see nothing, so he blamed it on his imagination and went back to bed. Over and over again it occurred, not only that night but for several nights, and thinking of Miss Katy, they got nervous.

Finally, the man got so skeered that he jumped out of a window ten feet high, leaving his wife and baby to the mercy of the haint. They were not harmed, but they were scared sick. So they went away and never came back to live in the house.

The old house was used to keep feed for the stock, and it was my unpleasant job to cut up the fodder and hay and to shuck the corn. Nothing happened for a good long time, and my nerves got in fair condition, and I was beginning to believe that the tales about Miss Katy were made up.

One day while in the barn cutting up the fodder, I turned to pick up something, and there she stood in the doorway, so near that she could have touched me. Her eyes were closed, and the bandage was still under her chin, and she was as white as a sheet. She stood with folded arms, as still as a statue, while I looked for a way of escape.

One door was barred, and my eye took quick note that there was a small cat hole cut into it, one window, too high to reach, and the door she was at present occupying. In a flash, I thought that I could get through the cat hole, and I did, though I never knew how I could have got through a stout door as easily as I could have broken a pipe stem, I got out somehow.

I'm not ashamed to say that I ran, and I didn't turn around to see whether Miss Katy was still there or not. I went to her son's house, resigned at first, and began breathlessly to tell him of the occurrence, when Uncle Ned, Miss Katy's favorite servant, laughed and said, "Lawd, Marsa Sampson, dat ain't nothin' at all. I sees de ole missus ever' mornin' go ter de smokehouse an' den come back ter de great house wid de keys in her hand."

121. THE HEADLESS HORSE

(WPA)

The remains of the old house are located about five miles from Raleigh, going west about a mile from the Leeville Highway, on the left, just after going up the hill.

I had heard that the house was haunted, and I knew that you could only see spooks after twelve o'clock on dark nights and that you must be quiet. One night, Estelle and I were going home from a dance, and it was about twelve, so we decided to stop for fun and see if we could see a ghost.

I drove up in the yard, forgetting to turn around, and parked with lights off, and we sat quietly for a long while. Just as we had about decided to go on home, we heard a noise. I can not describe it because it was a cross between a woman's wail and a cat's meow. It was circling the car, and it hollered four times as it circled. We were paralyzed and had no thought of moving, when a shadow appeared, and then on Estelle's side of the car, I see it. It was a horse without a head, and the long, bloody neck was pressed against the window, and the moaning went on.

Estelle screamed, of course, and fainted, and just then, I came to life, and backed out over the rail fence, punctured a tire, and went up the road as fast as the car would take us.

122. A HAUNTED HOUSE (WPA)

About the year 1860, there stood a mile from U.S. 70, back of the present State Fair ground, a large colonial mansion, with its numerous slave cabins. The owner's name has been long forgotten.

Sambo, an aged slave, and his Sulkey lived in the cabin nearest to the big house, as they were house servants. Sulkey had small respect for Sambo and often called him "Slow Pokey," or "Lazy Bones," because he moved so slowly. The old marster's son, while on a drunken spree, killed ole

Sambo on the front steps one night, and about a month afterward, while Sulkey was sitting there, she saw Sambo comin' around the house. She gave one look and fled toward the big house yelling, "Sambo, Sambo, lemme alone now! I know I called yo' 'Slow Pokey,' but yo' shore has got Sulkey in a gallop now!"

Sulkey refused to live in the cabin again, and so it was torn down after it proved to be too ghost infested for anyone to occupy. The family moved away, and the big house was torn down, and a small house erected in its place. On the hill is an old cemetery, and by it, and in front of the house, is an old trail that is said to be the trail of Cornwallis when he went to meet Green. Voices can yet be heard talking in dull monotony on still summer nights, and the neighborhood children are afraid of the old road after dark. They say that Sam and Sulkey are still talking.

123. The Lady of the Rose Garden (WPA)

Once I lived at a house where there was a rose garden located to the left of the front door steps. I used to sit on these steps and wash my feet after a hard day's work on the farm. One night, about dusk, I was sitting there when I saw a lady come up the path and pause in the garden. I saw one white hand reaching out toward the roses, and then while I was looking down, she disappeared; at least, when I looked up, she was gone. For several evenings, I saw her, and it began to get on my nerves. One day, I mentioned the incident to a neighbor who had been in that country for several years.

He told me a story of a young lady who was always frail, living there. Her delight was in roses, he said, and she planted the garden there. Her lover died, and after that, she grew daily more delicate. Finally, she died. Her last request was to have the cream rose bush planted on her grave. This was not done, and so she was often seen in the garden and always near the green rose bush. I saw her often after that but was never afraid or nervous anymore. In fact, I considered her a friend and neighbor.

124. The Legend of the Spinning Wheel (WPA)

In a little cove on Salola Creek, near Pinnacle Cove there can be heard until today the muted whirl of a spinning wheel. Year in and year out, she sets her wheel in its tireless [rhythm] as she waits for her husband who left so many years ago. When these mountains were a wilderness, a brave young pioneer and his wife built a cabin in Pinnacle Cove. While he hunted game, she sat spinning at her wheel. One day, she waited for his dear footsteps at sundown, but he didn't come. Was it the night cry of some bird, or the weird wail of a cat that she heard? She listened. The echoes died away, and all was still. In the morning, searchers found only a few bones over in Pinnacle Cove, where a bear had devoured him. He was buried close by Salola stream.

Soft winds drift over the Cove, and the years have passed away quietly, but in the evening, there can be heard the purring of her wheel as when she waited in bygone days for her husband's return.

125. Hospital Ghosts (WPA)

I has been workin' in de hospital now for four years, an' so I has seen a heap of men die an' seen deir ghosts come back too.

De wust one was a feller what had T.B. He was always havin' hemorrhages an' callin' me durin' de night. Way in de night one time, he gits up widout callin' me an' goes to de bathroom where he has a hemorrhage, an' de next mornin' he was found dead on de bathroom floor. Since dat time, he has stayed in de bathroom. I see him in de same corner, an' I often puts him a chair, an' he sets in it.

Lester Williams who expected to die fer several moths 'fore he finally did often comes back, an' sometimes in de dead o' night he talks to me.

I works mostly at night, an' sometimes I looks outen de window, an' I sees de yard full o' men an' women walkin' in two's an' three's. I know dat dey is haints from de way dey floats along. A man walks on de west wall, an' dey says dat dat post am hainted. I doan know 'bout dat, but I 'specks dat it is.

A feller by de name o' Jack was in de hospital sick. He come ter de penitentiary for murderin' a woman, an' while she was dyin,' she promised ter make him pay.

One night, I set at de desk, an' everybody was asleep but me. I heard a little fuss, an' lookin' up, I spied a yaller-skinned gal wid a blue dress on goin' down de aisle. I set still till she walked up ter Jack's bed an' was fixin' ter choke him when I yelled at her. De minute I yells, she disappears, an' Jack sets up an' says, "I was dreamin' de funniest dream!" I hears him out, den I tells him dat what he dreamt was real 'cept dat de woman ain't choked him lak she started ter do. De next day, he was well-enough ter leave de hospital.

CHAPTER NINE

SOUTH CAROLINA

✝

126. THE GRAY MAN

I guess the main ghost story from South Carolina that I would put any credence in is the Gray Man. I have a friend whom I consider to be very trustworthy whose parents moved to Pawleys Island in the last fifteen years. And they have either seen him or know somebody who has seen him. The pattern with the Gray Man is that he comes before inclement weather. I guess that in modern times, the first rash of sightings of him were in 1954 with Hurricane Hazel. He just walks up and down the Grand Strand of the South Carolina coast, and he appears to people before a hurricane comes. And some say that if he appears to you, your property or your life will be spared. You know, with the advent of early detection radar, it's no longer that big a deal, but I guess that before that, it could be quite something to have your life saved this way.

The only reason that this tends to stick in my mind is because one tends to be skeptical of these kinds of things. I have never seen anything like that, but here's a person who is a fairly trustworthy source who tells me that his parents have seen it, so one tends to put more credence in it.

127. THE PHANTOM COACHMAN

I remember how terrified I was as a child by this story. It was about—I want to say Greenville or Spartanburg. A woman who lived in Charleston was visiting her ancestral home of some sort—some relation of her family. There had been some change taking place, either at home or with her condition or her family. She was coming back to this home after some period of time and spent several days there during a holiday, like Christmastime or Thanksgiving. And she was spending her nights in an upstairs bedroom, and at a certain time every night, she would wake up to hear this noise below. And this was in modern times. And it's peculiar that what she would see coming up the circular drive in front of her home right there below her window was a coach. And the coach would stop below her window, and she would see the coachman look up at her with a ghastly smile and assure her that there was "room for one more" in the coach. And this happened several days while she was there.

Now this woman was a physician, and she got called back on an emergency for a patient. The only way she could get there in time was to take a flight from the Greenville/Spartanburg Airport to Charleston. She called to see if there were any flights, and when she called the ticket agent, the agent said, "Yes, we have a flight that will get you there in time, and it just so happens that we have room for one more on that flight." Of course, that horrified her, and she refused to take it, and everybody was killed.

One of the things that they like to do in Japan is tell ghost stories, and when I told this story in Japan, they assured me that they had a story just like it there.

128. THE VANISHING HITCHHIKER

This one is set around Lake Meridian, which is west of Columbia, and it's where a pastor is driving into Columbia and picks up this little old lady at the side of a road. She gives him an address of where she lives in Columbia. You know, he's busy with sermon preparations or whatever, and he doesn't pay any attention to her for thirty minutes. When he finally recollects that she's there, he turns around and looks to talk to her in the back seat, and she's gone.

So he goes to the address she gave him in Columbia, and the person inside says, "Yes, that's our mother who died five years ago, and she always reappears at this time each year. And Cindy [my wife] says this story is very common in Japan. She also says that she has heard this same story about the White Rock area.

129. LAND'S END

This one's about a place called Land's End in Beaufort County, South Carolina. It's thirty minutes from Charleston and Savannah. The story goes—I don't know how long it's been— there's a bus driving late at night with a bunch of kids and everything. The bus lost control and wrecked in Land's End.

[Now] you can go out there, and on some nights, there's a light that will appear like—I don't know—about seven feet off the ground. A big old light. And it will appear at a tree, and it will travel all the way down to a church, and what the story is is that it's the bus driver that's looking for the kids because apparently, everybody died [in the wreck].

You can go out there—and my mother says she has actually been out there to sit and drink on the double yellow line—to sit and wait and watch it [the light]. You can put your car right there and travel underneath the light. My grandmother said it could be swamp gas, but my mom once told me that they [scientists] have studied it and done everything, and it's not swamp gas. If it were swamp gas, why would it appear at one place? Every time, that's all it does. It hovers, and then it travels down to the church, and that's it.

130. AD'S PLAT-EYE (WPA)

Plat-eye, yas'm. De ole folks is talk 'bout plat-eye. Dey say dey takes shape ob all kind de critter—dawg, cat, hawg, mule, varmint, an' I is hear tell ob plat-eye takin' form ob 'gator. I ain' see dem 'scusin wan little time. You know dat leetle swampy place behind de Parsonage? Dem does call dat parsonage Branch. Well, wan time—I hab mah bloom on me en was clammin' dem days—en de tide been berry late in de ebenin'. Hit was dusky dark when I hit de Parsonage Lane—light dusky dark. I wasn't feared not 'tall. You see, ez I say, I hab meh bloom on me in dem days. En I pass de Cap'n's barn en stable. Dere he was wid Allan son milkin'. En I say, "Do ebens, Capn'n Bill!" En he gin me back ma word [replied, "Good Evening"]. En I bawg true dat deep white sand en I passes de graveyard entrance en I leabes de open en enters dem dark woods, whey de moss wabe low en bresh in yo' face. En I bin tink 'bout plat-eye. De mine come ter me it was good time tuh meet 'em.

Den I bresh dem weepin' moss aside, en I trabble de wet mud in mah bare feets en mah shoe bin tie ter mah girdle string. En, when I bin come ter de foot lawg, I could see same ez I see you now. I could see de foot lawg—dat same ole cypress what been dere now. He blow down in dat las' big September gale. En I been see Mr. Bull Frawg hit de water—"ker-plunk!" En a cooter slide ofen de lawg at meh feets. En, Miss, ah 'clare ter Gawd, I bin fer look up at dat cooter en den I turn mah eye up en deh was a cat—black cat wid he eye lak balls ob fire, en he back all arch up, en he tail twissin' en er switchin,' en he hair stan' on end. He move backward front ob me 'cross dat cypress lawg. En he bin big. He bin large ez mah little yearlin' ox. En I talk ter 'em en try fer draw close. En I say ter 'em, "I ain't fer fear nuttin'. Ain' no ghos'! Ain' no hant! Ain' no plat-eye. Ain' no nuttin'!"

En I'se try fer sing, "He carry me tru many ob danger. Because he fust lub me. He guard 'gainst hant en plat-eye. Because he fust lub me."

En dat plat-eye ain' gib me back mah word. He mube forward, en he tail swish en swish same lak big moccasin tail when he lash de rushes. En de sound come to me, "Child ob Gawd, doan you show no fear. . . ."

En den de mine come ter me, "De Lawd heps dem what heps deysef'." When I raise up mah rake en I come right 'cross dat critter haid. Ef dat had bin real cat, I'd er pin him er dat lawg. My rake bin bury deep, en de lawg hold 'em. En I 'clare ter Gawd, Miss, dat he up en prance right on der mah feets, dem eyes burnin' holes in me, en he tail swish, swish lak ole Sooky tail when de flies bad. En me ire bin raise. I fer struggle wid mah rake en de lawg loosen he grip, en I fer pray, "Gib Addie strent, O Gawd!"

En down I come straight tru dat critter middle. He stummick ball up same lak de leetle puffer toad-fish. But dat critter ain' feel mah lick. En I'se ressel lak Jacob wid de angel. I bin strong en hab mah bloom on me. It ain't 'vail nuttin'.

No, man. Mr. Plat-eye jest ez peart en frisky ez 'fore he bin hit. En I 'buse 'em en I cuss 'em en I say, "You debbil! Clare mah paat'!"

En ef dat critter didn't paw de air en jus' rise up dat big bamboo vine en me fer hi 'em ebery jump! So, Miss, den I tin, "Sinner, leble dat lawg?" Mah mind come tuh me, "Child ob Gawd, trabbel de woods paat'!"

En I turn back en mek hast. En I hit dat pat'. En I ain' bin tarry, en jes ez I was gibbin' Gawd de praise fer deliver me, dere dat cat! Dis time, he big ez mah middle size ox, en he eye bin blaze! En I lam en I lam. En dat rake hand bin wire en bin nail on. En jes ez I mek mah la' lam, dat critter rise up fore meh eyes, en dis time he bin big ez Cousin Andrew full grown ox. En he vanish up dat ole boxed pine ez you quits de deep woods. yas'm. I ain' b'leeve in plat-eye twil den, but I minds mah step since dem days.

131. THE SULPHUR RING (WPA)

I could tell when I near de door he been in dere, eben before' I put de key in de lock," she said, "My skin git prickly, and de flesh crawl on de back of my neck. I gone in, and I hear um rustle round. I ain't bodder to talk do [though] I mad t'rough. I grab de matches as quick as I kin, and I light two in each hand and swing dem 'round till I mek a streak like de comet tail. De speerit bin in sich a hurry to get out I hear um knock de houn' out eeself on de window sash when he gone t'rough. He 'fraid I gwine ketch um in dat sulphur ring. Soon as he gone t'rough I slam de window shet and lock um good. Den I light de light and look 'round to see what debbultry he do, but I can't find nothing, and I think to myself, "I been in luck dis time; I git home too soon for your."

It been a Saturday night, and while de water been hot for my baat [bath], I read my Bible. Ob cose, you know, I dan't rightly read reading, but I could hold de book and look at de page and say some de verse I hear in church. De whole time I duh wash, I been t'inking how good de bed going to feel. I got piller fer bed and a clean sheet. I put on my clean gown and outen delight; den I step in de bed. When I stretch out to enjoy de feel, I declare to Gawd if a pin didn't rake de whole side of my laig. Dat debbul of a ghost put um dere.

132. HANTS AND GHOSTS (WPA)

They's hant then they's ghost. Hant is a plat-eye. And a plat-eye some those old-timey people hat been ded a long time. Ghost just uh evil spirit.

Mattie see 'um. Well, first she saw, uh—let me see what color the cat was now—she saw a white cat, and next thing she saw was a big old white dog with red eye. Then after she saw all this, she leave out the house and was going next door to people she had farm with; and when she had step down the step and came out the door, she saw a woman dressed in white and ain't got no leg and had 'e arm fold up [at] the corner of the house.

Then as she was going off to Miss Jane house, she had the baby in her hand, and the boy was walking, and when she get a little piece down the road, she saw a woman standing upside the pump, and it followed her and walked between the little boy and her. And she told the little boy, "Look er there, Junior! Look at that ghost!" The little boy couldn't see it. And it follow her right on till it got jist about ten steps from the house. Then he

[she] turned 'round and went back. Mattie gone on to Miss Jane. She see that woman again. She and Gabe can see 'um and Alice Knox. She can see 'um better than all.

She see that same woman and a man, too. Somebody had got shot at the gate of that house. They called the place "Jack place."

133. The Haunting at Hull Street (WPA)

I was living at 123 Hull Street when I was terribly frightened by something [that] nearly took all of my nerves away. The people with whom I lived told me not to go out and stay out late at night, but I thought they were selfish and jealous, and I did not pay any attention to what they said. Night after night, I went out and stayed until 12 o'clock. Then one night came when my going was stopped without having to be told.

The house in which I lived is next to Avery Institute with a yard of beautiful shrubbery which makes it very haunted-looking at night. Very seldom are people seen passing in that somewhat secluded section of Charleston at night. Night after night, I would be the only one walking alone. Then on an eventful night just as I turned to go into the side entrance to my room in the rear, in the tree under which I had to walk, I saw a cat, which did not frighten me until it turned to a calf of about two years old. My hair stood straight on my head, and I became so weak that my voice was just above a whisper. Drops of perspiration fell from me. When I had recovered from the shock, I ran, and the animal must have followed me; I could hear it galloping behind me as I ran home a few rods from the scene. Looking back as I almost burst down the door, the peculiar thing was no longer visible.

134. Where Are You Going? (WPA)

There was once a young man about 18-years-old who lived in Mount Pleasant, South Carolina. His mother and father always spoke to him about staying out late at night. One night, he went to a girl friend's house and stayed until two o'clock in the morning. On his way home, he felt his hair rising. He saw a white object and started to run. He ran through the cotton field, looked back and saw the object following him, so he kept on running. When he looked back the second time, he heard a voice, "Where are you going?" He ran until he got to the next corner and heard the same voice again, "Where are you going?" So he said, I am going home. The voice asked, "Is your shoe sole good?" The man kept on running, and the object kept on following him. Then he came to an oak tree. A limb fell off the tree, and the voice said, "That one missed you, but the other one will get you." The other limb fell and hit him. He ran so fast that he knocked down the gate going into the yard. His mother heard the noise, and she came out to see what was the trouble. All he could say was, "A ghost! A ghost!" He was so frightened that his mother had to give him aromatic spirits of ammonia to quiet his nerves.

135. TOKENED (WPA)

Now I've heard my mother tell about that. Her grandmother was tokened! Her grandmother's brother worked turpentine. Rode the woods. He hadn't been home in eighteen months, and Ma's grandmother got a letter as how he was comin' home. He hadn't been home in over a year. And she read the letter and told everybody as how he said he was comin' home.

The day finally then come before the day he was due home. Mama's grandma, she was settin' out in the shade under a tree in the yard, and she seen somebody walkin' 'round the house corner, and she looked up, and it was her brother, and he went on 'round behind the house. So she called his name and said: "Come here! I'm 'round here!" And when he didn't come, she went on 'round the house, and there wasn't nobody nor nothin' there.

When her Pa come to the house, she told him they was goin' to hear bad news. Sure enough, next day, a letter come sayin' her brother was killed and throwed in the river.

This was way back there in turpentine days, and he rode horseback all over a big scope of woods. An somebody killed him and throwed him in the river. Mama used to always tell how her grandmother was tokened.

136. A TORMENTED MAN (WPA)

On John's Island, South Carolina, there was a man who was walking for many days, and occasionally, he stopped to rest when he had walked a long distance. So he stopped, stopped and stopped, for his journey was a long one. While he was going through a thick wooded section, he thought to rest again, so he did. There was an old oak covered with moss under which he stood a minute and then sat down. When he had wiped the perspiration from his brow, he said, "This journey is a long one." The object on which he sat and thought to be an oak tree, but instead, it was an aged rattlesnake, which said, "You bet it is." When the man turned around to see who was commenting, he saw the snake looking at him. As tired as he was, he took to his feet and did not stop running until he was out of the woods.

Then he stopped near where a cow was grazing, but he did not see the cow. Then he said aloud as though talking to someone, "I have never yet heard of an oak tree talking." The cow said, "Me neither." The man turned again to see who was commenting, but no one was to be seen, but there stood a cow that looked him right in the eye. He took to his feet again and ran almost a mile. Then when he was too exhausted to run any more, he stopped to rest. He was sitting no longer than five minutes when he said, "I have never heard of an oak tree talking nor a cow." At a little distance from where he sat stood a dog from which came the words, "Me neither." When the man turned and saw no one but the dog, he got up, this time more frightened than ever and took to his feet. The poor man ran and ran until his breath was almost gone. The man stopped near a ditch by which was a large rock. The man, still puffing and blowing, said, "In my whole life, I have not read nor heard of an oak tree talking nor a cow talking nor of a talking dog. Just as so as he was through, the rock said, "Me neither." The poor man started to rise but was too wore out. And so he died.

137. The Lady of the River

(WPA)

Early one winter morning, I was awakened by a peculiar noise in the near-by river. I lived right at the river's edge. I heard on the river, Splash! Splash! Splash! as though someone were casting shrimp or a sea-horse trying to catch fish. But the sound was more mysterious than that of a fisherman or a sea-horse. I was frightened; I went and flung the door open. When I looked into the river, there stood a woman dressed in white with part of her garment spread over the water as though it were a smooth, polished floor or a sheet of glass. Then all of a sudden, she took her head off and threw it toward me, and in a twinkle of an eye, she was gone into space. I went back to bed but did not sleep for fear of my two sons being tormented by the ghosts. The next two days, my healthy little boy died without any pain so far as anyone knew.

138. THE TALL GHOST (WPA)

In rural districts, the people usually say that after six o'clock in the evening, ghosts leave graveyards to go walking during the night. Some are said to be good and some bad. Two are usually together, a good one and a bad one. When one is frightened by a ghost, one is believed to have strayed from the good manner of living.

It was about 7:30 one winter night in the country when a friend and I were going to visit another. We had to cross a ditch which led to a long line of thickly clustered bushes and vines. When we were approaching this thicket, and about five feet from its entrance used by pedestrians, there appeared in the center of the path a man about nine feet tall whose feet were about a foot from the ground. This man had no face but stood erect like a soldier. We grabbed each other and began to run and scream when all of a sudden, a strong wind came and blew us to the ground before we could raise our voices high enough to be heard. It was about ten o'clock when we were discovered by a group of people passing while our nerves were still shattered.

This was not far from a graveyard. When we told of the tall man we saw, an old lady told us that that man with his feet above the ground was said to be the tallest man in the world when he was alive and that he guarded that place, for it was there that he had lost a girl he had loved.

139. SPECTRAL HAMMERING

(WPA)

Some carpenters were once sent to Landrum, South Carolina, to repair some houses which were to be occupied by mill employees. The houses were located in one section of the village and close together. It was noticed that the window glasses were broken out in all the houses except one, and in this house, none at all were broken. Upon inquiry as to how this one house had escaped injury done by mischievous boys, it was learned that the house was haunted. They were told that the man who had lived there a year or two before and was a maker of boxes had died after taking some laudanum while on a drinking spree. Since then, his spirit would return at night, and no one would go around there.

The carpenters made the necessary repairs to the house, and a family moved into it. The day after they moved in, they moved out again, stating that they heard the tapping of a hammer during the night as if boxes were being made. The carpenters were reluctant to believe in the house being haunted, so they returned the following night to investigate for themselves. They had not been in the place long before they heard the tapping noise, which sounded like a person striking a light stroke to start a nail, then a louder noise as if the nail were being driven into a box. After hearing this, they decided to not investigate the source of the tapping any further and left immediately for home.

140. Will-o'-the-Wisp (WPA)

It was a warm night during the winter of 1928. About dusk, we went out into the front yard to refresh ourselves and to take a little stroll down to the ferry after having finished the evening meal.

Buddy Watt, Gertrude and I were the only ones who went out into the yard. When we got out in front of the gate in the road, I saw a light in the shape of a ball not far away. It seemed to be about ten or fifteen feet above the ground and not far in front of us. We talked about it and wondered what it was. None of us knew, and so Bubby Watt and I decided to see what it was. Gertrude was not as interested as we were, so she went back to the fire.

It was a dark but a starry night and just cool enough for a light coat. Buddy Watt and I started out to get to that strange light. We followed it across the road and into a plowed field. I got my shoes all full of dirt and mud. We seemed to never get right up on the light. It kept the shape of a bell and stayed the same distance from the ground until we got to a lumber pile. It seemed to float over the huge pile of lumber. We went past the lumber until we reached a gully. We had gone about two miles without reaching the ball of light or will-o'-the-wisp.

141. Aunt Martha's Hant

(WPA)

Man, yes man! Hant was there in Tom Pryor house all right! Wouldn't give me no rest-tall, -tall! Turrible. Come in there and have more noise on that stove than enough. The noise sound peculious. He always come in the kitchen part. He stays in the kitchen part to the stove and cut up all he raziness in there. Don't come to the big half of the house and talk. Have more rattle up on that stove! Sound like he goin' break up the stove! Francis Gadsden and Georgie sit up with me more night than one for company.

They tell me when Tom Pryor die, they been a time in that house. He die a wicked death. Something terrible. They tell me they have to take and tie him on the bed! I could-a been there when he die. Everybody else been there. But I didn't choose to been there. If I'd a-seen how he die, I'd not a stay in that house.

One night, sumptin' talk to me in my room there from 'hind my room door. I got mad, and I say: "I want you to talk again so's I can hear you!" It didn't no more! Not that night. I been 'tween sleep and wake. And he talk kinder funny two time. And I say: "I want you to talk one more time so I can catch the voice!" Never had such a thing happen to me in my life before since I born from my Ma! Everybody tell me: "Martha, you got a mind to stay there!"

I gone two time to Parkersville and tell the root doctor good how that hant done me and he say: "Auntie, tell you, you wuk [work] dis here! Wuk you knee! [kneel down and pray!].

And I gone home and done some prayin'. If I didn't a-have the Lord in me, he would-a kill me!

CHAPTER TEN

Tennessee

142. The Orpheum Theater

Mary [the Orpheum's ghost] died in some kind of accident somewhere in Memphis, in either a street car accident or by a fall in 1921. I have never seen Mary, but I have gotten a spooky, cold feeling when I am in the balcony. Those who have seen her say she is about 12 years old, dressed in a white blouse or school uniform without shoes and has long, dark braids. She has been accused of unscrewing light bulbs and crying and laughing. She usually makes an appearance in the early morning hours when someone is playing the theater's organ. The ghost rarely appears during a performance.

We think Mary died suddenly and doesn't know what to do with herself. A lot of people, when they are going to die . . . really don't want to leave, but they do. They can't go forward or back and they get stuck. And the longer they stay, the harder it gets. Mary's nourishment is a certain energy left in the theater.

143. The Ghost of Walker's Valley

The area that we were in was just outside of Cades Cove, which is in the northwestern part of the Great Smoky Mountains National Park. We had an environmental school—we had dormitories, a cafeteria. We brought kids there basically for a week at a time. It's still in operation. Tremont is located at Walker's Valley. Will Walker settled that area in 1867. It's right in the middle part of a little river. And the ridge on either side is Lumber Ridge.

There's an interesting story. Will Walker came in there in 1867. His wife was Nancy—Nancy Taylor Walker. They had four children. Two of them died. One of the stories is supposed to deal with the two that died. He had two wives—common-law wives: Maude Stennet and Mary Ann Moore. They had a cabin—in fact, I lived where their original cabin was. You had the Maude Stennet cabin over here [pointing] and across that little pond he built the Mary Ann Moore cabin. And they built a little cabin. Mary Ann Moore's brother had built a little cabin up on the ridge there, and that became a school. I've got the diary of the original teacher [from that school]. Of course, all the kids from that school were Stennets, Moores, and a few Walkers. There were some people from the valley too. It was an interesting place to be.

Nancy Taylor had four children, and two of them died. And, of course, they had their own family cemetery up there. They were buried up on a little ridge above Walker Valley. In fact, it was Walker Ridge, which was basically right where our dorm sat. There were stories over the years. It was a Boy Scout Camp long before it became an Environmental Education Center. There were stories over the years of Nancy Walker roaming and looking for her children. Sightings of a woman all in white, floating around and looking for her children. This happened outside the dormitory. A lot of people claim that they have seen it. The story goes that that was Nancy Walker looking for her children that were buried up on that ridge. Once the cabin became a schoolhouse, it later became a church, and the graves are there from those folks. That was later. The original graves are supposedly up near the area of the dorm.

144. GHOSTLY CRIES

Another story that goes along with that is the fact that Mary Ann Moore lived across the river. There wasn't a bridge across that river. All they had across that river was a footlog. Of course, the kids went back and forth across that footlog. And one rainy, misty night—of course, everything has to do with a rainy, misty night—one of the Moore children fell off that log and drowned. And this is interesting because they claim that still on those rainy, misty nights that you can hear her crying and wailing. We lived right next to that river—wasn't more than just a short walk from it. We were where that original cabin was. And one night we did hear it—we could have sworn that it was a child crying. It was a rainy, misty night, and we'd go all over with a flashlight and find nothing, and I'm sure that it was an animal of some kind, but I can understand where they got the story from. Supposedly she cries on those rainy, misty nights where she fell into the river. This story was told thirteen years ago, and I'm sure they're still telling it.

145. The Hermit of Lumber Ridge

The hermit of Lumber Ridge is another one they tell. If you follow a trail that goes up the ridge, [it] follows an old oxen trail that used to go through the valley. There's an old cabin site up there. A depression is all that you can tell it was there. And, of course, the story of Lumber Ridge goes that the railroad came into this area, and they were logging this whole area. There were a lot of railroad people here around the early 1900s. One of 'em was missing. And a lot of stories in the park have to do with people missing.

But anyway, there was a railroad man missing, and they were looking for him, and they knew that he had a tattoo on his arm, a tattoo of Smokey Railroad. They were searching and searching, and the fellas from one of the towns in Tennessee came up in the mountains looking for him. And they came upon this cabin on the trail, and there was an awful stench from the cabin. There was no one there; they knocked, and they couldn't find anybody. They went in; there was still no one there. But they could see that there was a trap door [leading] to the cellar. So they went down, and all they found was some smoked meat, and that was where they were getting the smell from. As they started out, they bumped into one of the hams that was hanging there. They looked up, and there was a tattoo.

They knew who lived there; they called him the hermit of Lumber Ridge. As they came up, he was comin' in. When they saw him, and he saw them, he took off and fell down Lumber Ridge, and they could hear him rollin' over and over. Finally, [he] splashed into the river. And, of course, the story goes that they never did find him, never did find his body, and now anytime you're out on Lumber Ridge on these misty nights, and you hear something comin' down through that ridge in the woods makin' a lot of noise, it's the hermit of Lumber Ridge lookin' for more food. That's the only cannibalism story I know!

146. THE WHITE DOVE

There's a lot of stories about people gettin' lost in the park and never bein' seen again. The general feeling was that if you got lost in the park, you went to hell. The rhododendron and laurel thickets were called "hells," you see.

On the other side, there was a family that lived there named Kate, and they had a little girl called Mary. But over this ridge and down below—and this has to do with the feuds that go on, especially [between] highlanders and lowlanders—and there was a feud goin' on between the people livin' on the ridge there that Mary's family was a part of, and the people down in the valley known as "sugar makers" because of the maple trees. But there had been a feud goin' on between them for years. The people in the highlands would let their cattle go down there, and one day, they got together and decided they would burn out the lowlanders—set a fire and go down the ridge and just burn 'em out. Well, the wind changed, and instead of the fire goin' down, it started goin' back. It went back over the ridge toward the top of the ridge back toward Walker Valley. Mary was sittin' under a beech tree; beech typically are hollow. So the fire came up and went through that beech tree, and, of course, she didn't know that, and finally, it burned through the top, and the top of the beech tree fell off and fell on Mary.

So they picked up the girl—she was about five or six—and carried her back. Her grave is still at the cemetery at the school. You can go see her if you want to see her grave. So anyway, they carried her back to a little cabin, and the cabin's site is there if you know where to look for it, and the story goes that as far as the supernatural goes that they brought her in that afternoon and put her in a bed, and she was severely burned and injured from the limb fallin' on her, and that afternoon, late afternoon, a white dove lit on the windowsill, and the dove sat there for three nights and three days, and eventually, it flew away, and when it did, Mary was dead. When we talked to the kids about this, they said that it, the white dove, represented her soul, and especially her innocent soul.

147. The Haunted Cave

We used a cave there in the park, and there was a ghost story with it. Back around the early 1900s before the park came in, there was a cave around Cades Cove. And it was frequently used by kids, and, of course, they weren't supposed to. The parents told the kids, "Stay out of it. You'll get lost." Supposedly, these caves extend all the way up into Kentucky, and in their vast expanses, it was very easy to get lost. And anyway, these two young boys—Billy and Johnny, I'm not sure—went into the cave against their parents' wishes, and they got lost. And eventually, Billy found his way out, and Johnny never did, and his spirit still haunts the cave. You go into that cave now back into the back, you get into total darkness. You can at times, if his spirit wanders back that way, you can still hear him hollerin' for help. So we always took the kids back to the back of the cave and turned the lights out to see if they could hear him call for help.

I was director of the Environmental Education Center. I can get you a picture of Will Walker and all of his wives and all twenty-three of their kids.

148. The Bell Witch

John [Bell] had been courting Miss Kate Batts; they were planning to get married, but for some reason, they broke off the engagement. After a while since they had been broke up, John married another woman. Kate was very upset about their marriage, and she told John she would break up the marriage. She pulled all sorts of lies and dirty tricks on them to break it up. John could not take it any longer because his marriage was being destroyed by her. He told his wife the only way to get rid of her was to kill her. He got Kate over to his house and kept her captive until she starved to death. Then he buried her a ways behind the house in the woods. Before Kate died, she told John she would come back and make his life miserable. She said she would never let him live in peace.

After Kate's death, John was forever tormented. The ghost would scratch his body until it bled. Sometimes, he would barely make it home, taking off his boots and pouring out the blood. Kate never did let him live in peace, so John thought if he moved from the house where he killed her that she might not bother him anymore. He built a home down the road from his old home, but she did not stop the tormenting. John finally moved to Louisville, where he died. He died from the consistent torture which Kate put him through.

149. THE MYSTERIOUS CHURCH HOUSE (WPA)

On the road between Jacksboro and Oliver Springs stands an old church house which is surrounded by mystery. The doors are always open, and no one has ever been able to fasten them so securely that they will not open, apparently of their own accord. The people in the vicinity believe there is some great significance to the fact that the church always stands with wide open doors as if it were welcoming the people who pass that way.

A young girl in high school who doubted the stories she had heard became so curious that she thought she would test this unseen power that always opened the door. One day, she took a strong wire and a heavy beam of wood. With these, she fastened the door so firmly that it would have been difficult for human hands to unwind the wire and remove the barrier.

She went her way feeling sure that the door would remain closed. In about four hours, she returned; to her astonishment, the door stood wide open, with the wire and barring rod lying on the floor. She no longer doubted. For some reason, not explainable in terms of human understanding, the door refused to remain closed.

150. THE GHOST OF COAL CREEK (WPA)

Five miles east of Coal Creek, there once stood an old dilapidated house, which, though it was for many years not inhabited by human beings, was, nevertheless, not vacant; for the spirit of a good woman walked within it.

Almost half a century ago, a man and a woman lived alone in this house. They had no children and kept no servants. The woman was kind, beautiful, and good. Her husband was just the opposite. His nature was cruel, wicked, and vindictive. His temper was always on trigger's edge, and no one knew what he would do when aroused.

The good woman had prayed and hoped that she might influence him to improve his ways. When he was harsh and unkind to her, she would smile bravely and return his abuse with meek submission.

At times, when he seemed to be more amiable than usual, she would counsel with him; for she loved him in spite of his faults. Usually, she was very tactful when approaching him; and on a few occasions she almost believed that she had been able to make some impression on his stubborn disposition. But his outward calmness was only the closed crater of an inward seething volcano that eventually erupted.

One evening, when she was more earnest in her pleadings than usual, the dormant volcano became active and poured forth its molten lava of wrath. The man, in his frenzied state of mind, murdered the woman, believing that he would thereby be rid of the one person who was always reminding him of his wickedness.

However, his real torture had only begun, for soon the spirit of his murdered wife returned. Her mournful, pleading voice could be heard as her ghost wandered about the house. The mysterious noises became so frequent, that the husband, not wishing to be bothered by his dead wife's admonitions, disappeared from the community.

No one would ever live in the house, and many would walk miles out of their way to avoid passing it. They believed that the woman's spirit was still pleading with her wayward husband. In death, as in life, his salvation was her sole concern.

151. The Headless Horror

(WPA)

It happened on the second of October in the year 1899. On this particular night, a group of young people went to a party at the old Locke Place, which is four miles southeast of Summertown and two miles northeast of Henryville. The night was dark and very still. Only a few stars were to be seen between the clouds. The stars were so few that the young people could have counted them. However, no one did, for each believed the superstition that if one counts the stars, he will drop dead when the last star is numbered.

This group of young people, about 15, farmers mostly, were going from Henryville to the party. On the way, they had to pass through a wooded section called Horror Hollow. As they drew near this spot, all felt nervous.

Now, the party was over, and the young people were on their way home.

But just before leaving the party, Robert Fulton had twirled a chair around on one leg. Therefore, everybody knew that some bad luck would come to someone in the group. The nervous tension was now keener than when they were on their way to the party.

As they again drew near the flat, they began to sing in order to keep from hearing the whistling of the falling leaves. The group became separated. Seven of them were some distance ahead as they entered Horrow Hollow. Those who were in the lead made their way through the Hollow without anything going wrong. They were waiting on the opposite side of the flat when the horrible thing happened.

On the left of the road, abut 200 feet, there arose from a thick grove of bushes a series of barks and blood-chilling shrieks. A light was seen to rise, and then to fall. Again, it rose and fell. Finally, it emerged from the fringe of oaks and revealed a group of hunters.

The hunters ran up to the group of young people, who stood rooted to the spot. The leader of the hunters said, "We saw a figure dressed in black and absolutely headless."

The girls began to gather in the middle of the road and to try to comfort each other. Dogs with tails down, slinked around their masters. The youngest of the hunters was as pale as a ghost. The hunters and young people were standing in the road discussing "the man with no head" when they heard a mocking laugh that did not sound like a human's voice. It came from the bushes. The entire crowd turned to stare at the dreaded spot. Then they heard the "thump, thump, thump" of someone walking. The leader of the hunters threw his light in the direction of the sound.

Now, into the circle there came a horrible figure that was covered with blood. In his hands, he carried his head. He went limping across the road and disappeared into the night.

Terror seized the group. They bolted in every direction. Some of the girls fainted. The dogs tuck their tails and, howling with fear, went for home like a streak of lightning. The same spine-chilling laugh was heard to the right. Then there was a silence as still as death. The two groups went home, wishing their eyes and ears had deceived them, but they knew that their experiences were real.

All these young people have handed down this story and their superstitions to their children and their grandchildren.

152. THE BIRD-MAN (WPA)

There is a house in Gainesboro, now occupied by Mr. J. C. Reeves and family, that is said to be haunted. For the past few years, I have heard very little said about this house, but older residents who have formerly occupied this place tell of many things that have happened there. Strange noises like the clanking of chains are heard at all hours of the night. A few years ago, two different people saw a strange apparition in an upstairs room of this house. Neither was aware that the other had seen it. The apparition appeared about the height of an average man. Its body was about the size of that of a man. Its feet, legs, arms and hands were very similar to those of a bird, and it had small beady eyes and a long beak or bill like that of a bird. One of the people who saw it said it beckoned to her to follow it into a room. When she did so, the apparition disappeared behind a dresser. Another person told approximately the same story.

153. THE HAUNTED CAVE (WPA)

There is a story which was told to me by my grandmother before her death and concerns a haunted cave. This cave was located on the road which led from the mouth of Roaring River to Gainesboro. The road has been changed long since that time, and the cave filled up and destroyed. It seems that anyone passing the mouth of this cave any afternoon about sundown could see this apparition. It was a little girl apparently between the ages of four and six years. [Grandmother said], "She had golden brown hair, big blue eyes and the sweetest childish voice." She would be seen sitting on a rock in the mouth of the cave. As the rider passed, she would run out and holler, "Stop there! Stop there!" Many times, horses would become frightened and run away. One time, a person stopped to talk to the little girl, and she mounted his horse behind him and rode a long distance. The person never knew when she dismounted or where she went.

154. THE WOMAN IN BLACK
(WPA)

It is a belief among many of the older and more superstitious people of the county that the spirits of departed loved ones are often seen near the bed of people that are near death and that invariably the person will die on that night. A few years ago, a very prominent citizen of Gainesboro was lingering between life and death. On the night of his death, a number of his friends and relatives were gathered at his bed-side. Just a few minutes before he departed this life, a woman dressed in black came into the room and sat down on the bed beside him. She wore an old-fashioned sun-bonnet, and it was impossible to see her face. She sat there for some sec-onds with her hand on the dying man's brow and suddenly disappeared as would a shadow. She made no audible sound. It was later learned that an apparition, presumably the same, was seen by a number of people prior to her entrance into the room of the sick man. She came from the direction of what is known as the Gibson Hollow. She was said to be walking with a slow but steady step. She came down the hollow road, on down the main highway for a distance of some three-quarters of a mile, entered the house, and was gone. The same night just a few minutes later, the man died. One would have a hard time convincing many of the older people that she was not the spirit of some of his departed loved ones.

155. THE GHOST OF MOLLIE WOODRUFF

Two years ago I had a friend, Margo Ramsey, visiting me and helping catalog the costumes [at the Fontaine House]. Her daughter, Michelle, came down to where we were working and said someone had followed her down the stairs. But when she looked, no one was there.

Another day, Margo said that someone behind her said, "My dear." But when she turned around, no one was there.

One day I was escorting a visiting woman on a tour. As she walked into the bedroom, she said, "Oh, what a delightful room." Then she got very white and began trembling. The woman described herself as a medium, and she informed me that Mollie's room was arranged incorrectly and that the bed was on the wrong wall.

My own experience is confined to a door slamming. A friend and I were preparing for a party when we heard the door slam. I called out, [but] no one answered. Then my friend said, "Oh, that's just Mollie. She always comes back when we are getting ready to have a party."

[According to the story], Amos Woodruff knew that his daughter was about to marry and apparently planned the second floor of the house ac-cordingly. There was a master suite for him and his wife, Phoebe. Then across the hall was another suite for his daughter [Mollie] and her hus-band, and beyond that a nursery. Down the hall was another bedroom for the nurse or governess. [Mollie's] first and only child by Wooldridge, a son, was born and died almost immediately in the bedroom at the rear of the second floor, now called the Cabbage Rose room. This was February 13, 1875, and in May of that year, her young husband became ill on a fishing trip, was brought home and died within two or three days. Mollie lived as a widow with her parents until 1883 when she married James Henning. They also occupied the suite Woodruff had set aside for his daughter. On January 13, 1885, Mollie's and Henning's only child died on its day of birth. Mollie died 32 years later while she was visiting her younger sister.

156. A Ghost in the House

[Before buying our house] I asked [the previous owners] if there was anything wrong with the house, and they both sat there and kinda grinned at each other. They said the only thing is that you can hear people walking around in the living room at night. After living in the house a few weeks, we became convinced that the house is inhabited. It's definitely a ghost. The living room's the worst spot, but noises like opening doors, moving furniture and closing of dresser drawers have been heard throughout the house. You just have this feeling that someone's in the house with you. At first it kinda bugged me, but now I'm used to it.

After reading up on ghosts, I believe that it's probably a poltergeist. Right now, it's just playing games with us, so we aren't really scared of it at all. One of these games occurred when my children and I were in the yard, and we heard a pecking on the window, coming from the inside. There was no one in the house. We all heard it, the neighbor children heard it, but we still can't explain what caused it, unless it was a ghost. I feel that in due time, I'll either get in contact with it or it will show itself to let me know for sure that it's there.

157. The Houston House (WPA)

Not far from Mountain City, in a section called "The Bloody Third," stands the ruins of an old stone house. A strange legend is told about the place. After the Civil War, Dr. Houston bought the house and took up the surrounding mountain practice. Soon after moving into the house, the members of the Houston family were disturbed by queer noises. Early in the evening, with three distinct knocks, an invisible guest would enter. Then could be heard a patter of feet on the floor, ascending the broad oak stair and in the room above. Then the sound of steps could be heard returning down the stairway. Approaching the large fireplace in the living room, the unseen guest gave three farewell knocks and departed.

Mrs. Houston was not afraid of the ghost but was anxious to discover its origin. In an attempt to solve the mystery, she sprinkled flour over the stairsteps, hoping to get an imprint of the creature's airy feet. After listening to the patter on the steps, she went to look for the footprints in the flour, but none could be seen. She grew to expect the nightly visitor and accepted its coming with calmness. But if the doctor happened to be at home when the tapping occurred, he became disgruntled and would follow it upstairs and back, mumbling as he went.

One evening, when Dr. Houston was intoxicated, he decided that he would solve the problem. He sat with his pistol cocked, waiting for the ghost. As the three knocks sounded on the door, he jumped forward to meet it and, shooting and cursing, followed the ghost up the stairs. As the three farewell knocks sounded, Dr. Houston emptied his pistol into the darkness and closed the door.

This ghostly visitor never returned. Years later, when the huge fireplace was torn away, a skeleton was found underneath the hearthstone. A huge roll of Confederate bills was also found fastened to the ledge of a rock. It was thought that the unfortunate victim had been killed for his money and that the murderer was intercepted before he could return for his booty.

CHAPTER ELEVEN

Texas

✝

158. Aunt Neale and the Ghost

My big Aunt Jenny was my mother's aunt. She was the oldest of about five daughters. They were born in and around Denison, Texas. Their family members were Morrises, related to signers of the Declaration of Independence and that sort of thing. They finally migrated to the West, and my big Aunt Jenny who married a Thompson, they built a big house in Hereford, Texas, a little town west of Amarillo between Amarillo and the New Mexico border. And they went there in the 1880s. Theirs was the largest house in town. My great uncle owned a survey company, and he did surveys. In fact, the title company and survey company in Hereford, Texas, now is owned by their great-grandchildren, so it's been a family business. They were leaders in the community and went to the First Baptist Church every day, every Sunday, or every time the door was open.

But their house was a three-story Victorian house with a basement. In those early days, um, the shows, um, vaudeville, um, the opera singers, speakers, lyceum series would come and stay at big Aunt Jenny's house because there was no hotel, and it was just the thing they did.

Jenny had some children. They eventually grew up and moved away. She had a maiden sister, uh, Jessie was her name, Aunt Jessie, and she was the youngest of the Morris girls that lived there. My grandmother was in-between the two of them, along with a couple of others.

But, um this story also has to do with my mother's older sister, Neale. Now Neale Carter Fox was her name. Neale was an unusual woman. Neale had nerves of steel. She was very courageous. In later life she became a full professor at the University of Texas. She had four children. All of them were extremely successful and had names that might be familiar to some of us if we were in broadcasting.

But, um, Aunt Neale told the story to her daughter, and she also told it to me. When I was small, my mother was ill a lot. In fact, she died when I was seven, and Aunt Neale left a graduate student in charge and came over to New Mexico to take charge of me. And she told me that when she was about ten years old—now, Aunt Neale was a tomboy—all her cousins would be playing outside on a Sunday, and in those days, in the panhandle of Texas, little girls certainly did not play outside and roughhouse with the boys, particularly not on Sunday.

This particular story happened on Sunday, and Aunt Neale was about ten, she said, and all the old ladies, her mother and her mother's sisters, were sitting out on the front porch of this large Victorian house. And she just got too rowdy, and my grandmother sent her inside. She was very unhappy, and she was really angry about being a girl. She was angry about not getting to do what she wanted to. She was sitting on the bottom step of the stairs leading to the second floor, crying, and she walked on into the parlor and sat down in the middle of the floor and was really angry at the world when she looked up, and there was a little girl standing there, a little girl about four years old. Neale lived about a block and a half away. She'd never met this little girl before. The little girl had on a gingham dress, and she had panties to match, and Aunt Neale thought that that was really significant because that was a little unusual, and the way Aunt Neale knew it, the little girl had her thumb in her mouth and had the bottom of her dress up like this [pointing down], and so Aunt Neale could see her panties. She looked up, and she [Aunt Neale] said, "Who are you?" The little girl didn't say anything. And the little girl started up the stairs. Aunt Neale really got upset then because one of the rules that big Aunt Jenny had was that after the beds are made, you don't go upstairs and mess 'em up. And Aunt Neale was already in enough trouble, and she knew that if that little girl went upstairs and messed up Aunt Jenny's bed, things were going to get a lot worse. So she started up the stairs after the little girl, and about midway up, the little girl vanished.

Well, Neale came outside, and she said to her mother and her aunts,

"Did you see a little girl come out the door? Did you see a little girl go in the door? Did you see a little girl come around?" And she said, "No."

So Aunt Neale thought about it but didn't say much more about it for many, many years. One day, when Aunt Neale was a college professor at the University of Texas and big Aunt Jenny was probably on her last legs, they were over at my little Aunt Jenny's house for lunch, and there was my Aunt Jesse. She was probably in her seventies at the time. And they were just talking about things, and Aunt Neale told this story, and Aunt Jesse looked up at her, sort of surprised: "Oh, that little girl! She was there all the time, and she loved to go upstairs, and I would get after the broom, and every time on the same step, she disappeared." And, of course, Aunt Neale was very surprised that, um, this story was common knowledge between the old ladies and that nobody had really done anything with the story. And she got to checking, and there had been a little girl that met the description that she had remembered—about four years old—who had been brought to that house, um, with whooping cough, and she died there. So if you do believe that there are indeed ghosts, then perhaps this was the ghost of that little girl.

159. SARAH JANE LANE

This happened on a street called Sarah Jane Lane in, I think, it was the mid-1960s in Belmont, Texas. A girl who had been big-time into dope got a little bit too high, [got] took advantage of, and got pregnant. She decided to have the baby, and after she had it, she tried to take care of it, and the baby was starvin' to death basically, so she decided that the best way for this baby to go was to flat-out kill it. That way, it won't suffer. So she went down to Sarah Jane Lane. At the time, I think it was called Industrial Road or something. It was just a little road going up between two refineries. And there's a canal. She stepped on a bridge where the canal's waters went underneath it, chopped the head off [the baby], and threw the baby in. When she went to walk away, the paper said she felt terrible about it, so she killed herself and fell over [the side of the bridge].

Story goes that you can go down there and sit on the bridge for a second, kind of wait, and you'll see the head pop up. Wait til it goes on the other side of the bridge, turn around, [and] you'll see Sarah Jane kill herself and fall into the canal.

160. THE ABANDONED CEMETERY

At Saratoga, Texas, there's a little cemetery that's abandoned. There's a bridge goin' five hundred feet from it goin' over the cemetery. It's goin' over part of that land that—the cemetery didn't make it that far. As you're goin' over the bridge, you can look down and see the cemetery. As you're goin' over it, you can look to your right, and there's three lights that stop right at the fence.

I can't explain why. We don't know why. I didn't know the exact story behind it, but at the time that the cemetery was prominent, Saratoga used to be a rich city. These three men, like, the keepers of the cemetery, were walkin' through it. Either some lady had died—was executed, actually. She promised revenge. Well, they were walkin' the cemetery doin' their nightly routines, and when they reached the part of the cemetery where she was buried, she rose from the dead and killed them, and they left their lanterns there. And that's what the lights are supposed to be, from what I understand.

161. SPIRIT WARNINGS (WPA)

Yes ma'm, there's them that says there ain't no coming back, that when we pass on that, we don't ever come back to this earth, but I know different. The spirits have warned me too many times.

Why, when my sister was sick, everybody thought she was going to get well but me; I knew she wasn't. She called to me one night and asked me if I saw someone go from her room to mine. I told her "No," but when I got back in my bed, someone smoothed the covers down and started rubbin' my head like they was trying to soothe me to sleep. I knew then that the spirits was preparing me for the death. Sure enough, a week later, she passed away.

Later, when my husband took sick, the same thing happened, so I was warned and knew what to expect. Even last summer when I was in the hospital, I was awfully sick, but I knew I was going to get well, because the spirits held my hands to give me strength.

Scared of the spirits, did you say? Land o' mercy, child, they cain't hurt you. I'd whole lots rather have the spirits for company than a lot of these flesh and blood people I know.

162. THE GHOST OF GREGORIO HERNANDEZ (WPA)

As a little child, Senor Zertuche had a difficult time with an evil ghost who visited nightly and carried him out of his home. He grew ill and thin from the constant terror of being dragged out of his bed and left in the dooryard. The family was completely terrorized but unable to do a thing about it. The kicks and cries of the child were useless. The ghost continued to call. [His family knew] that if it kept up, there would soon be no little boy to carry out.

And then his mother remembered something she had once heard that if one made himself into the shape of a cross on the bed—arms flung wide, face upward [toward] heaven—no witch or ghost could possibly have power to harm. So as a last resort, the mother crept into bed with her child and awaited. Soon, a thing with claws reached out toward her. She felt a cold wind pass and realized that it was time she asked what the ghost wanted, for Christian people know that a ghost will not utter a word unless first spoken to. With much difficulty, she got the right words, of course, in Spanish: "For the love of Christ, if you are in trouble, tell me what it is, and then go in peace." The ghost answered, "I'm the spirit of Gregorio Hernandez and doomed to suffer for ages and ages." He talked of a buried treasure which he wished to find so that he could keep a promise made long ago to pay a certain sum for prayers and another to give to the poor, a promise which he had failed to keep. And he asked her help. The poor woman fainted away.

Next morning, she hurried to a house nearby, saying, "Calavera! Calavera! Last night, I talked with a ghost, and I want to ask your permission to dig for a saddle and two earthen pots which contain a treasure. They must be hidden in this house." So they dug in the corners, inside and out, and finally they found an old saddle, rotted from decay. Now they were sure of the treasure. Though it took more effort than they felt willing to put into it, they dug and found nothing but ashes. Because, as everyone knows, if a ghost tells you anything, you must not repeat it, or the gold will turn to coal or ashes.

All Socorro residents have heard the story about Senor Zertuche, but he will not talk to strangers. Acts a little crazy. The family picks cotton and is hard to find, but Senora Zertuche's rag-bound head is a familiar sight in the village. It is best not to question her too closely, for she has been known to take a hair and a feather, perhaps a piece of string, and concoct a charm for good or evil.

163. The House with a Secret (wpa)

On just such a night as this, my son and I drove into a tourist camp just outside San Antonio and asked for shelter. A man called to us through a closed door to move on, that he had no empty cabins. After much persuasion, he told us we might sleep in an old abandoned house on his property just down the road.

We were only too glad to have a place to sleep at all, so we quickly made our way in the rain to the old house. Outside, the house looked all right, but you can imagine my feeling when I discovered that no one had been inside for a very long time. Dust was so thick that our tracks were plain, even by the dim light of the candle.

The one room we were going to use had a bed still made as if expecting someone to use it. I was too tired to care much about what condition it was in, so I spread my own things out and made ready for bed. I had no sooner laid down and was dozing off than I heard someone walking slowly down the hall. I thought it must be the man who owned the place coming to see if we wanted anything, so I called my son and told him to open the door. We opened the door, and we saw nothing, nothing at all. Everything was quiet again, and we were trying to sleep when something screamed, and it seemed that the whole side of the house must be caving in. Then footsteps came pattering down the hallway and ran on up the stairs. I was afraid to go outside to see what it was and was afraid to go to sleep for fear of what might happen. All night long, I sat on the side of the bed listening to those ungodly things going on outside of my door. Daylight came at last, and we crept outside, almost afraid to glance back. You can imagine my surprise, then, when the owner told us that no one had slept in that house for five years.

Oh, yes, I know lots of people would laugh about it, but that house held a secret of some kind; something terrible had happened there, and the spirits were trying to tell it, and some day, it will come out. You watch and see!

164. The Dead Woman's Return (WPA)

About 1860, Mr. and Mrs. Morris settled on a piece of land near to the present town of Lipan. They built a log house, as most people did in those days. One morning soon after they had built their house, Mrs. Morris shot herself. Her husband was about a half-mile from home when the tragedy happened. Hearing the shot, he hurried home. When he saw what had occurred, he ran to the nearest neighbors for help. This man and woman returned with him to help with the burial. Soon after the funeral, the man left the place. This vacant house attracted newcomers to the settlement, and they would move into the vacant house to start their new home.

About eight o'clock each night, the dead woman would come back, dressed in white. She would come in at the window on the west side of the house. The first people would see of her would be her head. She would come in face downward, and her body would come in gradually until her feet would come through the window. She would slowly let her feet down to the floor and then start walking straight to the fireplace, which was on the east side of the room. Hastily gathering a few things, they would spend the night in the woods or at the neighbors'. The next morning, as quickly as they could gather their belongings and move, the house would again be empty. Soon, other new-comers would move into the house. Again, the woman would appear, and there would be another hasty move.

After this had happened a number of times, no one would spend even a night there. The citizens decided to hire some brave men to go on guard in the house to see for themselves what really happened. For there were many people who did not believe these tales about the house. Finally, two men agreed to spend the night in the house. They went there about dusk, built a fire in the fireplace. Promptly at eight o'clock, just as the reports had been, the woman appeared at the west window. The men were armed with pistols, and as the woman let herself down to the floor, they called to her to "Stop!" and she would stop when they told her to, but in about two minutes, she would advance a few steps farther on the way east to the fireplace. As she came farther into the room, the men would back toward the door. One of the men wanted to shoot her, but the other restrained him. When the men reached the door, they slid into the night, leaving the woman in full possession. They reported to the citizens who had hired them that the woman really did come. They had been promised ten dollars for laying the ghost, but since they did not spend the night in the house, they were not paid.

The citizens offered the men twice as much money to be returned to the house the next night and put their hand on the woman to be sure that it was her. But Mr. N. B. Self, Lipan, Texas, heard one of the men say that he would not put his hand on her for one hundred dollars.

Blood would rise in the chamber of the pistol with which the woman shot herself whenever that chamber was fired. This pistol was on exhibition at one time at a fair held in Wood County.

165. THE HAROLD HOUSE (WPA)

One of the earliest families to settle in Blanco County was a Mr. Harold and his family. The Harolds came from England and were highly respected and very learned people. The family consisted of Mr. and Mrs. Harold, four daughters and two sons. But at the time of this story, about 1919, there was living in the house just a mile north-west of the town Mrs. Harold, the two sons, Michael and Robert, and Robert's wife.

The two men were as different as could be in looks and temperament. Robert was the younger of the two and was an intelligent, seemingly normal young man. Michael was somewhat older and a bachelor. Some people thought that he was a little "queer," but he had never done anything out of the ordinary, being simply a quiet, old bachelor.

One cold winter night, the two brothers were sitting by the fire in the living room of their home. Michael had just gone outside to get more wood for the fire when Robert was evidently seized with a fit of insanity. As Michael stepped in the door, Robert picked up a stick of the wood and began beating his brother on the head with it.

Robert's wife and mother were aroused and phoned into town for help, but when some of the men got there, Michael was dead. No one could give any cause whatsoever for the act, not even the men's family.

However, Robert was committed to an asylum, and his wife and mother moved away. But the strange part of it was that they left the house they had always lived in just as it was that night. The key was given to a neighbor with the request that he keep the house in order. The bedding was left on the beds. The curtains were left hanging, and even the food was left in the kitchen.

The man with whom the key was left thinks, as do the other townspeople, that it is the craziest thing ever heard of. He enters the house when necessary, but it gives even him a spooky feeling to go in it. Rats have destroyed much of the clothes and papers in the house, but the furniture stands just as it was.

School children sometimes make the trip out to the house just for a lark, to peep through the window and imagine all sorts of wild stories; but since the time of the murder, no one except the caretaker has ever been inside the haunted house.

166. THE HAUNTED HUNTER

(WPA)

People nowadays don't believe in haunts, ghosts, or what have you. I don't myself, but there was a time when I came near being convinced. It was way back when I was just a young man. I had gone hunting, deep in the wooded hills of Spurger, Tyler County, Texas. Night was coming on, but I wasn't worried; I knew the county.

As it grew too dark to hunt anymore, I decided I would go home. Turning in the direction of home, I suddenly heard a noise sounding like the patter of soft paws on the leaves. At first, I just kept on going; then suddenly, I stopped. Immediately, the pattering stopped. Several times, I did this, and each time I stopped, the noise stopped. Finally, I turned in the direction of the noise and ran toward it. As I burst through the tangled leaves and branches, there pattering along ahead of me in the moonlight, her curly hair flying in the wind, was a little girl, who supposedly had gotten lost and had died in the woods. With a shout, I grabbed at her, only to grasp thin air and dead leaves.

There was nothing, absolutely nothing. You see, I don't believe in ghosts, but still—when the moon shines like it is tonight—I sometimes wonder.

167. THE BALL OF FIRE (WPA)

Now that you have mentioned it, I remember a crazy superstitious story that the old cattlemen, cowboys and scattered "nesters" over around

Bledsoe believed sincerely. They actually believed that there existed a Ball of Fire and swore time and again that they had seen it. I had not thought of that story in years, but I remember it now.

An old-timer who had lived over around Bledsoe for some 20 or 30 years first told me about this Ball of Fire and exactly how it appeared and disappeared. But I do not believe in the supernatural, and, of course, did not have much faith in such a fantastic yarn. But I could not offer any explanation, for the old squatters undoubtedly saw something to base their belief upon. I heard the incredible, nocturnal yarn quite frequently afterwards and talked to several old-timers that claimed to have actually seen the Ball of Fire. Really, I never thought much about the superstition at the time, merely taking it for granted that it was just another nester and rancher superstition, but since then, I have wondered many times just what it was that they based their belief upon, for they were so sincere and had so much faith that the Ball of Fire actually existed, I was greatly impressed by their belief.

This old-timer took great pains in explaining just exactly how it happened. The best I remember, he said it just suddenly appeared—a large, immense ball-like fire, rolling slowly along or above the horizon in the south or southeast and sometimes in the southwest. Sometimes, it did not look more than a mile away, and again it would appear to be many miles away. When asked if it had flames leaping from it, the old-timer said that it did not; [it] seemed to be just a big coal of fire, glowing as it rolled along. The Ball of Fire had no certain time to appear, except that it usually appeared on the darkest nights when there was no moon. Sometimes, it could be seen for hours, appearing and disappearing along the horizon. Sometimes, it would just bob up and go out, appear again in a few moments, miles from the spot. On some occasions, it had scintillating rays of light flashing from it.

Well, he just thought it was simply a ball of fire. He thought it was an omen. Some thought it was an evil omen, others a good omen. They had different beliefs for its cause. Along about this time, a meteor fell, landing in the southern part of Citron County, and many people thought that the meteorite had something to do with this Ball of Fire. Government geologists said this territory was rich in minerals, and some of the people thought that the Ball of Fire was caused by gases escaping from the earth. Other people had other fantastic ideas about its cause. Some even thought it was a night mirage. People living around Bledsoe now sometimes relate the story as told to them by their parents who saw the Ball of Fire.

168. HALLOWEEN MADNESS

(WPA)

It was twenty years ago, this past Halloween night, that the thing that made me a wanderer happened. Jerry Barclay, my best friend, and me started out on our horses from our farm home near Cuero, Dewitt County, Texas, to town. Jerry's horse was a gentle old stallion he had been riding for years. He hadn't gone far when, at my suggestion, we decided to go by an old graveyard to see if we could see a ghost

Lady, I can tell you, something happened that night that'll stay with me as long as I live. We were laughing and talking, when out of nowhere, it seemed, there came a thousand devils, each squawking or groaning in a different voice.

My horse froze in his tracks, and I couldn't move. All of a sudden, one of the devils made for Jerry's horse, and that gentle old stallion seemed to go wild. I'll never forget the horror in Jerry's eyes as he tumbled from the saddle. With screams and yells, them devils went after him. I don't care what people say. I saw the best friend I ever had in my life torn to pieces while his life's blood covered the ground. Jerry gave one awful scream, and my horse bolted away from the place.

I don't remember much about that wild ride, with a thousand devils at my heels. but when I finally came to my senses, my old man was shaking me and yelling, "What's the matter!" I couldn't talk, just jabbered out the story. Finally, he got my brother and went back to that graveyard. They said Jerry broke his neck when he fell off the horse, and the only blood they found was from a cut on his head where he struck it when he fell. I knew better, and so did Jerry's horse. Nobody could handle him, and one night, he had some kind of a spell and died. Them devils killed him, I know they did, 'cause they're still after me. I left that part of the country, and I ain't been back. Still, at night, when I hear Jerry's scream, I know they're coming, so I just up and leave for another part of the country.

169. FISHERMAN'S SURPRISE

(WPA)

One night, my step-son and another fellow went floundering on Pelican Island. They weren't having much luck, so they seen another fellow floundering a little farther down from them. My step-son couldn't see him very well, but he thought it was old man Travis, so him and the other fellow waited for him to catch up with them. When he did come up close, they took one look and lit out. By gad! The fellow didn't have a head.

I kidded them about it and, of course, I didn't believe it. So the next day, they made me go over there and look for tracks. I went over and found the tracks all right, but I could only find two sets. I seen where the fellows left the water and went to the log. Then seen where they stood and waited for the other fellow. Then I seen where they started running. That was the only tracks there was, and sometimes they were so far apart, I'd lose them. But other people claim to have seen this fellow too.

170. THE HOUSE OF GREGORIO HERNANDEZ (WPA)

One half mile from the little house where I live is the big house of 20 rooms, where no one who enjoys his sleep at night ought to live, for many people have tried it. It's the house of Gregorio Hernandez, the richest man in Socorro before his death. He thought only of making a lot of money and keeping it. He would not tell anyone where he hid his money and failed to keep a sacred pledge, so now he comes to the big house. A light moves from room to room, as one carrying a candle. At night, the cupboard turns over, and dishes are thrown out on the floor, but never broken.

And Mike Lujan, a bus driver, has dug all over the place with no success. One night, he and others were digging when they heard the sound of a horse galloping, and they heard the horse man get off the horse and come near. They had piled a lot of dirt against a certain door. The door was suddenly pushed open, and the dirt packed back into the hole. They all ran away. Mercy of God! They wouldn't want to return for anything.

171. THE GROANING CEMETERY (WPA)

My cousin suggested that we go over and get some honey as he could handle the bees if I could make friends with the dog. Tom, my brother-in-law, had a very bad dog. I told him that I could handle the dog because the dog was familiar with me. I had hunted with him several times before. We started on the trip, which was about two miles. Sleet and ice was very deep on the ground, and since this was a hilly country, the trip was a very tiresome one, but we made the trip over, and each got a bucket of honey and were returning home.

This was a sparsely settled country, and at the time, there was only one house to be passed on making this trip, and that was an old abandoned house that had been built in the early part of the nineteenth century but had not been used as a residence in many years. There was an old cemetery near the house containing the graves of the former settlers of this farm. Being tired from sliding over the ice-covered hills, I told my cousin that I was going to stop and rest near the cemetery. He said he was going on down the hill as he had heard too many ghost stories about this place. I informed him that I did not believe in ghosts because I had never seen one.

He continued on down the hill, and I stopped to rest. He had not been gone long until I heard something which sounded like a groan of someone in distress. The groan seemed to be out in the cemetery, and I was at the edge of the cemetery. I did not feel that I was a believer in ghosts, and I could not see anything, yet this moaning [was] like someone in great agony.

I picked up my bucket of honey and started down the hill in pursuit of my cousin. In my haste to get going, my feet slipped on the ice, and I started sliding down the hill but managed to hold on to my bucket of honey but had no control over my course and not only slid down the hill but into the creek at the bottom of the hill. Lucky for me, the creek was frozen so deep that I was saved an ice-cold bath. My cousin said, "I told you that place was haunted!"

The next morning, I went to investigate the old cemetery, and over on the opposite side from where I had stopped to rest, I found one of my neighbors' cows had slipped into a deep gully and frozen to death. Later on, I bought this place and moved the house to another part of my farm but did not see or hear another "ghost."

172. The Woman at the Fence (WPA)

One night, a Mr. Thorn was riding home down a lane fenced on each side with barbed wire. The moon shone so brightly that he could see everything distinctly. Something attracted his attention, and he looked to the left of the road. There, he saw a woman of middle age approaching one of the wire fences. She had on a checked gingham dress; her hair hung in a plait down her back. Something in general was appalling about the sight. A feeling of terror was in the very air. The nearer he came to the fence, the greater his terror until his hair actually stood up-right and nearly pushed his hat off his head. When she reached the fence, she didn't climb over it nor crawled under it; she passed right through it! Mr. Thrall swore afterward that he had not been drinking and was as wide-awake as ever in his life. When the woman vanished in thin air, he dashed home and in a few days, as soon as he could, he sold out his farm and moved to another farm several miles away. He always said that he had had a vision, but he could not tell what it meant other than that it was a warning for him to move.

CHAPTER TWELVE

VIRGINIA

✝

173. A RUDE AWAKENING

Now this is not a folktale. This is something that really happened. Well, he [my friend] was house-sitting, and he was in a small bungalow next to the big house, if I can remember correctly, and he kept hearing all these banging and walking sounds. And he went back to sleep, and the next night, it happened again. Well, it happened again, and he talked, I guess, to the person living in the big house. He [the person living in the big house] said there was some spirit—a ghost—around there. And he went [back], and he was awakened again, and he got up, and said, "I don't know who you are, but you have got to be quiet so I can get some sleep." And he never heard anything else.

This house is in Albermarle County right outside Charlottesville. His name is John Joseph Van Halloween, and he works for the Salvation Army in the Washington, D.C., area. It'd be easy to trace him through the Salvation Army. He worked as a volunteer coordinator, and I was director of the Volunteer Center, so we knew each other.

174. WALKING GHOST

Well, something happened to me that really made me feel uncomfortable. I work at the United Way Building, and I was there alone at 7:30 at night, and I kept hearing these footsteps overhead. Finally, I got up and looked out in the parking lot. There were no cars there but mine, and I thought, "Who could be up there?" And they [the footsteps] kept walking back and forth, back and forth.

The next day, I went on in and finished what I was doing and left. And the next day, I said something to my boss about it, and she said, "And you didn't tell me?" And so I mentioned it to one of the men that works in the investment firm upstairs, and he said, "Oh yeah, there's supposed to be a ghost here." And I said, "Well, I certainly heard him walkin' last night!"

The Professional Center is the name of this building. The United Way is in this building. It's next to Birdwood, which is an old antebellum home which is kind of like the Moon House here [at the University of West Alabama]. People can stay there and have parties there and stuff. I don't know if it was the janitor, and maybe they dropped him off and came back later and picked him up. I didn't investigate. But last night when you were talkin' to the ADK [Alpha Delta Kappa teaching honorary society in Livingston], I said to myself, "I wonder if that was an experience with a ghost?" And I guess it could have been. This possibility is very real. This is in Charlottesville, Virginia. Now the office building is located in Altamont County just over the county line.

175. A Night in a Haunted House (WPA)

In a certain neighborhood in Scott County, Virginia, there lived a family by the name of Loveall, in a small cottage by the side of a lane. The wife of this home on a certain night became a mother, and a certain woman in the neighborhood, who was a midwife, was in attendance there too. The mother passed away the next morning, strange to relate, because she seemed to be getting along so well.

In those days, the people had no coffee mills. They bought their coffee green, parched it, tied it in a cloth, and then beat it up with a hammer, thus converting it into pulverized coffee. The coffee that was used that night was beaten by the midwife who was in attendance.

Soon after the death of this mother, the home became vacant, the remainder of the family moving away. In passing to and from by that house, the neighbors could hear a noise—somebody hammering in the deserted house. Thus, it became known as a haunted house. Not many people cared to pass that way at night.

Uncle Elias Rhoton, a justice of the peace in that neighborhood, a man who was unquestioned for truth and veracity, decided he would go there one night and investigate the situation. The time was set at after midnight, and he went there alone.

He stepped inside the gate to a tall apple tree that stood on the lawn and put his arms around the tree. Immediately, he heard the knocking or hammering commence inside the house. He said, "In the name of High Heaven, what or who is that in there?" A woman stepped to the door and replied, "I am Nancy Loveall." "Well, then what do you want and why are you here?" "Three things I want done; if you'll do the three things and never reveal but one, I'll go away and you'll see me no more." She then told him what the three things were, one of which she said, "I want you to go and fix my grave as I shall here tell you." He agreed and promised to do it. She then stepped down off the little narrow porch, went up the hill, through an old field to the graveyard and suddenly vanished from his sight.

He said it was a bright moonlight night and that he knew it to be Nancy Loveall, because he knew the dress that she usually wore and which she was wearing that night, and that he didn't believe that he could have been mistaken in what he saw there that night.

All the neighbors believed that the two things she requested him not to tell and which he never did were that she told him the midwife who made the coffee that night poisoned her and told him why she poisoned her, but Mr. Rhoton never said that these guesses were correct.

176. THE HEADLESS MAN ON BIRCHFIELD ROAD (WPA)

I'ze never hyerd many things in my life that I didn't fin' out what was, but thar's a hainted place right down hyer on Birchfield road where Lewis Medley used to live. I've passed thar at all hours of the night an' haint never seed or heard anythin,' but I've heared lots of people tell about seeing an' hyerin' things thar time after time.

One man had to quit his job on account of seein' sumpin' thar. Hit was old man Peaks; I can't remember his first name now. Been dead a long time. He's workin' for Big Milbourn Gilliam, an' he got to gittin' thar late every mornin'. Milbourn he got to kickin' about him gittin' thar so late, an' he told Milbourn he jes' couldn't git thar before day 'cause up thar at the Lewis Medley place was sumpin' that he jes' wouldn't pass in the dark. He said that every mornin' as he went by that, he'd hear sumpin' jes' a-slippin' down the bank inter the road, an' he'd look, an' thar'd come a man walkin' right toward him with no head, an' hit looked every time like his head had jes been cut off fresh an' the blood was jes' a-streamin' down over his shoulders. He said hit made the hair stan' up on his head, an' he'd have to reach up an' pull hit down to keep hit from fallin' off'n his head. So before he'd put up with sich as that, he jes quit his job.

Lewis Medley lived up on the hill jes above where Peaks seed that thing. He had some girls, an' Emmett Blevins was a-goin' thar to see one of 'em. He told me that one night, he'd started that to see his gal, an' jes as he's leavin' the main road, he heard sumpin' slippin' down the bank by his side. He looked but didn't see a thing, but jes then, somethin' took a-holt of his shoulder. He said he sorter stepped up, an' the further he got, the harder hit bore down on him. Before he got to the house, hit had him around the shoulders an' was bearin' down on him so hard that he jes' couldn't go. He tried to wranch himse'f loose from hit, but hit helt him that much tighter, an' he finally had to holler for some Medley's folks to come down an' he'p him up the bank. 'Bout the time they's comin' outer the house with a light, hit let him loose, an' he went on to the house all right.

Thar was a lot of people seed an' heard sumpin' thar, but I can' think of 'em right now.

177. THE GHOST THAT SCRATCHES IN THE ASHES (WPA)

Long, long time ago, there was a man and his wife and three little children living away back in the woods, far off from anybody else. I don't know where it happened, but somewhere in the country, I guess.

One day, the man cut a turn on his horse and started off to the mill. It was a long ways to the mill, and he would be gone all day.

He hadn't been gone but a little while till his wife heard somebody a-coming riding up the rocky road. She looked out and saw two Indians coming riding on their ponies. She told the children to crawl in the closet and no matter what happened to stay there and not cry.

The woman didn't have a thing to fight with. They had but one gun, and her husband had took it with him, and the axe was sticking in the chop block out in the yard. So she got down on knees and began to pray.

The Indians come on up and got down and knocked on the door. She wouldn't open it. Then the chief broke it down. They come in and found her kneeling there on the hearth a-praying. They took her up and tied her hands and feet and carried her down to the edge of a high cliff and danced around her and then threw her over the bluff into the river. Then they went back and got everything out of the house they wanted and burnt the house down on the three little children.

That night when the man come back from the mill, he found his house in ashes. He soon found the burnt bones of his three little children and their hearts. You know, they say a person's heart won't burn. He hunted and hunted for his wife's heart, but of course couldn't find it. So he went crazy and run off in the woods and jumped over a cliff and killed himself. A few days later, somebody found his wife's body in the river.

And now they say that ever since then, the ashes of that cabin stays right there and nothing will grow in there, and that many a person passing there of a night have seen an old man with a long gray beard and a stick in his hand hunkered down there stirring the ashes hunting for his wife's heart.

178. Light Around the Corner (WPA)

I lived on Birchfield Creek. Hit's been about thirty-five, maybe forty years ago. I'd been off from home one day. Late in the night when I got back, I opened the gate and walked up the walk. Just as I went to turn the doorknob, I heard something like somebody sort o' sobbin' or cryin'. I looked around, an' there, comin' right around' the house to my left side was somethin' that looked like a blaze of fire but in the shape of a person. Hit was comin' right round the corner, first the head part an' then the rest of it. Jes sort of been around the corner of the house, hit seemed. I couldn't see any features or anything like that, but hit had the outline of a person. I looked off a minute by some means, an' when I looked back, it was gone. That's the only thing I ever seed that I never found out was.

No, nothin' followed it that I know of.

179. The Haunted Spinning Wheel (WPA)

I used to go around and visit with first one of my children and then to the others, one at a time, and stay a good spell before I went on to one of the other places. I recollect that Maude, my oldest daughter that lived out in a far end of Wise here, had a spin' wheel they'd bought from a old man whose wife had died up in the hurricane, and then he'd sold most of the stuff out as he didn't need but just enough to furnish a couple of rooms for hisself. One night when I was at her house and sleepin' in the room I always slept in when I was there—it was the room by the grate—and I'd seen it before and never paid much attention to it, only that it had been polished and cleaned. Anyway, it is a long time now as that was in 1912 some time in the late fall, and the nights was gettin' cool. Along 'bout 12:00 I was woke up by something I didn't know just what. Anyway, I knowed I'd been woke up and lay there wondering if some prowler had been 'round the house or what or maybe some dog or cow had made a noise somewhere near. The way I was layin' my eyes were on that old spin' wheel and naturally, I got to thin' 'bout it. Well, sir, as I laid there a-lookin' at it, I thought I saw the wheel give a turn around right fast, and I thought I heard a little noise. Then I thought I'se 'bout half asleep and at first never paid no attention to it but tried to think why I'd been woke up. Try as hard as I could, I couldn't, though, and kept lookin' back towards that old spin' wheel and blamed my soul if it didn't turn clear 'round the next time I looked at it. If I'd been drinkin,' I'd swore it was the jimmies bit. I hadn't been drinkin,' and I knowed it was really turnin' 'round, or that is, I saw the wheel turn 'round right fast-like. Well, I ain't no coward myself, and I just decided to stay awake and watch it and see if I could find out more about it. Well, every time I'd turn my head and look back, it'd turn around at least one time and sometimes more. Then the cold sweat stood out on my head, and I had a feelin' that everything wasn't all right around me. I got up, and I called Maude and told her and she said that I'd have to put up with it and I wouldn't notice it any more. But I couldn't sleep that night no more.

In the mornin' at the breakfast table, she told me that the man's wife that sold it to her had worked herself to death nearly spin' for things they needed at home, and it had caused her to lose her eyesight, and later she died, broken in spirit and health. She said the old spinnin' wheel just couldn't keep still. She guessed as she'd heard some folks tell her that was the reason the old man sold it for nearly nothing. Well, it was enough for me, and I never stayed in that room any more. Although I went back lots, I stay shy of that old time spin' wheel. Even if it didn't disturb them, it did me. I can't stand to get the jimmies over a little thing like that, but it got my goat right then and there, and I ain't aimin' to deny it either. I could almost see the old woman spin at the wheel after I'd heard about it, and if I'd slept in a room in where it was after that, I didn't know but what she'd come around herself, so I steered shy of it. They say the tale's the truth, though, sure.

180. QUILT-PULLING GHOST

(WPA)

Yes, I believe in haints. I can't help believin' in 'em. I've seed an' heard too much not to believe in 'em. You know, if they'uz sich things back yanner in Bible times, they would be now.

Hit 'uz jes a while after Glamorgan started up. I was workin' thar an' got me house on Tank Hill an' moved thar. Hit was the third day of July. I remember that very well. Think hit was in 1905.

We brought some chickens, an' I had 'em in a coop, an' I jes slid 'em under the edge of the floor that night. Well sir, jis before I went to go to bed, I stepped out on the front porch, like you'd do, ye know, when thar set a man with a white shirt on right at the edge of the floor. Looked like he was stoppin' down an' reachin' under the floor. My fust thought was that hit 'uz somebody tryin' to steal my chickens. I turned an' run back in the house to git my shotgun. Thought that I'd took hit upstairs, an' run upstairs an' got hit. When I got back he 'uz gone. An' you know what I done? I sot down right thar with the gun across my knees an' sot thar til after midnight. But 'e never showed up again.

I never thought about hit bein' sumpin' come back from the other world. Nair time I didn't. Ain't the woman that lived in the next house had axed my wife when we 'uz movin' in if we 'uz afeared of boogers, an' she said, "No, why?" "Well," she said, "thought if you was that you wouldn't like that house. Hain't been anybody that lived in hit long. Hear an' see all sorts of things they tell me."

Well sir, that night as soon as I come back in the house an' put my gun up an' went to bed, hit stared in. Jes jerkin' a' pullin' at the kiver. Couldn't keep hit over me a-tall.

An' ever' night, hit got worse. Jes like a man 'ud take holt of the two corners of the kiver at the foot of the bed, like he 'uz goin' to fan wheat or sumpin' an' I've twisted the other en's in my hands, but I could hold hit. Very minute I'd turn on the lights or strike a match, hit 'ud quit. Thar would lay the kiver at the foot of the stairs, jes like hit 'ud started to drag hit upstairs, but not a sign of anything to be seed. I could even hear the kiver bein' drug across the floor. Sometimes, I've scratched a match right quick an' thought I see whatever hit was, but no sir, thar'd lay the kiver at the stairs an' nothin' else to be seed anywhere. I'll tell ye, folks, hit made a person feel quare.

We told people about hit, an' lots of our folks an' neighbors come an' stayed all night with us to hear hit or feel hit. For that's what we done, we felt hit, except hearin' the kiver goin' slitherin' over the floor, thar wasn't nothin' to hear.

Never a thing til we'd blow out the lamp. But very minute the light went out an' we got in the bed, I'd begin to feel hit start tuggin' at the kiver. I got so I'd grab the kiver, an' my wife would, too, an' we hol' on with all power we had in us, but hit 'd pull hit out o' hants in spite of all we could do. If we let the light burn, hit wouldn't bother us.

We stayed thar a little over a month. Stayed til the tenth day of August an' jes could work an' lose so much sleep an' I told the super I wanted another house, an' he let me have another'n, an' we moved. But I never felt right thar an' I soon looked me up another job an' moved out of the camp.

I don't know what hit was or why hit done that, but hit must o' been God's work. Sumpin' must o' happened thar, although I axed Around' an' thar hadn't been anybody killed or died thar as far as anybody knowed of. But we can't tell what might o' been done thar some night in secret. House might o' been built on an Indian grave. You know, they say if ye build a house on a grave, hit'll be hainted.

Yes, I believe thar's things been seed an' heard. They seed 'em an' heard 'em back yanner, ye know. He's the same God today He was then.

181. A True Story of a Haunted House (WPA)

It was an old mountain plantation near Lynchburg. The owner had been a owner of slaves. The house had large windows all across the front. It was a very large mountain home with a long lawn, and for generations, a large rocking chair had been left in the large living room in front of the open fireplace. No one was ever known to sit in it. When it was left alone, it would begin to rock, and a pale light would appear over this rocking chair, and as different families would move out of the house, they always left the rocking chair there. It seemed that everyone was afraid to have anything to do with it, and at the time my father saw it, he was not married, and he was going to see a girl who lived there with her family. They would go to church, and when they would come home after dark, they could see the chair through the window. They didn't use shades then, but there were hanging draperies over the window, and they could see the chair rocking with its blue light over it. He said they weren't afraid. It has never hurt us, she said, but, of course, we never use it. Never sit in it.

As soon as anyone opened the door, the chair would instantly be still. People around Amherst County came from far and near to see that old rocking chair rock. My father said he had seen it oh so many times. He said the chair had a high back that was covered with tapestry, and the cushion was of red flowers design. It never wore out as no one over-used it, and the family said, "We are afraid to move the chair; we think it must have been used by an old lady after the war. She sat in it, and when she died, her chair began to act like this." It has never been moved from in front of the fireplace.

182. THE HAUNTED RIFLE (WPA)

When I was a boy about thirty years ago, my daddy lived in the same house you live in now. One day, he was over on the point—you know, the hill just over from where you live. He was going along there near the fence that runs up the hill by a cliff and found a rifle barrel sticking out of the ground. Just the end of the barrel was all that was sticking out. He caught hold of it and pulled and it come out. He got a stick and dug and found the trigger and hammer in the dirt too. The gun was in pretty good shape except being rusty. He brought it down to the house and laid it on a shelf under the window.

Well sir, that night, we heard something knock, knock, knock around the window. Daddy got up and went to the window, and something was knocking on the old rifle. He moved it to another place and went back to bed, and the knocking started again, right where he'd put the rifle. It was an old war rifle like they used in the Civil War. He moved the thing from place to place, and everywhere he'd move it, the knocking would follow. He told mother he was going to take it back where he found it and leave it there. I let home about this time and was gone a long time. I don't know what he did with rifle, whether he took it back or what, but I guess he took it back where he found it.

183. The Headless Teamster

(WPA)

I've heard my grandma tell about seeing something when she lived at the old Richmond place out from Wise. Back then, there wasn't any cars. The house she lived in sets on the side of the road leading from Wise to Kentucky, and people traveling along couldn't make the trip in a day, and they always stopped over and stayed all night at grandma's.

One evening, grandma said it was about dusk when she heard a wagon drive up and stop. She could hear the wagon chains rattling, and she didn't look out but just waited for whoever it was to come to the door and knock. In a few minutes, she heard someone come upon the porch, heard them walk across the porch and knock on the door. She went to the door and opened it, and there stood a man. She said when she opened the door, she looked first down at his feet and then slowly up to his head, and when she looked at his head, she saw he was headless. He didn't have a sign of a head from his shoulders up. She looked at him for a moment, and he just disappeared, and nobody was there and no wagon in front of the house either.

184. The Haunted Maple (WPA)

Willard Roberts knows more haint tales than anybody. I heard him tell one the other night that happened to him. You know his uncle, Owen Roberts, built the house where Letty Chizenhall lives, and he died there.

Willard said he was a boy like when his uncle died. One day, he went down to see him, and he was pretty bad off. He said that his uncle told him that he was going to die and that when he died, he wanted 'em to bury him back of his house under a big maple that stood there.

Well, his uncle died not long after that. He said he told 'em what he had said about burying him under the maple, but they wouldn't bury him there. Took him to the regular family graveyard.

Then Willard said that one day, he was going down the road and got right against the maple tree, and he heard something out there just like somebody had throwed down a load of boards. He'd about forgot about his uncle's request to be buried there. So he thought it might be somebody makin' boards out there. He went out and didn't see a thing, but as he got under the maple, he heard something just like somebody diggin' down under the ground. Then he thought of what his uncle told him, and he started to leave, and as he was leaving, he heard something like clods falling on a coffin.

He said that every time he passes that place until this day, he hears something like somebody digging a grave.

185. The Ghost of Dug Hill

(WPA)

I don't know how come Dug Hill to be ha'inted. No sir. Guess somebody's been killed there. Don't you? My pap allus said he b'lieved somebody been kilt there in the old war. Maybe that's so. It would a been a mighty good place to kill a body.

I'd allus heard tell that somethin' had been seed on Dug Hill. Pap seed somethin' like a goose there one time, he said. Hit went flappin' off down the steep hill below the road. He said he never seed anything like hit before.

Yes, musta been somebody kilt there sometime. You know, if a body is kilt an' nobody find hit out, the place will be haunted til they do find out about hit. I don't know whether people can come back after they die or not. Sometimes think they can. Some folks say they don't. They say if they're in heaven, they don't want to come back, an' if they're in torment, they can't come back. Me, I don't know.

But I'll tell you just what I seed at Dug Hill one night, an' you can judge for yourse'f. I had been workin' down the road, b'lieve hit was fer Cicero Addington. Maybe somebody else. Anyway, I'd been a-workin' fer somebody down the road. Jes after me an' Jane had moved up here. Well sir, I was a-comin' along up Dug hill an' was about to the top thar, an' allus at once, I heard somethin' like somebody a-walkin' behin' me. I turned my head an' looked around,' an' there come a woman dressed in white an' without any head. If she had any head, I couldn't see it. Now sir, hit's funny. I'd been feelin' sort of lonesome coming along thar by myse'f an' knowin' the place was said to be hainted, but soon's I seed that woman a-standin' thar, I din't seem to be scared a bit. I just looked at her an' started walkin'. Not runnin'. Not even a-pickin' up my gait. Walked along jes like I hadn't seed anythin'. I kept my head turned an' watched her. She come right along after me. She's about ten steps behin' me an' seemed to be steppin' right in tracks. Well sir, she kept comin' right on til she got right where that awful steep place is below the road. Then all at once, she just seemed to lift up her hands and went tumblin' right over an' over down the bank. She went out of my sight about the time she struck the bottom. Nor sir, I didn't hear a sound. But when she was rollin' over and over, hit seemed like blazes of fire was squirtin' out of her head or where her head ought to been.

Next day, I went back thar an' examined the bank whar she went down an' couldn't see no sign of her a-tall. Musta been something. I'll allus b'lieve hit was something, an' that hit wanted to tell me something. Wish I'd spoke to hit.

186. HAUNT TALE (WPA)

Once there was a girl married to a man who had been married before she was married to him. He took her to his home, and one day while he was away, she was standing on the hearth by the fire. All at once, there was a woman came and stood by her on the hearth. She said, "I was your husband's first wife, and he killed me and buried me under this hearth. I want you to bury my bones, and then I won't bother you anymore." It was night, and the last wife said, "I have no light. I can't go out and bury your bones because it's dark." The other wife said, "I'll give you a light." And she held out the prettiest candle the other wife had ever seen. It was so bright she could see everywhere. She took the candle and raised the hearth stones and there saw a pile of human bones. She got a sack, scooped up the bones, and buried them. She never saw the other wife's ghost anymore.

187. KNOCKING SPIRIT (WPA)

John Moore, my brother-in-law's brother during the Civil War, was laying out from the Yankee's. They lived on Laurel Ridge way down on Elkhorn (Kentucky). He wasn't strong; [he was] little and pale. He had consumption, I reckon. The Yankees was out hunting him and run upon him. He fell down behind a log, and they shot him. He begged them not to shoot him anymore. He said, "This shot will kill me. Don't shoot me anymore! Let me go home and see my wife and little children once more." They said, "Yes, you can see your wife and children once more," and bang! They shot him twice more.

Now Emory, such things can be so, for he wanted to see his wife and children so bad. It tormented him because he couldn't see them. His spirit or something could have come back because he wanted to see them so bad. After this, something got to bothering around Uncle Aaron's house. They couldn't keep the door shut. They lived in an old-time log house. In them days, they had latches for the doors with a string run through a hole to the outside. You could pull the string down on the outside, and it lifted the latch on the inside. Well, they just couldn't keep the door latched.

My daddy could talk to spirits, and they sent after him to come and see what he could do. Daddy went, and they got supper. Then nearly everybody got supper after dark. In them old time log houses, they ate and slept in the same room. They was sitting around before supper, talking. Caroline got supper and was waiting on the table. A pine torch was sticking up here [she points to the mantel]. They didn't have any lights them days but pine torches. Caroline walked around the table, and the door flew open and hit her in the back. She said, "Oh, that hurt!" She shut it back, but they couldn't keep the door shut. It'd fly open every time they shut it.

After supper, they talked a little while, and then it was way in the night. Uncle Aaron said he was going to bed, and they all went to bed. Daddy was going to set up and watch. They had left the door stand open. They couldn't keep it shut. Daddy had prepared him some little pine splinters to make him a quick light. Daddy was going to lay down before the fire. He had his pine splinters ready to stick in the fire. He shut the door and stuck his splinters in the fire to make a good light. The door flew open, and he kept his eyes on the door. The splinters lit up, and there in the door stood a man with no head on. Daddy said it shore did frighten him, and he said the man stood there with no head in his white shirt sleeves and his hands in his pockets. He said he was pretty scared, and instead of using the three highest names—"Why in the name of the Father, the Son, and the Holy Ghost are you here?"—he said, "What in the hell are you doing here?" And in just a jump or two, he was in the bed. He lit right in behind Uncle Aaron. He said when he asked that, the man stepped backwards off the steps and was never seen nor heard anymore.

Πotes

In the following notes, as much information is given on the informants as was available. This information includes the name, age, place of collection and place of residence, attitude toward the narratives, and other biographical material. Additionally, all information was collected by the author, except as noted.

Motif numbers are included at the end of the comments about the informants. References are keyed to the numbering systems employed in Ernest Warren Baughman's *Type and Motif-Index of the Folktales of England and North America* (The Hague: Mouton, 1966). These items are marked with an asterisk (*) to distinguish them from the numbering system employed by Stith Thompson in his *Motif-Index of Folk Literature* (Bloomington: Indiana University Press, 1955). Most of the references are Baughman's because he is more directly concerned with American folk narratives. In those cases where he does not list parallel material, Thompson's numbers are given. Whenever similar accounts of these tales were located, the title of the collection and the page numbers were given.

1. Collected on 21 February 1996 in Livingston, Alabama, from Margaret Sullivan, a retired English teacher and part-time college instructor from Eppes, Alabama. Because the story is told by her son, Sullivan is convinced that it really happened. Motifs include *E281, "Ghosts haunt house"; E338, "Non-malevolent ghost haunts building"; E338 (b), "Female ghost seen in house"; E338.1(h), "Miscellaneous activities of ghosts in house."

2. Collected on 14 August 1996 in Livingston, Alabama, from Jean Aubey, a retired resident of Mobile, Alabama. Aubey reference to the acorns in Boyington's ears suggests that she does not believe in the supernatural elements of the tale. The only relevant motif is E274(a), "Ghost haunts scene of unjust execution."

3. Collected on 27 June 1995 in Livingston, Alabama, from George Snow, about forty years old. Snow is the comptroller at the University of West Alabama. Although Snow is certain that he saw and smelled a ghost in Webb Hall, he suggests in the end that some of the ghost stories about the administration building have arisen because of the creaking of the wood in the framework. Motifs include E280, "Ghost haunts building"; E424.1, "Revenant as woman."

4. Collected on 2 October 1996 in Livingston, Alabama, from Linda Campbell, about forty years old. Campbell is a freelance journalist who lives in Livingston. Campbell accepts the supernatural explanation for the strange events in her house. Motifs include *E281, "Ghost haunts house"; *E402.1.2, "Footsteps of invisible ghost heard."

5. Collected on 24 June 1996 in Livingston, Alabama, from Jeffrey Beasley,

about thirty years old. He is a middle-school teacher from Tuscaloosa, Alabama. Because of the newspaper accounts, Beasley has no doubt that the principal was beheaded. Motifs include E338.7, "Ghost haunts educational institution"; *E402.1.2, "Footsteps of invisible ghost heard"; *X916(m), "Remarkable eyes."

6. Collected on 25 October 1996 in Livingston, Alabama, from Scott Bonjean, about forty years old. Bonjean is a computer salesman from Leeds, Alabama. Because he has not personally experienced any supernatural occurrences in the house, he reserves comment on the veracity of the stories. Motifs include *E281, "Ghosts haunt house"; E338.1(H), "Miscellaneous activities of ghosts in house"; E421.5, "Ghost seen by two or more persons; they corroborate the appearance"; E425.1, "Revenant as woman"; *E521.1, "Ghost of dog."

7. Collected in 1955 by Mrs. David N. Oates in Toxey, Alabama, from her father, who received the tale from his grandfather. The story was given to me by my graduate assistant, Charlotte Hernandez. Hernandez is about thirty years old and is a resident of Toxey. Motifs include E338.1(h), "Miscellaneous activities of ghosts in house"; *E402.1.4, "Invisible ghost jingles chains"; E402.1.8, "Miscellaneous sounds made by ghost of human being"; E421.5, "Ghost seen by two or more persons; they corroborate the appearance."

8. Collected on 28 January 1997 in Livingston, Alabama, from Carey Moore, about forty years old. Moore, a resident of Livingston, is a physics professor. Motifs include *E 281, "Ghosts haunt house"; E338.1(h), "Miscellaneous activities of ghost in house"; E421.5, "Ghost seen by two or more persons; they corroborate the appearance."

9. Collected on 21 June 1996 in Rainesville, Alabama, by David Campbell from Kathy Bethune, an eighteen-year-old college student. She received the story from her grandparents, who live in Flat Rock. Bethune's interpretation of the apparition as an angel is quite possibly the result of her religious beliefs and the ghost's kindness. Motifs included *E425.1, "Revenant as woman"; *E575, "Ghost as omen of calamity or ill fortune"; V230, "Angels."

10. Collected on 29 February 1995 in Livingston, Alabama, from a forty-year-old administrative assistant in a state university. She clearly believes that her family home is haunted. Motifs include E38.1(h) "Miscellaneous activities of ghost"; E402.1.8, "Miscellaneous sounds made by ghost of human being"; E421.5, "Ghost seen by two or more persons; they corroborate the appearance."

11. Collected on 19 May 1995 in Livingston, Alabama, from David Leverett, a twenty-four-year-old graduate student and resident of Emelle, Alabama. Leverett believes in the story because of his faith in the sanity of most of his family members. Motifs include M341, "Death Prophesied"; M341.1, "Prophecy: Death at a certain time."

12. Collected on 12, July 1995 in Livingston, Alabama, from Howard Turner, a forty-five-year-old employee of Bryce Mental Health and resident of Eppes. Alabama. Turner appears to believe the tale because of the character of his informant. Motifs include *E425.1, "Revenant as woman"; *E435.2, "Revenant as man."

13. Collected on 21 October 1995 in Livingston, Alabama, from Ray Jordan, a twenty-four-year-old graduate student and resident of Livington. Jordan's sincere belief in the truthfulness of his story was evident in his words and in his quavering tone of voice. Motifs include E338.8, "Ghost haunts library"; *E425.1, "Revenant as woman."

14. Collected on 13 February 1997 in Livingston, Alabama, from Claire Smith, around fifty years old. Smith is a retired university librarian who lives in Livingston. Smith's belief in the story is produced primarily by the existence of the shack and the discovery of Indian artifacts on her property. Motifs include E337.1(e), "Death sounds of mother and baby re-enacted"; E421.5, "Ghost seen by two or more persons; they corroborate the appearance"; *E425.1, "Revenant as woman."

15. Collected on 2 October 1996 in Livingston, Alabama, from Linda Campbell, (see note on informant in story 4). Campbell appears to put credence in the story because of her friendship with the Munoz family. Motifs include E338.1(h), "Miscellaneous activities of ghosts in house"; E413 "Murdered person cannot rest in grave"; E421.5, "Ghost seen by two or more persons; they corroborate the appearance"; *E425.1, "Revenant as woman."

16. Collected on 29 October 1997 in Livingston, Alabama, from Angelia Willis, an eighteen-year-old college student. Willis tends to believe in the tale because she has seen the hole in the ground. The only relevant motif is *F974 "Grass refuses to grow in certain spot." For another version of the hanging of Bill Sketoe, see "The Hole that Will not Stay Filled" in Windham's *Thirteen Alabama Ghosts and Jeffrey* (87) and "A Tale and Five Variations: Always a Hole" in Jack and Olivia Solomon's *Ghosts and Goosebumps* (74).

17. Collected on 13 March 1996 in Meridian, Mississippi, from Stephen Lance. Lance is about thirty years old and is a college professor from Knoxville, Tennessee. This story and the one that follows are part of Lance's family folklore. Motifs include *E272, "Road ghosts. Ghost which haunts road"; E421.5, "Ghost seen by two or more persons; they corroborate the appearance"; *X916 (m), "Remarkable eyes."

18. Collected on 13 March 1996 in Meridian, Mississippi, from Stephen Lance (see note on informant in story 17). Motifs used in this very common story are M341, "Death Prophesied"; M341.1, "Prophecy: death at a certain time."

19. Collected on 9 February 1996 in Livingston, Alabama, from Michelle Gothard, an eighteen-year-old college student. Michelle is certain that she and her friends had an encounter with the supernatural. Motifs include E421.5, "Ghost seen by two or more persons; they corroborate the appearance"; *E530.1, "Ghost-like lights."

20. Collected on 3 August 1936 for the WPA in Little Rock, Arkansas, by J. C. W. Smith from Elberta Bailey, a resident of Little Rock. Motifs include *E371. "Return from dead to reveal hidden treasure"; *E425.2, "Revenant as man."

21. Collected on 22 August 1936 for the WPA in Little Rock, Arkansas, by J. C. W. Smith from Elberta Bailey, a resident of Little Rock. Motifs include *E281, "Ghost haunts house"; *E279.2, "Ghost disturbs sleeping person."

22. Collected on 22 August 1936 for the WPA in Little Rock, Arkansas, by J. C. W. Smith from Charlie Longs, a resident of Little Rock. Motifs include *E360, "Friendly return from the dead"; *E371, "Return from the dead to reveal hidden treasure"; E421.5, "Ghost seen by two or more persons; they corroborate the appearance"; *E425.1, "Revenant as a woman."

23. Collected on 22 August 1936 for the WPA in Little Rock, Arkansas, by J. C. W. Smith from John Wade (black), a resident of Little Rock. Motifs include *E281, "Ghost haunts house"; *E279.2, "Ghost disturbs sleeping person"; *E425.2, "Revenant as man."

24. Collected on 8 August 1936 for the WPA in Little Rock, Arkansas, by J. Pettigrew from Lewis Allen, a sixty-nine-year-old resident of Tucker, Arkansas. Tucker is the son of a slave and an Indian. He believes in the ghost because he, his brother, and his sister saw it. Motifs include E279, "Malevolent revenants; miscellaneous; *E279.2, "Ghost disturbs sleeping person"; *E371, "Return from dead to reveal hidden treasure"; *E425.2, "Revenant as man."

25. Collected on 8 August 1936 for the WPA in El Dorado, Arkansas, from Mrs. Effie Allen, a resident of El Dorado and a participant in the Home Helper's Project. Motifs include *E272, "Road ghosts. Ghost which haunts road"; E421.5, "Ghost seen by two or more persons; they corroborate the appearance"; *E424.1, "Revenant as woman."

26. Collected on 22 August 1936 for the WPA by Carol Graham in El Dorado, Arkansas, from Mrs. J. R. Wilson, a resident of El Dorado. Motifs include *E281, "Ghosts haunt house"; *E402.1.4, "Invisible ghost rattle chains"; *E425.1, "Revenant as woman."; E421.5, "Ghost seen by two or more persons; they corroborate the appearance."

27. Collected 5 December 1936 for the WPA by Odessa Miles (black) in El Dorado, Arkansas, from the Reverend R. B. Riley, a resident of El Dorado. This story is clearly a folktale. Motifs include D1812.5.0.3, "Behavior of fire as omen"; *E281, "Ghosts haunt house."

28. Collected on 16 November 1936 for the WPA by J. C. W. Smith in Little Rock, Arkansas, from Mrs. V. E. Sample, a resident of Blytheville, Arkansas. Sample gives no indication whether or not she accepts the wash woman's explanation. Motifs include *E281, "Ghosts haunt house"; E338.1(h), "Miscellaneous activities of ghost in house"; *E360, "Friendly return from the dead".

29. Collected on 21 November 1936 for the WPA by Annie L. LaCotts in St. Charles, Arkansas, from Jonas Brone. Motifs include *E279.2, "Ghost disturbs sleeping person; *E281, "Ghosts haunt house"; E337.1.3(b) "Sounds of dance in haunted house"; E421.5, "Ghost seen by two or more persons; they corroborate the appearance."

30. Collected on 22 August 1936 for the WPA in El Dorado, Arkansas, by Carol Graham from Mrs. A. Goodwin, a resident of El Dorado. Motifs include *E281, "Ghosts haunt house"; *E402.1.1 "Vocal sounds of ghost of human being"; *E402.1.2, "Footsteps of invisible ghost heard"; E421.5, "Ghost seen by two or more persons; they corroborate the appearance."

31. Collected on 21 November 1936 for the WPA in St. Charles, Arkansas, by Annie L. LaCotts from Adeline Burris (black) a ninety-one-year-old resident of DeWitt, Arkansas. Motifs include E280, "Ghosts haunt house"; E38.1(c), "Ghost opens doors and windows repeatedly"; *E545.12, "Ghost directs man to hidden treasure"; *E545.19.2(b), "Proper means addressing ghost: person must ask, 'In the name of the Lord, why troublest thou me?' "

32. Collected in 1936 for the WPA in Little Rock, Arkansas, by S. S. Taylor from W. H. Morley. Motifs include *E279.2, "Ghost disturbs sleeping person"; *E281, "Ghost haunts house"; *E425.1, "Revenant as woman."

33. Collected on 21 November 1936 for the WPA in Fayetteville, Arkansas, by Mary E. Overholt from R. M. Casey, forty years old. The only relevant motif is *E334.2.1, "Ghost of murdered person haunts burial spot."

34. Collected on 21 February 1995 in Livingston, Alabama, from Keaton Willis, an eighteen-year-old college student from Panacea, Florida. Keatons seems to put some credence in the story because it came from his father. Motifs include *E272, "Road ghosts. Ghost which haunts road"; *E422.1.1, "Headless revenant."

35. Collected on 17 May 1995 in Livingston, Alabama, from James Mercer. Mercer is a forty-year-old resident of Port Charlotte, Florida. Mercer's belief in his family's psychic abilities suggests that he feels that the story is real. Motifs include *E 545.12, "Ghost directs man to hidden treasure"; *X916(m), "Remarkable eyes."

36. Collected on 3 October 1996 in Livingston, Alabama, from Charles Loveless, a fifty-two-year-old college professor from Livingston, Alabama. Loveless does not seem to be ready to accept the story as more than just a local legend. The only relevant motif is *E432.2, "Revenant as animal."

37. Collected on 15 November 1996 in Livingston, Alabama, from Tom Hambright. Hambright is about forty years old and is a librarian at the Key West Public Library. Motifs include *E279.2, "Ghost disturbs sleeping person"; E280, "Ghosts haunt buildings"; E415, "Dead cannot rest until certain work is finished." For more information on the ghost of Maria de Gutsens, see "Nurse's Ghost Still Makes Nightly Rounds," *Midnight Magazine*, 18 January 1977.

38. Collected on 5 November 1996 in Livingston, Alabama, from Jennifer Santiago, an eighteen-year-old college student from Lakewood, Florida. Motifs include *E344.4, "Ghost of suicide seen at death spot"; E338.7, "Ghost haunts educational institution." A variant of this tale entitled "The Roommate's Death" can be found in Jan Harold Brunvand's *Vanishing Hitchhiker* (57) and in Joel D. Rudinger's "Folk Ogres of the Firelands: Narrative Variations of a North Central Ohio Community," *Indiana Folklore* 9 (1976): 41–93.

39. Collected in December 1972 by Mrs. Janice Simmons, a resident of Glasgow, Kentucky, and a student in a folklore class. The story is based on her personal experience and is taken from the folklore archives at the Western Kentucky University. Motifs include *E272, "Road ghosts. Ghost which haunts road"; E421.5, "Ghost seen by two or more persons; they corroborate the appearance"; *E530.1, "Ghost-like lights."

40. Collected on 9 January 1997 in Livingston, Alabama, from Cynthia Infinger, a twenty-year-old college student from Lynnhaven, Florida. Infinger's personal experiences, as well as those of her relatives, tend to make her believe in the stories about the house. Motifs include *E279.2, "Ghost disturbs sleeping person"; *E402.1.1, "Vocal sounds of ghost of human being"; *E402.1.2, "Footsteps of invisible ghost"; *E402.1.1.3, "Ghost cries and screams."

41. Collected on 9 January 1997 in Livingston, Alabama, from Cynthia Infinger (see note on informant in story 40). Infinger's experiences with the Ouija board seem to have convinced her of the ghost's existence. Motifs include D1812.0.1, "Foreknowledge of death"; *E279.2, "Ghost disturbs sleeping person"; *E281, "Ghosts haunt house"; M341, "Death prophesied."

42. Collected on 9 January 1997 in Livingston, Alabama, from Cynthia Infinger (see note on informant in story 40). The only relevant motif is E338.1(hg), "Ghost causes rocking chair to rock."

43. Collected on 9 January 1997 in Livingston, Alabama, from Cynthia Infinger (see note on informant in story 40). Infinger suspects that her grandmother may have imagined the phenomena. Motifs include *E338(b), "Female ghost seen in house"; *E402.2, "Sound of ethereal music."

44. Collected on 15 December 1938 for the WPA in Jacksonville, Florida, by Veronica E. Huss from Izzelly Harding, a sixty-three-year-old resident of Riviera, Florida. Harding was born in Long Island Bahamas; her father was white and her mother was black. Most of her youth was spent in the islands. Harding's superstitious nature is probably the result of growing up in the Bahamas in the nineteenth century. Motifs include *E530.1.0.1, "Ghost light as ball of fire"; F491.4, "Will-o'-wisp hops about."

45. Collected on 15 December 1938 for the WPA in Jacksonville, Florida, by Veronica E. Huss from Izzelly Harding (see note on informant in story 44). There is no relevant motif.

46. Collected on 15 December 1938 for the WPA in Jacksonville, Florida, by Veronica E. Huss from Izzelly Harding (see note on informant in story 44). Interestingly enough, Harding is skeptical about the effectiveness of the magic. There is no relevant motif. For more information on the use of grave dust in obeah and hoodoo, see Lewis Spence's *Encyclopedia of Occultism* (Secaucus, N.J.: University Books, 1960) and Harry Middleton Hyatt's *Hoodoo, Conjuration, Witchcraft, Rootwork* (Hannibal, Mo.: Western Publishing, 1970). Zora Neale Hurston explains how grave dust, known as "the dust of Goofer," is employed in voodoo rituals in New Orleans in *Mules and Men* (New York: Random House, 1990), 196.

47. Collected on 7 March 1996 In Livingston, Alabama, from George McRae, an eighteen-year-old college student from Eutaw, Alabama. The trust McRae has in his friends' honesty accounts for his belief in the tale. Motifs include *E334.4, "Ghost of suicide seen at death spot or near by"; *E338.1(ca), "Ghost opens door or window and looks out"; *E402.1.2, "Footsteps of invisible ghost heard."

48. Collected on 19 May 1938 for the WPA in Augusta, Georgia, by Louise Oliphant from Frances Cade (black), a resident of Augusta. Cade's belief in the phenomenon is bolstered by the fact that her child had witnessed the same thing. Motifs include *E272, "Road ghosts. Ghost which haunts road"; E421.5, "Ghost seen by two or more persons; they corroborate the appearance"; E423.1.3.4, "Actions of ghostly horse."

49. Collected on 19 May 1938 for the WPA in Augusta, Georgia, by Louise Oliphant from Hallie Hanson (black) a sixty-three-year-old resident of Augusta. Hanson sincerely believes that she saw a ghost. Motifs include *E422.1.1, "Headless revenant"; *E521.2, "Ghost of dog."

50. Collected on 19 May 1938 for the WPA in Augusta, Georgia, by Louise Oliphant from Hattie Hanson (black), a resident of Augusta. Hanson's belief in the phenomenon is bolstered by the fact that her father also saw the ghost and that the field had not been plowed. Motifs include *E338(a), "Male ghost seen"; E415, "Dead cannot rest until certain work is finished"; E421.5, "Ghost seen by two or more persons; they corroborate the appearance"

51. Collected on 19 May 1938 for the WPA in Augusta, Georgia, by Louise Oliphant from Mary Jackson (black), a resident of Augusta. Jackson believes she saw a ghost because her hair stood on end. Motifs include *E415, "Dead cannot rest until certain work is finished"; *E425.1, "Revenant as woman."

52. Collected on 12 May 1938 for the WPA in Augusta, Georgia, by Louise Oliphant from Almira Heath (black), a resident of Augusta. Heath seems to agree with the generally held opinion that a ghost forced a confession out of the murderer. Motifs include *E272, "Road ghosts; Ghost which haunts road"; E273, "Churchyard ghosts"; *E332.3.3, "Ghost asks for ride in automobile"; *E332.3.3.1, "The Vanishing Hitchhiker"; E334.2.3, "Ghost of tragic lover haunts scene of tragedy."

53. Collected 1937–38 for the WPA in Augusta, Georgia, by Louise Oliphant from Alberta Thurmond (black), an elderly resident of Augusta. Motifs include *E281, "Ghosts haunt house"; E337.1.3(b), "Sounds of dance in haunted house"; *E402.1.3, "Invisible ghost plays musical instrument."

54. Collected 1937–38 for the WPA in Augusta, Georgia, by Louise Oliphant from Alberta Thurmond (black) (see note on informant in story 53). Thurmond believes she saw a ghost because her brother and sister saw it too. Motifs include *E272, "Road ghosts. Ghost which haunts road"; *E413 "Murdered person cannot rest"; E421.5, "Ghost seen by two or more persons; they corroborate the appearance"; E423.1.2, "Revenant as cat"

55. Collected in 1937–38 for the WPA in Augusta, Georgia, by Louise Oliphant from Alberta Thurmond (see note on informant in story 53). Thurmond sincerely believes the cow was the ghost of the dead woman. Motifs include *E272, "Road ghosts. Ghost which haunts road"; *E423.1.8, "Revenant as cow, bull, calf or steer."

56. Collected 1937–38 for the WPA in Augusta, Georgia, by Louise Oliphant from Alberta Thurmond (see note on informant in story 53). Thurmond sincerely believes that she saw her husband's spirit. Motifs include *E334.2, "Ghost haunts

burial spot"; *E338(a), "Male ghost seen"; *E360, "Friendly return from the dead"; *E402(d), "Ghostlike noises causes owners to abandon farm"; *E402.1.5, "Invisible ghost makes rapping or knocking noise."

57. Collected in 1937–38 for the WPA in Augusta, Georgia, by Louise Oliphant from Alberta Thurmond (see note on informant in story 53). Thurmond seems to believe the story because it happened to her sister. Motifs include *E272, "Road ghosts. Ghost which haunts road"; *E432.1.2, "Revenant as cat."

58. Collected in 1937–38 for the WPA in Augusta, Georgia, by Louise Oliphant from Cora Elam (black), an elderly resident of Augusta. Motifs include E273, "Churchyard ghosts"; *E423.1.1, "Revenant as dog."

59. Collected 1937–38 for the WPA in Augusta, Georgia, by Louise Oliphant from Louise Crawford (black), a fifty-eight-year-old resident of Augusta. Crawford sincerely believes that a ghost walked into her bedroom. Motifs include *E279.2, "Ghost disturbs sleeping person"; E280, "Ghosts haunt building"; E338.1(ca), "Ghost opens door or window and looks out"; E338.1(f), "Ghost haunts bedroom"; *E421.5, "Ghost seen by two or more persons; they corroborate the appearance"; *E425.1, "Revenant as woman."

60. Collected on 6 May 1938 for the WPA in Augusta, Georgia, by Louise Oliphant from Lucy Burke (black), a resident of Augusta. Motifs include *E423.1.1, "Revenant as dog"; *E423.1.1.2, "Revenant as cat"; *E425.1, "Revenant as woman."

61. Collected 1937–38 for the WPA in Augusta, Georgia, by Louise Oliphant from Susie Brown (black), an eighty-nine-year-old ex-slave and resident of Augusta. Brown sincerely believes that she was confronted by two ghosts on the street. Motifs include *E272, "Road ghosts. Ghost which haunts road"; *E338(a), "Male ghost seen"; *E422.1.1, "Headless revenant."

62. Collected in November 1972 by Janice Simmons, a folklore student from Western Kentucky University in Bowling Green, from Gloria Godby, an eighteen-year-old switchboard operator for Holiday Inn of Somerset, Kentucky. Motifs include E423.1.1.1(b), "Ghostly black dog"; M341, "Death prophesied."

63. Collected in November 1972 by Janice Simmons, a folklore student from Western Kentucky University in Bowling Green, from Lloyd T. Godby, a forty-nine-year-old truck driver and chief of the Science Hill Fire Department. Godby may have heard the story from his father, who was a foreman on the Southern Railway. Motifs include E338.1(hg), "Ghost causes rocking chair to rock"; *E422.1.1, "Headless revenant"; *E422.1.1.5, "Miscellaneous actions of headless ghost." For a similar story about a headless railroad ghost, see "Michael and the Ghost Light" in Richard and Judy Young's Ghost Stories from the American Southwest (40).

64. Collected in December 1971 by Terry Hicks, a student in a folklore class at Western Kentucky University in Bowling Green, from Brian R. Loader, an eighteen-year-old college student from Louisville, Kentucky. Loader tends to believe the stories about Van Meter Auditorium because he heard them from his father, an engineer. Motifs include E280, "Ghosts haunt building"; *E530.1, "Ghost-like lights"; *E411.1.1, "Suicide cannot rest in grave"; *E422.1.11.5.1(a), "Ineradicable bloodstain in stone or wood floor after bloody tragedy at spot."

65. Collected in October 1972 by Donna Smith, a folklore student from Western Kentucky University in Bowling Green, from Linda Reeves, a resident of Louisville, Kentucky. According to Jan Harold Brunvand, this tale, which he calls "The Boyfriend's Death," is clearly related to two older yarn "The Hook" and "The Roommate's Death," and has been told by teenagers as a separate story only since the 1960s. There is no relevant motif for this story. Variants of the story may be found in Brunvand's *The Vanishing Hitchhiker: American Urban Legends and Their Meanings* (5) and in Joel D. Rudinger's "Folk Ogres of the Firelands: Narrative Variations of a North Central Ohio Community," *Indiana Folklore* 9 (1976): 41–93.

66. Collected on 28 October 1972 by Donna Sue Smith, a folklore student at Western Kentucky University in Bowling Green, from Nora Farnem. Motifs include *E220, "Dead relative's malevolent return"; *E235.4, "Return from dead to punish theft of part of corpse." For another version of this well-known jump-tale, see "Who's Got My Liver?" in Jack and Olivia Solomon's *Ghosts and Goosebumps: Ghost Stories, Tall Tales, and Superstitions from Alabama* (60).

67. Collected on 28 October 1972 in Bowling Green, by Donna Sue Smith, a folklore student at Western Kentucky University in Bowling Green, from Dennis Elzey, an eighteen-year-old college student. Elzey is convinced that he saw a ghost. Motifs include *E273, "Churchyard ghosts"; *E402.1.2, "Footsteps of invisible ghost heard"; *E422.1.1(b), "Headless woman, appearance only."

68. Collected on 5 December 1987 by Dana Albrecht, a folklore student at Western Kentucky University in Bowling Green, from Mary Long, a nineteen-year-old college student from Portsmouth, Virginia. The footstep that Long heard convinced Long that Potter Hall really is haunted. Motifs include *E338.1(h), "Miscellaneous activities of ghosts in house"; E338.7, "Ghost haunts educational institution"; *E402.1.2, "Footsteps of invisible ghost heard."

69. Collected in 1977 by Mary Gail Abell, a folklore student at Western Kentucky University in Bowling Green, from M. K. Hendrick, a fifty-eight-year-old farmer from Hardinsburg, Kentucky. Motifs include E273, "Churchyard ghosts"; *E402.1.8, "Miscellaneous sounds made by ghost of human being."

70. Collected in Summer 1971 in Louisville, Kentucky, by Glenn E. Groebli, a folklore student at Western Kentucky University in Bowling Green, from James R. Kettner, a seventy-eight-year-old resident of Louisville. Kettner, who did not go beyond the fifth grade, worked on the railroad and in construction. Motifs include *E272, "Road ghosts. Ghosts which haunt road"; *E 273, "Churchyard ghosts"; *E423.1.1.1(c), "Ghostly white dog."

71. Collected in 1972 by Odell S. Crockett, a folklore student at Western Kentucky University in Bowling Green, from Virginia Sizemore, a twenty-two-year-old college student from Hyden, Kentucky. Motifs include *E272, "Road ghosts. Ghost which haunts road"; *E332.3.1, "Ghost rides on horseback with rider."

72. Collected in 1972 in Russellville, Kentucky, by Mike Burchett, a folklore student in Western Kentucky University in Bowling Green, from Beulah Whitsett, a seventy-six-year-old resident of Russellville. Motifs include *E532(a), "Ghost-like

portrait etched in glass"; M414.1, "God cursed." For a more famous example of a face etched in glass, see the accounts of the face in the Garrett window of the Pickens County Courthouse in Carrolton, Alabama, in stories 29a and 29b in W. K. McNeil's *Ghost Stories from the American South* (68–69), "Face in the Window" (four versions) in Alan Brown's *The Face in the Window and Other Alabama Ghostlore* (77–79), and "The Face in the Courthouse Window" in Kathryn Tucker Windham and Margaret Gillis Figh's *13 Alabama Ghosts and Jeffrey* (63). For a different "face in the window" story from Kentucky, see the six variants of "The Russellville Girl" in William Lynwood Montell's *Ghosts Along the Cumberland* (212) and "The Russellville Girl" from "Haunted Kentucky" on the American Ghost Society's Web site (www.prairieghosts.com).

73. Collected in 1965 by Patrick John Fuller, a folklore student from Western Kentucky University in Bowling Green, from Anna Belle Daves, seventy-one years old, from Christian County, Kentucky. Daves is descended from plantation slavers. Motifs include *E220, "Dead relative's malevolent return"; *E402.1.1, "Vocal sounds of ghost of human being"; *E424.1, "Revenant as woman."

74. Collected in November 1973, by Isaac Hinkle, a folklore student from Western Kentucky University in Bowling Green, from Mrs. Bell Fitch from Richardson, Kentucky. Hinkle says in a note, "I have tried to disprove some of these stories, such as the one about the girl killing herself at the river. Ring and Steeple, where she killed herself, is now one of the best fishing spots in the area. One night, several of my friends and I were fishing there and decided to stay until midnight just to see if she would jump into the river. She never jumped by midnight, so we left just as soon after midnight as we could. However, we decided after leaving that since we were on Daylight Savings Time when we were there that she didn't jump until one o'clock. We never went back after that to check out our theory." Motifs include *E334.4, "Ghost of suicide seen at death spot or near by"; E334.2.2(c), "Ghost of drowned person"; *E402.1.1, "Vocal sound of ghost of human being."

75. Collected in June 1988, by Gary Reesor, a folklore student from Western Kentucky University in Bowling Green, from Mrs. Ivy McBride, an eighty-three-year-old retired teacher from Shepherdsville, Kentucky. Motifs included are *E281, "Ghost haunts house"; *E334.4, "Ghost of suicide seen at death spot or near by"; *E338(a), "Male ghost seen"; *E402.1.1, "Vocal sounds of ghost of human being.

76. Collected in Spring 1974 in the Albany quadrangle by Mildred B. Byrd, a folklore student at Western Kentucky University, from Elvin Byrd, a fifty-eight-year-old carpenter and farmer from Albany, Kentucky. Byrd is certain that the story is true because he believes Walter Groce, one of the witnesses to the phenomenon. Motifs include *E272, "Road ghosts. Ghost which haunts road"; *E272.4, "Ghost chases a pedestrian on road"; *E530.1, "Ghost-like lights."

77. Collected on 6 December 1977, in Henderson, Kentucky, by Kim Goheen, a folklore student at Western Kentucky University, from Hardin Dome Whitworth, fifty-six years old. Whitworth lives on a houseboat on the Ohio River; he makes his living by fixing boat motors. Whitworth, who did not go beyond the fifth grade,

is mostly self-educated. Motifs include 419.7.1, "Ghost returns to search for head"; *E422.1.1, "Headless revenant"; *E545.19.2(b), "Proper means of addressing ghost: person must ask, 'In the name of the Lord, why troublest thou me?' "

78. Collected on 27 December 1967, in Edmonson County by Harold W. Elmore, a folklore student at Western Kentucky University in Bowling Green, from George Elmore, a resident of Brownsville, Kentucky. Although the person who told George Elmore the story swore that it is true, Elmore does not indicate whether or not he believes it. Motives include *E272, "Road ghosts. Ghost which haunts road"; *E272.4, "Ghost chases pedestrian on road"; *E433.1.1, "Headless revenant."

79. Collected in October 1977 in Brooks, Kentucky, by Philip Pitchford, a folklore student in Western Kentucky University in Bowling Green, from Mrs. James Edward Creighton, forty-one years old. Creighton sincerely believes that she saw a ghost. Motifs include *E282, "Ghost haunts house"; *E324, "Dead child's friendly return to parents."

80. Collected on 12 November 1997 in Livingston, Alabama, from Steven Guillbeau, an eighteen-year-old college student from Broussard, Louisiana. Guillbeau's belief that he saw a ghost is bolstered by his friends' witness of the same event. Motifs include *E334.2, "Ghost haunts burial spot"; *E334.4, "Ghost of suicide seen at death spot or near by"; *E425.1, "Revenant as woman." For an account of the haunting of T-Frere in Lafayette, Louisiana, see "T-Frere's Amelie" in Christine Word's Ghosts Along the Bayou (102).

81. Collected on 28 February 1995 in Livingston, Alabama, from Brock Muse, an eighteen-year-old college student from Kentwood, Louisiana. "Roo-Garoo" is a Cajun pronunciation of "Loupe Garou," the French word for "werewolf." There is no relevant motif for this story. For additional information on Louisiana werewolves, see "The Loupe Garou" from Christy L. Vivano's Haunted Louisiana (23).

82. Collected on 3 March 1995 in Livingston, Alabama, from Robert Gaspard, an eighteen-year-old college student from West Memphis, Arkansas. Gaspard seems to be torn between the possibilities that the lights are ghosts and that they are swamp gas. Motifs include *E530.1, "Ghost-like lights"; F491.4, "Will-o'wisp hops about." For another account of the Fifolet, see "Fifolet" in J. J. Reneaux's Cajun Folktales (141).

83. Collected on 31 October 1996 in Livingston, Alabama, from Jaime Smith, an eighteen-year-old college student from Preston, Mississippi. Smith is convinced that she saw ghosts in the house, although she admits that she was very young when she witnessed the events. Motifs include *E275, "Ghost haunts place of great accident or misfortune"; *E281, "Ghosts haunt house"; *E334.2.1, "Ghost of murdered person haunts burial spot"; *E337.1.3, "Sounds of revelry heard"; E338.1(h), "Miscellaneous activities of ghosts in house"; *E402.1.8, "Miscellaneous sounds made by ghost of human being."

84. Collected on 9 February 1996 in Livingston, Alabama, from Michelle Gothard, an eighteen-year-old college student from Bastrop, Louisiana. At the time of the interview, Gothard had only lived in Louisiana for two years. The expression

"they say" suggests that Gothard is not totally convinced that the story is true. Motifs include *E272, "Road ghosts. Ghosts which haunt road"; *334.2.2, "Ghost of person killed in accident seen at death or burial spot"; *E422.2.4, "Revenant in black."

85. Collected on 9 February 1996 in Livingston, Alabama, from Michelle Gothard (see note on informant in story 84). Gothard makes it clear in the beginning of the story that she is not convinced that her friend was stalked by a ghost. Motifs include *E272, "Road ghosts. Ghost which haunts road"; *E272.4, "Ghost chases pedestrian on road"; *E402.1.2, "Footsteps of invisible ghost heard."

86. Collected on 9 February 1996 in Livingston, Alabama, from Michelle Gothard (see note on informant in story 84). Expressions like "I think" indicate that Gothard has not actually heard the ghostly screams. Motifs include *E272, "Road ghosts. Ghost which haunts road"; *E275, "Ghost haunts place of great accident or misfortune"; *E402.1.1.3, "Ghost cries and screams."

87. Collected on 15 April 1997 in Livingston, Alabama, from David Mazel, a forty-one-year-old college professor from Livingston, Alabama. Mazel attended Louisiana State University as an undergraduate and made frequent trips to New Orleans. Mazel recalls all of the ghost stories he has heard about New Orleans as being folklore and nothing more. Motifs include *E281, "Ghost haunts house" *E334.2.1, "Ghost of person killed in accident seen at death or burial spot"; *E425.1, "Revenant as woman"; *E337.1.1, "Murder sounds heard as they must have happened at time of death." For additional information on the Lalaurie house, see "La Maison Lalaurie" in Victor C. Klein's *New Orleans Ghosts* (7); "Lalaurie House" in Dennis William Hauck's *Haunted Places* (192); and "The Haunted House" in Lyle Saxon's *Fabulous New Orleans* (202).

88. Collected on 15 April 1997 in Livingston, Alabama, from David Mazel (see note on informant in story 87). Motifs include *E275, "Ghost haunts place of great accident or misfortune"; *E281, "Ghosts haunt house"; E411.10, "Person who dies violent or accidental death cannot rest in grave"; *E425.1, "Revenant as woman"; *E425.2, "Revenant as man." For another account of the death of the octoroon girl, see "The Octoroon Mistress" in Victor C. Klein's *New Orleans Ghosts* (61).

89. Collected on 15 April 1997 in Livingston, Alabama, from David Mazel (see note on informant in story 87). Motifs include *E275, "Ghost Haunts place of great accident or misfortune"; *E281, "Ghosts haunt house"; *E337.1.1, "Murder sounds heard just as they must have happened at time of death"; E402.1.8, "Miscellaneous sounds made by ghost of human being." For additional accounts of the hauntings in the Beauregard-Keyes House, see "The Beauregard-Keyes House" in Victor C. Klein's *New Orleans Ghosts* (55) and "Beauregard House" in Dennis William Hauck's *Haunted Places* (191).

90. Collected on 15 April 1997 in Livingston, Alabama, from David Mazel (see note on informant in story 87). Motifs include *E275, "Ghost haunts place of great accident or misfortune"; *E38.2, "Non-malevolent ghost haunts church"; *E402.1.2, "Footsteps of invisible ghost heard"; *E402.1.1.3, "Ghost cries and screams"; *E413,

"Murdered person cannot rest in grave"; *E425.2, "Revenant as man." For another account of "The Sultan's Murder," see "The Sultan's Retreat" in Victor C. Klein's *New Orleans Ghosts* (65).

91. Collected on 15 April 1997 in Livingston, Alabama, from David Mazel (see note on informant in story 67). Motifs include *402.1.1, "Vocal sounds of ghost of human being"; *E402.4, "Sounds of ethereal music." For another account of the haunting outside the St. Louis Cathedral, see "Pere Dagobert" in Victor C. Klein's *New Orleans Ghosts* (51) and "Ghosts" in Saxon et al.'s *Gumbo Ya-Ya* (294).

92. Collected on 25 July 1936 for the WPA by Susie Heather from Evelyn Brown, supervisor of the Home Helpers Project. The explanation of the phenomenon in the end of the tale indicates that Brown did not believe the story. Motifs include *E272, "Churchyard ghosts"; *E421.3, "Luminous ghosts"; *E530.1, "Ghost-like lights." For another account of the glowing tomb in the Metairie Cemetery, see "The Flaming Tomb" in Victor C. Klein's *New Orleans Ghosts* (1).

93. Collected on 5 December 1936 for the WPA in El Dorado, Arkansas, by Carol Graham from Fay Goodwin, owner of Goodwin's Gas Station in El Dorado. Motifs include 1676(b) "Clothing caught in graveyard"; *N384.2, "Death in graveyard; person's clothing is caught, the person thinks something awful is holding him; he dies of fright." For a variant of this well-known graveyard folktale, see "Fork in a Skirt" (four versions) in William Lynwood Montell's *Ghosts Along the Cumberlands* (199–201).

94. Collected on 12 December 1995 in Meridian, Mississippi, from Fonda Rush, historical preservationist and neighborhood-development specialist from Meridian. Rush, an authority on the history of local landmarks, has been instrumental in the preservation of such antebellum homes as Merrehope and has entertained local civic groups with her storytelling for many years. Although Rush believes the history behind the tale, she appears to agree with her grandmother that the supernatural aspects of the story are folklore. Motifs include E274 (a), "Ghost haunts scene of unjust execution"; *E530.1, "Ghost-like lights."

95. Collected on 12 December 1995 in Meridian, Mississippi, from Fonda Rush (see note on informant in story 94). Rush, who found this story in a 1904 article in the *Meridian Star* and tells it at a children's Halloween celebration every year, stresses the humor in the line, "Oh Lordy! Lordy! There's Missouri!" Motifs include *E334.2.2, "Ghost of person killed in accident seen at death or burial spot"; *E334.2.2(c), "Ghost of drowned person haunts spot of drowning"; E4425.1, "Revenant as woman."

96. Collected on 11 March 1996 in Livingston, Alabama, from Don Hines, president of the University of Western Alabama. Hines, who grew up in northern Mississippi, laughed as he told the story, an indication that he did not take it very seriously. Motifs include E423.2, "Revenant as wild animal"; *E520, "Animal ghosts." For another ghost possum story, see "Possum as Ghost" in Ray B. Browne's *"A Night with the Hants" and Other Alabama Folk Experiences* (197).

97. Collected on 24 June 1994 in Meridian, Mississippi, from Beth Cagle, a

thirty-five-year-old college student from Scuba, Mississippi. Cagle makes it clear in the beginning that she regards the story as nothing more than a humorous tale. The only relevant motif is F585ff, "Phantoms."

98. Collected on 24 June 1996 in Livingston, Alabama, from Delissa Davis, a twenty-one-year-old graduate student from Sweet Water, Alabama. Davis, who grew up in Meridian, believes her grandmother's story. Motifs include E423.2, "Revenant as wild animal"; E423.2.7, "Revenant as wolf"; *E575, "Ghost as omen of calamity or ill fortune."

99. Collected on 14 March 1997 in Livingston, Alabama, from Crystal Tanner, a forty-year-old college student and former nursing home employee. Tanner definitely believes that the Queen City Nursing Home is haunted, primarily because of what she has seen and the testimony of her patients and fellow employees. Motifs include *E2165, "Meeting host carries misfortune"; *E338(a), "Male ghost seen"; *E360, "Friendly return from dead"; *E575, "Ghost as omen of calamity or ill fortune."

100. Collected on 18 January 1995 in Livingston, Alabama, from Christopher Shelton, an eighteen-year-old college student from Toombsooba, Mississippi. Shelton is convinced that he saw a ghost at the house. Motifs include *E281, "Ghosts haunt house"; *E334.2, "Ghost haunts burial spot"; *E413, "Murdered person cannot rest in grave"; *E425.1, "Revenant as woman"; *E530.1.0.1(c), "Building seen to light up strangely at night when unoccupied"; *E530.1.3, "Ghost light haunts burial spot."

101. Collected on 22 June 1994 in Livingston, Alabama, from Nyaz Khan. Originally from Bangladesh, Khan received his graduate degrees from Mississippi State University and was a college professor. Khan's quivering tone indicated that he really believes that a ghost rode with him in the car that night. Motifs include *E332.3.3, "Ghost asks for ride in automobile"; *E332.3.3.1, "The Vanishing Hitchhiker"; *E422.4.4, "Revenant in female dress." For additional versions of "The Vanishing Hitchhiker" story, see "The Doctor in Elba" in Jack and Olivia Solomon's Ghosts and Goosebumps (27); "The Lady of White Rock Lake" in Richard and Judy Young's Ghost Stories from the American Southwest (70); "The Vanishing Hitchhiker" (118) and "The Vanishing Girl" (126) in William Lynwood Montell's Ghosts Along the Cumberland; "The Vanishing Hitchhiker" in Jan Harold Brunvand's The Vanishing Hitchhiker (24); and "Highway 365" from "Haunted Arkansas" on the American Ghost Society's Web site (www.prairieghosts.com).

102. Collected on 23 May 1995 in Meridian, Mississippi, from Carlene Barkley, a fifty-year-old middle school gym teacher from Meridian. Barkley is convinced that a ghost appeared to her and moved her keys. Motifs include *E279.2, "Ghost disturbs sleeping person"; *E281, "Ghosts haunt house"; *E360, "Friendly return from the dead."

103. Collected on 28 June 1995 in Livingston, Alabama, from Earl C. Stennis, dean of the College of Business at the University of West Alabama and nephew of Senator John Stennis. Stennis is certain that this tale was concocted by camp coun-

selors down through the years to frighten the Boy Scouts. Motifs include E419.7.1, "Ghost returns to search for head"; *E422.1.1, "Headless revenant"; *E422.1.1.5, "Miscellaneous actions of headless ghost"; and "The Golden Arm" from Jack and Olivia Solomon's *Ghosts and Goosebumps* (61).

104. Collected 30 June 1995 in Meridian, Mississippi, from Robert Matheny, a seventy-nine-year-old retired preacher from Meridian. Matheny is very much aware that this jump tale, which was told by his elementary school principal in 1925, is a folktale. He suspects, correctly, that the tale possibly originated with the slaves who lived in the area. Motifs include *E235.4, "Return from dead to punish theft of part of corpse"; *E235.4.1, "Return from dead to punish theft of golden arm." For additional versions of this tale, see "The Golden Arm" in William Lynwood Montell's *Ghosts Along the Cumberland* (209). For a version of a similar tale, see "The Big Toe" in Jack and Olivia Solomon's *Ghosts and Goosebumps* (58). See also John Burrison's study of this tale, *"The Golden Arm."*

105. Collected on 12 December 1995 in Meridian, Mississippi, from Fonda Rush (see note on informant in story 94). The collective testimony of the people on the tour, Elliot Street, and her children has convinced her that she heard a ghost in the Grand Opera House. Motifs include *E402.1.1, "Vocal sounds of ghost of human being"; E402.1.6, "Crash as of breaking glass, though no glass is found broken"; E402.4, "Sound of ethereal music"; *E421.5, "Ghost seen by two or more persons; they corroborate the appearance." For additional stories about the Grand Opera House, see " 'The Lady'—Meridian's Grand Opera House" in Sylvia Booth Hubbard's *Ghosts! Personal Accounts of Modern Mississippi Hauntings* (77) and "Grand Opera House" in David William Hauck's *Haunted Places* (238).

106. Collected on 24 June 1995 in Meridian, Mississippi, from Beth Cagle (see note on informant in story 97). Cagle appears to accept the scientific explanation for the apparition: foxfire. Motifs include *E422.1.1, "Headless revenant"; *E530.1, "Ghost-like lights"; Ff491.4, "Will-o'-wisp hops about."

107. Collected on 22 June 1994 in Livingston, Alabama, from Nyaz Khan (see note on informant in story 101). Khan and his roommate seem to have accepted the supernatural explanation behind the strange events in their apartment. Motifs include *E279.s, "Ghost disturbs sleeping person"; E280, "Ghosts haunt buildings"; *E402.1.1, "Vocal sounds of ghost of human being"; *E402.1.8, "Miscellaneous sounds made by ghost of human beings"; *E421.5, "Ghost seen by two or more persons; they corroborate the appearance."

108. Collected on 12 December 1995 in Meridian, Mississippi, from Fonda Rush (see note on informant in story 94). Rush draws from the sightings by other visitors to Merrehope to support her conclusion that the antebellum home is haunted. Motifs include *E338(b), "Female ghost seen in house"; E338.1(h), "Miscellaneous activities of ghost"; *E360, "Friendly return from the dead"; *E421.5, "Ghost seen by two or more persons; they corroborate the appearance." For additional stories about Merrehope, see "Merrehope" in Sylvia Booth Hubbard's *Ghosts! Personal Accounts of Modern Mississippi Hauntings* (121).

109. Collected on 12 December 1995 in Meridian, Mississippi, from Fonda Rush (see note on informant in story 94). Rush tends to believe the legendary haunting of city hall because Mayor Kemp witnessed the same phenomena. Motifs include E280, "Ghost haunts building"; E338.1(h), "Miscellaneous activities of ghosts."

110. Collected on 12 December 1995 in Meridian, Mississippi, from Fonda Rush (see note on informant in story 94). Rush's belief in the ghostly occurrences appears to be lessened by the fact that they occurred in the presence of other people, not her. The only relevant motif is E338.1(h), "Miscellaneous activities of ghosts."

111. Collected on 22 June 1994 in Livingston, Alabama, from Patricia Hewitt, a forty-year-old college professor and resident of Meridian, Mississippi. Hewitt received this tale from her mother, Mary Lancaster Bradley, who heard it from her grandmother, Mary Hines Lancaster. Hewitt treasures this tale as an important part of her family folklore. Motifs include *E321, "Dead husband's friendly return"; E338.1(c), "Ghost opens doors and windows repeatedly"; *E402.1.1, "Vocal sounds of ghost of human being"; *E451.5, "Ghost laid when treasure is unearthed"; *E545.12, "Ghost directs man to hidden treasure."

112. Collected on 21 April 1997 in Livingston, Alabama, from Tim Ballard, a twenty-year-old college student from East Flat Rock, North Carolina. Ballard's belief that he had an encounter with the supernatural is bolstered by the fact that he shared this experience with his friends. Motifs include *E;;272, "Road ghosts. Ghost which haunts road"; *E338.1(h), "Miscellaneous activities of ghost"; *E421.5, "Ghost seen by two or more persons; they corroborate the appearance."

113. Collected on 21 April 1997 in Livingston, Alabama, from Tim Ballard (see note on informant in story 112). Ballard believes that the house is haunted because the lights came on in the house when the only occupant was standing in the doorway. Motifs include *E281, "Ghost haunts house"; E338.1(h), "Miscellaneous activities of ghost."

114. Collected on 15 November 1995 in Livingston, Alabama, from Stephen Slimp, about thirty-five years old. Slimp, a resident of Livingston, has taught on the college level in Siler City, North Carolina, and Japan. He received these tales from his students and regards them as nothing more than local folklore. Brown Mountain is not in the Great Smoky Mountain National Forest; it is near Linville, approximately sixty miles from the Smokies. The only relevant motif is *E530.1, "Ghost-like lights." For another version of this story, see "Brown Mountain Lights" in Dennis William Hauck's *Haunted Places* (311) and "The Brown Mountain Lights" in Nancy Roberts's *Southern Ghosts* (13).

115. Collected on 15 November 1995 in Livingston, Alabama, from Stephen Slimp (see note on informant in story 114). Motifs include E280, "Ghosts haunt buildings"; *E338(a), "Male ghost seen."

116. Collected on 15 November 1995 in Livingston, Alabama, from Stephen Slimp (See note on informant in story 114). The only relevant motif is *F974, "Grass refuses to grow in certain spot." For another version of this story, see "Devil's Tramping Ground" in Dennis William Hauck's *Haunted Places* (318). For a similar

story, see "The Bare Spot" in William Lynwood Montell's *Ghosts Along the Cumberland* (178). See also John Hardin's *Devil's Tramping Ground.*

117. Collected on 23 June 1937 for the WPA in State Prison by Mary A. Hicks from Melvin McLong (black), a prisoner formerly of Scotland County. Because McLong is reporting a local legend that he has not personal experience of, it is difficult to determine his level of belief in the tale. Motifs include *E281, "Ghosts haunt house"; *E402.1.2, "Footsteps of invisible ghost heard"; *E402.1.4, "Invisible ghost jingles chains."

118. Collected in 1938 for the WPA by Mary A. Hicks from Nettie Grimshaw (black), a resident of Raleigh, North Carolina. Grimshaw's humorous editorial comment at the end of the tale suggests that she does not take the story very seriously. Motifs include *E281, "Ghosts haunt house"; *E334.1.1, "Ghost of person killed seen at death or burial spot"; *E337.1.1, "Murder sounds heard just as they must have happened at time of death"; *E402.1.1.3, "Ghost cries and screams."

119. Collected on 7 July 1937 for the WPA in State Prison by Mary A. Hicks from John Lowry, a prisoner formerly of Pasquotank County. Lowry suggests that he sincerely believes that he and his comrades witnessed ghosts, but one cannot be sure because the tale bears evidence of having been heavily rewritten. Motifs include *E338(b), "Female ghost seen in house"; *E338.1(b), "Miscellaneous activities of ghost in house"; E419.10, "Concern of ghost about belongings of its lifetime." For more information on the activities of Edward Teach (a.k.a. Blackbeard the Pirate) in the American South, see "The Devil's Brother: Scourge of the Spanish Main" in E. Randall Floyd's *Great Southern Mysteries* (154) and "The Return of Blackbeard" in Michael Norman and Beth Scott's *Historic Haunted America* (257).

120. Collected in July 1936 for the WPA in Raleigh, North Carolina, by Mary Hicks from B. E. Rogers of Franklin County, who received the tale from his father, Sampson Rogers. The fear Rogers conveys in the end of the tale indicates that he believed that he had had a confrontation with a spirit. Motifs include *E279.2, "Ghost disturbs sleeping person"; *E279.3, "Ghost pulls bedclothing from sleeper"; *E281, "Ghost haunts house"; *E338(b), "Female ghost seen in house."

121. Collected in 1927 for the WPA in Raleigh, North Carolina, by Mary Hicks from N. C. Blake. Blake sincerely believes that he and his girlfriend encountered a headless horse. Motifs include *E281, "Ghosts haunt house"; *E421.5, "Ghost seen by two or more persons; they corroborate the appearance"; *E422.1.1, "Headless revenant"; E423.1.3.3, "Revenant as headless horse"; E521.1, "Ghost of horse."

122. Collected in 1928 for the WPA in Raleigh, North Carolina, by Mary Hicks from B. W. Medley. Although Medley gives no indication that he believes the tale, Hicks adds in a note that she has heard the voices. Motifs include *E218, "Ghost haunts house"; *E402.1.1, "Vocal sounds of ghost of human being."

123. Collected on 22 January 1941 for the WPA by Mary Hicks from Alfred Smith of Wake County. Smith not only claims to have seen the ghost but considers it his friend and neighbor. The only relevant motif is *E425.1, "Revenant as woman."

124. Collected in 1938 for the WPA in Western North Carolina by L. Santutlah from Sadie S. Patton. Motifs include E534, "Phantom spinning wheel makes noise"; *E338(b), "Female ghost seen in house."

125. Collected on 17 August 1937 for the WPA in State Prison from Napoleon Scott (black), a prisoner formerly of Forsythe County. Scott sincerely believes that he has seen ghosts because they were floating at the time. Motifs include E280, "Ghosts haunt buildings"; *E338(a), "Male ghost seen"; *E360, "Friendly return from the dead"; *E425.1, "Revenant as woman."

126. Collected on 15 November 1995 in Livingston, Alabama, from Stephen Slimp (see note on informant in story 114). Slimp tends to be less skeptical about this story than some of the others he told because it came from a trusted friend. Motifs include *E425.2, "Revenant as man"; *E575, "Ghost as omen of calamity or ill fortune." For additional accounts of this well-known tale, see "The Gray Man" in Nancy Roberts's *South Carolina Ghosts: From the Coast to the Mountains* (68) and "The Gray Man's Warning" in Nancy Roberts's *Ghosts and Specters of the Old South* (41).

127. Collected on 15 November 1995 in Livingston, Alabama, from Stephen Slimp (see note on informant in story 114). Slimp, who remembers this story from his childhood, was surprised by the fact that he found the same tale in Japan. He seems to regard it as a widely circulated folktale. Motifs include *E425.2, "Revenant as man"; *E575, "Ghost as omen of calamity or ill-fortune."

128. Collected on 15 November 1995 in Livingston, Alabama, from Stephen Slimp (see note on informant in story 144). Slimp regards this tale, like the previous one, as a widely circulated folktale. Motifs include *E332.3.3, "Ghost asks for ride in automobile"; *E332.3.3.1, "The Vanishing Hitchhiker"; *E425.1, "Revenant as woman." See also story 101 in this volume.

129. Collected on 5 May 1995 in Livingston, Alabama, from Angela Howard, a twenty-one-year-old college student from Livingston. Motifs include *E530.1, "Ghost-like lights"; F491.4, "Will-o-the-wisp hops about." For an additional account of this tale, see "The Mysterious Land's End Light" in Nancy Roberts's *South Carolina Ghosts* (7).

130. Collected on 18 July 1936 for the WPA by Genevieve Chandler from an elderly informant known only as "Ad." Chandler describes Ad: "Constantly expectorates between each sentence. Hair plaited down and tightly wrapped with white twine. Splay feet unshod. Never clean. And yet? My hat's off to her. Why? Fourteen other souls she keeps alive with her two hands. Undernourished. Half-naked. All in one room. Unmoral. Once a dead baby lay hidden under its sick mother's bed for a week." Ad sincerely believes that she encountered a "Plat eye." Motifs include *E272, "Road ghosts. Ghost which haunts road"; *E272.4, "Ghost chases pedestrian on road"; *E423.1.2, "Revenant as cat."

131. Collected on 6 October 1937 for the WPA in Charleston, South Carolina, by Jessie A. Butler from Fannie Lucas (black), a former resident of Charleston. Although Lucas clearly feels that the cold temperatures in her room indicated the

presence of a spirit, Butler adds that Lucas had forgotten to close the window before she left for work. The only relevant motif is *E281, "Ghost haunts house."

132. Collected on 12 May 1937 for the WPA by Genevieve Chandler from Thelma Knox, described by Chandler as a fifteen-year-old "low-country Negro" from Murrelle's Inlet, South Carolina. Motifs include E422.4.3, "Ghost in white"; *E423.1.2, "Revenant as cat"; *E425, "Revenant as woman"; *E521.2, "Ghost of dog."

133. Collected on 6 October 1936 for the WPA in Charleston County by Augustus Ladson from unnamed informant, thirty-six years old, who worked as a maid and lived in Charleston, South Carolina. Motifs include *E272, "Road ghosts. Ghost which haunts road"; *E272.4, "Ghost chases pedestrian on road"; *423.1.2, "Revenant as cat."

134. Collected on 5 October 1936 for the WPA in Charleston County by Laura Middleton from Louis Beckett, a forty-nine-year-old resident of Charleston, South Carolina. *E272, "Road ghosts. Ghost which haunts road"; *E272.4, "Ghost chases pedestrian on road."

135. Collected on 17 October 1938 for the WPA in Georgetown County, South Carolina, from an informant referred to only as "Mr. Blanton's neighbor, a resident of Loris, South Carolina." The informant tends to believe the story because he heard it from his mother, who received it from her grandmother. Motifs include *E338(a), "Male ghost seen"; *360, "Friendly return from the dead"; *E575, "Ghost as omen of calamity or ill fortune."

136. Collected on 6 October 1936 in Charleston County by Augustus Ladson from Abram Ward a resident of Adams Run and Johns Island, South Carolina. Ward gives no indication that he accepts this story as being more than a folktale. Motifs include *E272, "Road ghosts. Ghost which haunts road"; *E272.4, "Ghost chases pedestrian on road"; E423.1.8, "Revenant as cow, bull or calf"; *E521.2, "Ghost of dog."

137. Collected on 6 October 1936 for the WPA in Charleston County, South Carolina, by Augustus Ladson from unnamed informant, an eighty-six-year-old resident of Charleston, South Carolina. Motifs include *E422.1.1(b), "Headless woman, appearance only"; E422.4.3, "Ghost in white"; *E575, "Ghost as omen of calamity or ill fortune"; J1495.1, "Man runs from actual or supposed ghost."

138. Collected on 6 October 1936 for the WPA in Charleston, South Carolina, by Augustus Ladson from Joe Williams, an eighty-six-year-old resident of Charleston. Williams's shared experience with this ghost is bolstered by the old lady's story. Motifs include *E272, "Road ghosts. Ghost which haunts road"; *E273, "Churchyard ghosts."

139. Collected on 27 April 1937 for the WPA in Spartanburg, South Carolina, from W. J. Gilbert, a resident of Spartanburg. Motifs include *E281, "Ghosts haunt house"; *E402.1.5, "Invisible ghost makes rapping or knocking noise."

140. Collected on 4 December 1938 for the WPA by Caldwell Sims from Estell Mathis, a resident of Union, South Carolina. Mathis believes that she and her

friends actually saw a ball of light, although the supernatural explanation for the phenomenon is implied. Motifs include *E530.1, "Ghost-like lights"; *E530.1.0.1, "Ghost light as ball of fire"; F491.4, "Will-o-wisp hops about."

141. Collected in 1938 for the WPA in Georgetown County, South Carolina, by Genevieve Chandler from Martha Wright (black), a seventy-year-old resident of Murrells Inlet, South Carolina. Wright sincerely believes that she lived in a haunted house. Motifs include *E281, "Ghosts haunt house"; E338.1(h), "Miscellaneous activities of ghost in house"; *E402.1.1, "Vocal sounds of ghost of human being"; *E402.1.8, "Miscellaneous sounds made by ghost of human being."

142. Collected on 21 October 1985 in Memphis, Tennessee, by *Daily News* arts editor Nancy R. Randall from Vincent Aster, theater director of the Orpheum Theater. Although Aster has never seen Mary's ghost, he seems to sense that there is a ghostly presence in the theater. Motifs include E338.1(h), "Miscellaneous activities of ghost"; *E402.1.1, "Vocal sounds of ghost of human being"; *E425.1, "Revenant as woman." For additional versions of the ghost of the Orpheum Theater, see "Phantom in the Memphis Orpheum" in James Ewing's *It Happened in Tennessee* (74); "Orpheum Theater" in Dennis William Hauck's *Haunted Places* (389); and "Orpheum Theater" from "Haunted Tennessee" on the American Ghost Society's Web site (www.prairieghosts.com).

143. Collected on 16 July 1996 in Livingston, Alabama, from Tommy DeVaney, a forty-five-year-old college professor from Livingston. DeVaney's knowledge of the lore from the northwestern part of the Great Smokies National Park is derived from his work as director of the Environmental Education Center. DeVaney and the other instructors told these tales to entertain the students in the camp. DeVaney regards this story as a folktale because he has not seen the apparition. Motifs include *E323, "Dead mother's friendly return"; *E323.1, "Dead mother returns to see baby"; E422.4.3, "Ghost in white"; *E424.1, "Revenant as woman."

144. Collected on 16 July 1996 in Livingston, Alabama, from Tommy DeVaney (see note on informant in story 143). DeVaney is certain that the strange sound he heard came from an animal, not a ghost. Motifs include *E334.2.2(c), "Ghost of drowned person haunts spot of drowning"; *E402.1.1, "Vocal sounds of ghost of human being"; *E402.1.1.3, "Ghost cries and screams."

145. Collected on 16 July 1996 in Livingston, Alabama, from Tommy DeVaney (see note on informant in story 143). DeVaney smiled as he told this tale, an indication that he did not take much of it, especially the supernatural elements, very seriously. Motifs include *E334.2.2(c), "Ghost of drowned person haunts spot of drowning"; *E402.1.8, "Miscellaneous sounds made by ghost of human being"; *E425.2, "Revenant as man."

146. Collected on 16 July 1996 in Livingston, Alabama, from Tommy DeVaney (see note on informant in story 143). DeVaney made it clear in his delivery that he regards this as nothing more than a colorful story. The only relevant motif is *E575, "Ghost as omen of calamity or ill-fortune."

147. Collected on 16 July 1996 in Livingston, Alabama, from Tommy DeVaney

(see note on informant in story 143). DeVaney told this tale to scare his students during his tours of the cave. Motifs include *E334.2.2, "Ghost of person killed in accident seen at death or burial spot"; *E402.1.1, "Vocal sounds of ghost of human being."

148. Collected on 1 May 1978 in Adams, Tennessee, by Heidi Miller, a folklore student at Western Kentucky University in Bowling Green, from W. M. Eden Jr., a lifelong resident of Adams and an authority on the Bell legend. He claims to have received much of his information from descendants of the Bell family who assured him that they had told him the "real" story. Eden, who lived for ten years in the second house Bell built, swore that he had heard ghostly knocking on his front door. He also found the cave where Kate Batts and her friends played when they were children. Motifs include M430, "Curse on person"; M451, "Curse: Death." For additional versions of the Bell Witch, America's most famous ghost story, see "The Bell Witch of Tennessee" in E. Randall Floyd's *More Great Southern Mysteries* (26); "The Bell Witch" in Phyllis Raybin Emert's *Ghosts, Hauntings and Mysterious Happenings* (88); "The Bell Witch of Tennessee and Mississippi: A Folk Legend" in Arthur Palmer Hudson's *Humor of the Old Deep South* (433); "Family Troubles" in Michael Norman and Beth Scott's *Historic Haunted America* (318); "Return of the Bell Witch" in Nancy Roberts's *Ghosts of the Southern Mountains and Appalachia* (12); "John Bell Farm" in Dennis William Hauck's *Haunted Places* (382); "Horrific Hauntings" in Time-Life's *Hauntings* (93); "The Witch Who Tormented the Bell Family" from Kathryn Tucker Windham's *13 Tennessee Ghosts and Jeffrey*; "Ghosts and Spirits" from Reader's Digest's *Into the Unknown* (177); and "Bell Witch Cave" from "Haunted Tennessee" on the America Ghost Society's Web site (www.prairieghosts.com).

149. Collected in 1938 for the WPA in Jacksboro, Tennessee, by Lena Lipscomb from Alma Davis, an eighteen-year-old high school student in Jacksboro, Tennessee. Davis believes the story because she has seen the door. Motifs include *E281, "Ghosts haunt house"; *E338.1(c), "Ghost opens doors and windows repeatedly."

150. Collected in 1938 for the WPA in Jacksboro, Tennessee, by Lena Lipscomb from Katie Copeland, a high school student from Jacksboro, Tennessee. Motifs include *E220, "Dead relative's malevolent return"; *E425.1., "Revenant as woman."

151. Collected in 1945 for the WPA by Lena Lipscomb from Jack Furham, an eighth-grade student from Summertown, Tennessee. Durham is certain that this local legend is true. Motifs include *E272, "Road ghosts. Ghost which haunts road"; *E272.4, "Ghost chases pedestrian on road"; *E402.1.1, "Vocal sounds of ghost of human being"; *E422.1.1, "Headless revenant"; *E433.1.1.5, "Miscellaneous actions of headless ghost."

152. Collected in 1938 for the WPA in Gainesboro, Tennessee, by John H. Vernon from himself. Vernon was a resident of Gainesboro. The fact that two people told the same story leads Vernon to believe that it is true. Motifs include *E281, "Ghosts haunt house"; *E402.1.4, "Invisible ghost jingles chains"; *E421.5, "Ghost

seen by two or more persons; they corroborate the appearance"; *E425.2, "Revenant as man."

153. Collected in 1938 for the WPA in Gainesboro, Tennessee, by John H. Vernon (see note on informant in story 152). Motifs include *E332.3.1, "Ghost rider on horseback with rider"; *E402.1.1, "Vocal sounds of ghost o human being"; *E425.1, "Revenant as woman."

154. Collected in 1938 for the WPA in Gainesboro, Tennessee, by John H. Vernon (see note on informant in story 152). Vernon's statement that this story is believed by older people suggests that he does not put much credence in it. Motifs include *E272, "Road ghosts. Ghost which haunts road"; *E360, "Friendly return from the dead"; *E422.4.4(e), "Female revenant in black dress."

155. Collected on 5 May 1980 in Memphis, Tennessee, by *Press-Scimitar* writer Dorothy Ward from Elizabeth Dow Edwards, the great-granddaughter of Mollie's sister Sarah. Edwards, who moved to Topeka, Kansas, lived in Memphis for several years and coordinated the costumes at the Fontaine House. Edwards seems to feel that her experiences and those of the visitors to the house are genuine encounters with the supernatural. Motifs include *E281, "Ghosts haunt house"; *E338.1(c), "Ghost opens doors and windows repeatedly"; E338.1(h), "Miscellaneous activities of ghost"; *E402.1.1, "Vocal sounds of ghost of human being."

156. Collected on 26 July 1975 in Memphis, Tennessee, by an unidentified *Press-Scimitar* writer from Mrs. Kenneth Parks, a thirty-year-old resident of Memphis, who sincerely believes that her house is haunted. Her belief is supported by that of the previous owner of the house at 3200 Given Street, Mrs. Johnny Addison, who was also sure that the house was haunted, citing her dog's bizarre reaction to unseen presences as proof. Mrs. Parks said that she went to a palmist who suggested that she have a seance, but she wasn't able to get enough people together. Motifs include *E281, "Ghosts haunt house"; *E338.1(c), "Ghost opens doors and windows repeatedly"; *E338.1(h), "Miscellaneous activities of ghost in house"; *E402.1.2, "Footsteps of invisible ghost heard"; *E402.1.5, "Invisible ghost makes rapping or knocking noise."

157. Collected on 19 August 1936 for the WPA in Mountain City, Tennessee, by Lena Lipscomb from Mrs. Harrison Donnelly, an elderly resident of Shouno, Tennessee. Motifs include *E334.2.1, "Ghost of murdered person haunts burial spot"; *E402.1.2, "Footsteps of invisible ghost heard"; *E402.1.5, "Invisible ghost makes rapping or knocking noise."

158. Collected on 15 April 1994 in Livingston, Alabama, from Cathleen Pittman, about fifty years old. Pittman, a college professor and longtime resident of New Mexico, lives in Tuscaloosa. Pittman is convinced that this is a true story because of the admiration she has for her aunt's intelligence. Motifs include *E281, "Ghosts haunt house"; *E338(b), "Female ghost seen in house."

159. Collected on 7 November 1995 in Livingston, Alabama, from Bobby Dickerson, an eighteen-year-old resident of Beaumont, Texas. Dickerson's belief in the tale seems to be bolstered by the fact that a newspaper article was written on it.

Motifs include *E334.2.2(c), "Ghost of drowned person haunts spot of drowning"; *E334.4, "Ghost of suicide seen at death spot or near by"; *E425.1, "Revenant as woman."

160. Collected on 7 November 1995 in Livingston, Alabama, from Bobby Dickerson (see note on informant in story 159). Dickerson's belief in the story is bolstered by the fact that he has seen the phenomenon. Motifs include *E273, "Churchyard ghosts"; *E425.1, "Revenant as woman"; *E530.1, "Ghost-like lights."

161. Collected on 9 November 1936 for the WPA in Houston, Texas, from an unnamed, elderly female informant who clearly believes that spirits have played an important part in her life. The only relevant motif is *E575, "Ghost as omen of calamity or ill fortune."

162. Collected in 1936 for the WPA in El Paso, Texas, by Vera Elliott from Aurora Valdez, a thirty-year-old resident of Socorro, Texas. Valdez implies that the story might be true because of Senora Zertuche's reluctance to talk about it. Motifs include *E281, "Ghosts haunt house"; *E402.1.1, "Vocal sounds of ghost"; *E545.12, "Ghost directs man to hidden treasure."

163. Collected on 3 December 1936 for the WPA in Houston, Texas, by Margaret Beane from Essie Miller, a fifty-seven-year-old resident of Houston, Texas. Motifs include *E279.2, "Ghost disturbs sleeping person"; *E281, "Ghosts haunt house"; *E402.1.2, "Footsteps of invisible ghost heard."

164. Collected in 1936 for the WPA in Hood County, Texas, by Mary Agnes Davis from Mr. N. B. Self, a resident of Lipan, Texas. Self tends to believe the tale because he received the tale from one of the men who spent the night in the haunted house. Motifs include *E34.4, "Ghost of suicide seen at death spot or near by"; *E422.4.4(a) "Female revenant in white clothing"; *H1411, "Fear test: staying in haunted house."

165. Collected on 11 February 1941 for the WPA by Marjorie Durham Kidder from Mr. Plum McCullough, a resident of Blanco, Texas. Motifs include E226, "Dead brother's return"; *E281, "Ghosts haunt house."

166. Collected on 6 November 1936 for the WPA by Margaret Beane from S. Macmillan, a fifty-three-year-old resident of Anahuac, Texas. Despite McMillan's statement that he does not believe in ghosts, he seems to harbor some suspicion that the story might be true. Motifs include *E272, "Road ghosts. Ghosts which haunt road"; *E425.1, "Revenant as woman."

167. Collected in 1936 for the WPA by Pierce Welty from G. A. Graham, a judge from Norton, Texas. Graham seems to be somewhat skeptical of the tale because he received it from an "old-timer." Motifs include *E530.1, "Ghost-like lights"; *E491.4, "Will-o-wisp hops about."

168. Collected on 7 November 1936 for the WPA in Houston, Texas, by Margaret Beane from H. K. Walters, whom Beane refers to as a "vagrant found in rooming house." Walters attributes his becoming a wanderer to this traumatic experience. Motifs include *E272, "Road ghosts. Ghost which haunts road"; *E272.4, "Ghost chases pedestrian on road"; *X424, "The Devil in the cemetery."

169. Collected on 21 October 1936 for the WPA by Mary Liberato from Leonard Bliss, a resident of Galveston, Texas. Bliss's initial skepticism in his son-in-law's tale seems to have been somewhat diminished by the fact that other people have seen the ghost as well. Motifs include and *E338(a), "Male ghost seen"; *E422.1.1, "Headless revenant."

170. Collected in 1936 for the WPA by Vera Elliott from Aurora Valdez (see note on informant in story 162). Motifs include *E281, "Ghosts haunt house"; *E530.1, "Ghost-like lights."

171. Collected on 7 December 1936 for the WPA in Pleasant Grove, Texas, by Leonard Browning from William B. Browning, a resident of Pleasant Grove. Browning implies that he believed that he had heard the moans of a ghost until he found the cow. Motifs include *E273, "Churchyard ghosts"; *E402.1.1.3, "Ghost cries and screams." For another version of the story of the cow in the graveyard, see "Devil in the Graveyard" in Jack and Olivia Solomon's *Ghosts and Goosebumps* (68) and "The Cow in the Graveyard" in William Lynwood Montell's *Ghosts Along the Cumberland* (193).

172. Collected in 1936 for the WPA in Lampasas County by Ada Davis from W. B. Hensley, a resident of Lampasas, Texas. Motifs include *E272, "Road ghosts. Ghosts which haunt road"; *E425.1, "Revenant as woman."

173. Collected on 4 October 1996 in Livingston, Alabama, from Cherry Rubio, a forty-year-old employee of the United Way and resident of San Luis Potosi, Mexico. Rubio believes that this incident really occurred because it happened to a trusted friend of hers. Motifs include *E281, "Ghost haunts house"; *E402.1.8, "Miscellaneous sounds made by ghost of human being."

174. Collected on 4 October 1996 in Livingston, Alabama, from Cherry Rubio (see note in story 173). Rubio is not entirely sure that she had an experience with the supernatural. Motifs include E280, "Ghosts haunt building"; *E402.1.2, "Footsteps of invisible ghost heard."

175. Collected in 1938 for the WPA in Wise, Virginia, by Emory L. Hamilton from his father, Dr. J. M. Hill. Both father and son are convinced that this story is true. Motifs include *E281, "Ghosts haunt house"; *E338(b), "Female ghost seen in house"; *E402.1.8, "Miscellaneous sounds of ghost of human being."

176. Collected on 4 November 1940 for the WPA in Big Laurel, Virginia, by James Taylor Adams from Perry Bullion, an eighty-eight-year-old resident of Wise, Virginia. Even though he has never seen or heard the ghost, Bullion is willing to believe in the headless ghost because he had heard the stories from other people who have seen it. Motifs include *E272, "Road ghosts. Ghosts which haunt road"; *E402.1.8, "Miscellaneous sounds made by ghost of human being"; *E422.1.1, "Headless revenant."

177. Collected on 14 November 1940 for the WPA by Eva Fair Pegram from her great-uncle, Samuel Simpson Adams, who received it from his mother, Celia Church Adams, seventy-five years before. In a note at the end of the story Pegram says that this story may have been based on the Hamlin family tragedy near the

present village of Hamlin in Russell County, Virginia. Mrs. Hamlin and her children were massacred by Indians. Adams adds that this tale also resembles a story in song from Alabama in which a woman was drowned and her children were burned in a house by Indians, but he does not give the name of the folk song. Motifs include *E411.1.1, "Suicide cannot rest in grave"; *E415, "Dead cannot rest until certain work is finished"; *E425.2.1, "Revenant as old man"; *F974.1, "Grass will not grow where blood of murdered person has been shed."

178. Collected on 27 August 1941 for the WPA by James Taylor Adams from William Collins, a resident of Wise, Virginia. Collins was born on Birchfield Creek on 11 May 1863. Collins states in the end that this is his only encounter with the supernatural. Motifs include *E402.1, "Ghost cries and screams"; E421.3, "Luminous ghosts."

179. Collected on 30 September 1941 for the WPA in Wise, Virginia, by James M. Hylton from Dan Fraley, a forty-one-year-old resident of Wise. Fraley was a high school friend of Hylton's who had regaled his friends on campus with tales that he had heard from the old-timers in the area. Fraley received this tale from George Beverly, an uncle through marriage. In a note, Hylton says, "Dan likes to hear a good tale of the olden times and can often be found sitting among a group of old timers exchanging tales with them. I went to high school with Dan and am well acquainted with him." Fraley seems to believe that the story is true. Motifs include *E402.1.8, "Miscellaneous sounds made by ghost of human being"; E415, "Dead cannot rest until certain work is finished"; E534, "Phantom spinning wheel makes noise."

180. Collected on 14 July 1941 for the WPA by James Taylor Adams from Noah Hamilton, a native of Bland County, Virginia, and a descendant from some of the earliest settlers in the area. Hamilton states in the beginning that he believes in ghosts and that a ghost interrupted his sleep. Motifs include *E270.2, "Ghost disturbs sleeping persons"; *E279.3, "Ghost pulls bedclothing from sleeper"; *E338(a), "Male ghost seen"; E338.1(h), "Miscellaneous activities of ghost"; *E422.4.3, "Ghost in white."

181. Collected in 1940 for the WPA by John W. Garrett from Mrs. Dalton, a fifty-year-old resident of Hopewell, Virginia. In a note at the beginning, Garrett states that Dalton is not superstitious but that she knows for a fact that the story is true. Motifs include *E281, "Ghosts haunt house"; E338.1(hg), "Ghost causes rocking chair to rock"; *E530.1, "Ghost-like lights."

182. Collected on 1 November 1940 for the WPA in Wise, Virginia, by Emory Hamilton from Sullivan Vanover, a resident of Wise. Vanover believes that the knocking noise that he and his family heard in their house was made by the owner of the Civil War rifle. Motifs include *E281, "Ghosts haunt house"; *E338.1(h), "Miscellaneous activities of ghost"; *E402.1.5, "Invisible ghost makes rapping or knocking noise."

183. Collected on 11 December 1940 for the WPA in Wise, Virginia, by Emory Hamilton from Etta Kilgore, a resident of Wise. Kilgore seems to believe that her

grandmother actually saw a ghost. Motifs include *E338(10, "Male ghost seen"); *E402.1.2, "Footsteps of ghost heard"; *E402.1.4, "Invisible ghost jingles chains"; *E422.1.1, "Headless revenant"; *E422.1.1.5, "Miscellaneous activities of headless ghost."

184. Collected 8 December 1941 for the WPA in Big Laurel, Virginia, by James Taylor Adams from Mrs. W. J. Kilgore, a resident of Big Laurel. Kilgore received this tale from Willard Roberts, who swore that this incident really occurred. Motifs include *E402.1.8, "Miscellaneous sounds made by ghost of human being"; E410, "The unquiet grave. dead unable to rest in peace"; E419.8, "Ghost returns to enforce its burial wishes or to protest disregard of such wishes."

185. Collected on 14 October 1940 for the WPA in Big Laurel, Virginia, by James Taylor Adams from Patton Kilgore, a resident of Big Laurel. Adams notes in the beginning that Dug Hill is in a deep forest two miles east of Big Laurel. Kilgore believes that his experience in Dug Hill supports the tales that he and others had told about the place. Motifs include *E272, "Road ghosts. Ghost which haunts road"; *E272.4, "Ghost chases pedestrian on road"; *E272.4, "Ghost chases pedestrian on road"; *E421.3.9, "Ghost with ball of fire for head"; *E422.1.1(b), "Headless woman, appearance only"; *E425.1.1, "Revenant as woman in white".

186. Collected on 24 January 1940 for the WPA in Wise, Virginia, by Emory Hamilton from Goldie Hamilton, a resident of Esserville, Virginia. Motifs include *E221.1, "Dead wife Haunts husband on second marriage"; *E402.1.1, "Vocal sounds of ghost of human being"; E419.8, "Ghost returns to enforce its burial wishes or to protest disregard of such wishes."

187. Collected on 23 September 1940 for the WPA in Wise, Virginia, by Emory Hamilton from Polly Johnson, a resident of Wise. Johnson's statement "his spirit or something could have come back" and her belief that her father could communicate with the dead suggest that she believes John Moore's ghost caused the disturbances in their house. Motifs include *E338.1(c), "Ghost opens doors and windows repeatedly"; *E402.1.5, "Invisible ghost makes knocking or rapping noise"; *E422.1.1, "Headless revenant"; *E451, "Ghost finds rest when certain things happen"; *E545.19.2(b), "Proper means of addressing ghost: person must ask, 'In the name of the Lord, why troublest thou me?' "

SELECTED BIBLIOGRAPHY

Barden, Thomas E., ed. *Virginia Folk Legends.* Charlottesville: University Press of Virginia, 1991. *Virginia Folk Legends* is a collection of folk materials gathered by the WPA in Virginia during the 1930s. This is a scholarly text that uses motifs and tale type numbers from Ernest Warren Baughman's *Type and Motif Index of the Folktales of England and North America* (The Hague: Mouton, 1966) and Stith Thompson's *Motif Index of Folk Literature* (Bloomington: Indiana University Press, 1955). The book also has an excellent introduction, which outlines the history of the Federal Writers' Project and examines the distinguishing characteristics of legends. Fifty-one stories are contained in the chapters entitled "Conjure and Witchcraft," "Ghosts," "Haunted houses," "Spirit Dogs," and "Supernatural Events." The book's only flaw, the lack of biographical information on the informants, can be traced to the collecting practices of many of the WPA workers.

Brewer, J. Mason. *American Negro Folklore.* Chicago: Quadrangle Books, 1968. Brewer, who was one of the leading black folklorists of his day, has devoted one chapter in this book to ghost tales. The use of dialect in these tales suggests that he tried to record the stories exactly as he heard them. However, he offers no comparative data.

Brown, Alan. *The Face in the Window and Other Alabama Ghostlore.* Tuscaloosa: University of Alabama Press, 1996. This book is the second scholarly collection of ghost stories from Alabama. The introduction discusses folktales in general and ghostlore in particular. The notes in the end provide background information on the informants and motif numbers keyed to the numbering systems employed in Baughman's *Type and Motif-Index of the Folktales of England and North America* (The Hague: Mouton, 1966) and Stith Thompson's *Motif-Index of Folk Literature* (Bloomington: Indiana University Press, 1955). Variants of the tales are also noted. The annotated bibliography lists all collections of Alabama ghost tales that are currently in print. Ten photographs are contained in the book, including a picture of the fabled face in the window of the Pickens County Courthouse.

Browne, Ray E. *"A Night with the Hants" and Other Alabama Folk Experiences.* Bowling Green, Ohio: Bowling Green University Popular Press, 1977. This was the first scholarly collection of oral ghost stories from Alabama. Browne includes comparative data, biographical data on the informants, and a transcript of an actual storytelling session. Most of Browne's informants were elderly country people. Unfortunately, Browne made no effort to reproduce subtleties in dialect, making it difficult to distinguish between the narratives of blacks and whites. On the whole, though, this is a fairly scholarly work.

Brunvand, Jan Harold. *The Vanishing Hitchhiker: American Urban Legends and Their Meanings*. New York: Norton, 1981. *The Vanishing Hitchhiker* is the first of Brunvand's highly influential collections of urban folktales. Unlike many popular volumes of folktales, Brunvand's definitely qualifies as a scholarly work. Both the preface and afterword serve as a sort of introduction to the themes and terminology found in many folktales. The chapters, which are arranged thematically, contain urban folktales provided by informants and by newspapers and magazines. Each oral narrative is followed by an in-depth analysis of the tale. A comprehensive notes section is included at the end of each chapter. Although most of the tales originate in the large urban centers of the Midwest and Northeast, several of the WPA tales were collected in southern states.

Burchill, James V., Linda J. Crider, and Peggy Kendrick. *The Cold, Cold Hand: Stories of Ghosts and Haunts from the Appalachian Foothills*. Nashville, Tenn.: Rutledge Press, 1997. Most of these stories collected from the foothills of southern Appalachia consist of first-person narratives of encounters with ghosts. The names of the informants are provided with little or no biographical data. Still, this nonscholarly book comes closer to being a folklore text than many of the other books written for the popular press.

Burchill, James V., et al. *Ghosts and Haunts from the Appalachian Foothills: Stories and Legends*. Nashville, Tenn.: Rutledge Hills Press, 1993. Written by four members of the First Draft Writers Group, this collection of southern Appalachian ghost stories is based on oral tales that the writers heard from both old and young local residents. No comparative data or biographical information about the informants is provided. The states in which the stories take place are not identified.

Burrison, John A. *"The Golden Arm": The Folk Tale and Its Literary Use by Mark Twain and Joel C. Harris*. Atlanta: Georgia State College, 1968. In this sixty-five-age pamphlet, Burrison presents a scholarly analysis of the famous folktale. The four chapters include "Origins of the Tale" (3), "Literary Use: Twain and Harris 'Steal' 'The Golden Arm' " (9), "Form, Function, and Diffusion of 'The Golden Arm' " (15), and "Appendix of Tale Variants" (25). This booklet is a must for anyone who is interested in the evolution of folktales.

―――. *Storytellers: Folktales and Legends from the South*. Athens: University of Georgia Press, 1989. Drawing from the student-recorded folktales deposited in the Georgia Folklore Archives, Burrison's book focuses on tales from Georgia, although stories from the six states of the Lower Southeast are also included. Most of the informants are elderly residents from rural areas. The author provides the name, age, and hometown of each informant at the beginning of each story. A large number of the tales in the "Legends" section are ghost stories. The excellent introduction is a scholarly analysis of the nature of the material that qualifies as folklore. Burrison also discusses storytelling as performance and storytelling events.

Dorson, Richard. *American Negro Folktales*. Greenwich, Conn.: Fawcett Publications, 1967. This is a compilation of his two earlier books: *Negro Folktales in Michigan* (1956) and *Negro Folktales from Pine Bluff, Arkansas, and Calvin, Michigan* (1958). Several supernatural tales are presented from Arkansas. Dorson provides informant and collection data as well as comparative notes. The introduction's primary value lies in its analysis of the art of Negro storytelling.

Duffey, Barbara. *Angels and Apparitions: True Ghost Stories from the South*. Eaton, Ga.: Elysian, 1996. Like Duffey's previous book, *Banshees, Bugles, and Belles*, this collection recounts the standard legends connected with historic buildings in the South. Even though the book claims to contain stories from the entire South, it actually includes stories from only Alabama, Georgia, Louisiana, Mississippi, Tennessee, Texas, and west Georgia. The bulk of stories are set in Georgia, Duffey's home state. The Georgia stories are also developed in much more detail than the tales from the other states, primarily because of the interviews Duffey conducted with people who have seen or heard the ghosts. The chapter entitled "Supernatural" contains several stories dealing with ghostly photographs, cold spots, and angels.

―――. *Banshees, Bugles, and Belles: True Ghost Stories of Georgia*. Berryville, Va.: Rockbridge, 1995. This fascinating volume of ghost stories focuses primarily on historically haunted buildings in Georgia. Although the title suggests that this is a comprehensive collection of Georgia ghost tales, the narratives in this text are taken from only Milledgeville, Macon, Piedmont, and Tidewater. Each chapter begins with the history of a building and ends with a narrative from someone who has had a personal encounter with a ghost. The author also indicates whether or not the buildings are open to the public. Some of the photographs allegedly depict the images of spirits.

Emert, Phyllis Raybin. *Ghosts, Hauntings, and Mysterious Happenings*. New York: Tom Doherty Associates Book, 1992. This little book of unexplained events from Europe and America is written primarily for children. The chapter on the Bell Witch is a good introduction to one of America's most famous hauntings.

Ewing, James. *It Happened in Tennessee*. Nashville, Tenn.: Rutledge Hill Press, 1986. A former columnist for the *Nashville Banner*, Ewing has compiled a collection of tales of strange but true events from Tennessee that were submitted by readers of the newspaper. The names and hometowns of the writers are provided. The supernatural stories included in this volume are "The Wampus Cat" (69), "Tales My Grandmother Told Me (70), "Phantom in the Memphis Orpheum" (74), "Ghost in the Cemetery" (77), and "The Moonshine Still Ghost" (79).

Floyd, E. Randall. *Great Southern Mysteries*. Little Rock, Ark.: August House, 1989. Floyd's provocative collection of little-known myths and legends from the American South is written for the general public but is especially valuable to anyone interested in southern folklore. The extensive bibliography at the end of the book indicates the source of most of the tales, although several of them are spin-offs of articles Floyd has written for various newspapers and magazines over the years. The chapter entitled "Specters and Spells" includes three ghost tales: "Miracle in the Clouds" (100), "Voodoo and the Walking Dead" (104), and "The Surrency Haunting" (109).

———. *More Great Southern Mysteries.* Little Rock, Ark.: August House, 1991. The sequel to *Great Southern Mysteries* includes more tales gleaned from the public library and Floyd's personal collection of books. Most of the stories are traditional tales that have been passed down by generations of southerners. The supernatural stories in the book include "Entertaining Satan in the Old Dominion" (13), "The Mystery of Marie Leveau's Tomb" (63), "The Curse of Barnsley Gardens" (83), "Ghost Lights in the Forest" (86), "The Ghost That Came to Stay" (93), "Better Run When the 'Man in Grey' Comes Calling" (97), "Gifts from Beyond the Grave" (101), "The Portrait That Came to Life" (105), and " 'Dead' Men Do Tell Tales" (108).

Harden, John. *The Devil's Tramping Ground and Other North Carolina Mystery Stories.* Chapel Hill: University of North Carolina Press, 1949. This book is an outgrowth of a weekly radio program presented for sixteen months over radio station WPTF in Raleigh, North Carolina, in 1946 and 1947, featuring Harden's versions of strange legends and mysteries from North Carolina's past. The supernatural tales in this volume include "The Ghost Ship Mystery of Diamond Shoals" (1), "The Devil's Tramping Ground" (53), "The Strange Hoof-Marks at Bath" (69), "The Brown Mountain Lights" (127), and "The Strange Killer of Turkey Hollow" (147).

Hauck, Dennis William. *Haunted Places: The National Directory.* New York; Penguin Books, 1996. Hauck, an expert on paranormal activity, has compiled a fairly complete collection of the nation's most haunted sites. Although the book does not treat texts from a folklore perspective, folklorists who are interested in finding the addresses of such places as Alabama's Boyington Oak and New Orleans's Lalaurie House may find the book to be useful.

Hubbard, Sylvia Booth. *Ghosts! Personal Accounts of Modern Mississippi Hauntings.* Brandon, Miss.: QRP Books, 1992. The twenty-five stories included in this book are personal interviews with people who have had supernatural experiences in some of the state's most haunted houses, such as King's Tavern on the Natchez Trace and Vicksburg's Cedar Grove. Hubbard appears to have paraphrased parts of the interviews for the sake of brevity. No comparative data and very little information on the informants is given.

Hudson, Arthur Palmer. *Humor of the Old Deep South.* New York: Macmillan, 1936. This is essentially a compilation of articles reprinted from newspapers and journals. The tales analyzed in this book are taken primarily from Mississippi and Alabama. The chapter entitled "Ha'nt's" includes two tales: "The Bell Witch of Tennessee and Mississippi" (433) and "A Ghost Story 'As Is' a Ghost Story" (446).

Klein, Victor C. *New Orleans Ghosts.* Chapel Hill, N.C.: Professional Press, 1993. Klein's book is essentially a tour guide of haunted places in New Orleans. He gives the names and some background information of his informants but does not allow them to speak in their own words. He has also provided maps, photographs, and addresses to assist the reader in locating these haunted places in the city. The book also has an extensive bibliography pertaining to books about New Orleans. *New Orleans Ghosts* is the best collection of New Orleans ghost stories in print and an excellent guide to haunted places in the city.

Longo, Jim. *Ghosts Along the Mississippi*. St. Louis: St. Anne's Press, 1993. Longo's book is a collection of haunted houses along the Mississippi River from St. Paul, Minnesota, to Natchez, Mississippi. Seven of the book's twenty-one stories deal with southern ghosts. Each chapter is devoted to a lengthy interview with a local authority on the haunted site. Longo identifies his informants and allows them to tell the stories in their own words. No comparative data or motifs are provided. Southern stories featured in the book include "Woodruff-Fontaine House" (Memphis, Tennessee) (132); "Five Generations of Hauntings" (Helena, Arkansas) (140); "Willie and the Police Department" (Vicksburg, Mississippi) (150); "Vicksburg's Perfume Lady" (Vicksburg, Mississippi) (156); "Longwood Plantation" (Natchez, Mississippi) (160); "The House on the Bluff" (Natchez, Mississippi) (166); and "Spirited Traditions of New Orleans" (New Orleans, Louisiana) (176).

McNeil, W. K., ed. *Ghost Stories from the American South*. Little Rock, Ark.: August House, 1985. This is by far the most scholarly collection of ghost stories from the entire South. Nt only does the excellent introduction delineate the characteristics of folktales but also the book contains a very comprehensive annotated bibliography of all the scholarly books of oral ghost tales that had been collected in the United States up to that time. Most of the stories are taken from archives throughout the South. The comparative data in the notes section use the motifs of Ernest W. Baughman's *Type and Motif-Index of the Folktales of England and North America* (The Hague: Mouton, 1966) and Stith Thompson's *Motif-Index of Folk Literature* (Bloomington: Indiana University Press, 1955).

Mead, Robert. *Haunted Hotels: A Guide to American and Canadian Inns and Their Ghosts*. Nashville, Tenn.: Rutledge Hill Press, 1995. Although essentially a guidebook, *Haunted Hotels* is also a collection of ghost tales from twenty-seven states and Canada. Assembled by travel writer Robin Mead, this book provides no comparative data or information on informants. However, the traveler might find the phone numbers, addresses, and price range of each hotel to be useful.

Meyer, Arthur. *The Ghostly Gazetteer: America's Most Fascinating Haunted Landmarks*. Chicago: Contemporary Books, 1990. This volume contains firsthand accounts of spectral sightings but makes no attempt to use them as proof of man's continued existence after death. Although the book contains no comparative data, it does provide notes on the informants and additional data, such as the histories of the houses, the identities of the ghosts, and the names of the witnesses.

Miller, Elaine Hobson. *Myths, Mysteries, and Legends of Alabama*. Birmingham,

Ala.: Seacoast, 1995. Miller, a journalist and freelance writer, has collected strange Alabama tales that are reputed to have a basis in fact. Although there are no true ghost stories in the book, some of the tales, such as "Railroad Bill: Shape-Shifting Train Robber" (37) and "The Indian Who Caused an Earthquake" (21), do deal with the supernatural.

Montell, William Lynwood. *Ghosts Along the Cumberland: Deathlore in the Kentucky Foothills.* Knoxville: University of Tennessee Press, 1975. This was the only truly scholarly collection of southern ghost stories until the publication of W. K. McNeil's *Ghost Stories from the American South.* Unlike most collections of ghost tales, Montell's book focused on a very small region, an area in southwestern Kentucky known as the Eastern Pennyroyal. Montell supplies the reader with ample information regarding background of informants, comparative data, and motifs. Like McNeil and Brown, Montell employs the two standard motif indexes: Ernest W. Baughman's *Type and Motif Index of the Folktales of England and North America* (The Hague: Mouton and Co., 1966) and Stith Thompson's *Motif Index of North America* (Bloomington: Indiana University Press, 1955). The only drawback to the book is that the inclusion of the scholarly apparatus after each tale could possibly discourage the general reader.

Norman, Michael, and Beth Scott. *Historic Haunted America.* New York: Tour Books, 1985. In this book, the authors have brought together the most compelling true stories from their previous volume, *Haunted America.* Every state in the union is represented, as well as the District of Columbia and many Canadian provinces. Although interviews were conducted with park service employees and owners of the haunted houses, much of the historical information appears to have been taken from books. The fine bibliography contains books and articles about ghosts throughout North America.

Randolph, Vance. *Ozark Magic and Folklore.* New York: Dover, 1947. This compilation of folk beliefs from the hill country of Missouri and Arkansas has long been considered a folk classic. Although Randolph, a largely self-trained folklorist, names his informants, he provides no biographical information. For the most part, his tales are rewritten summaries. The book is notable for its two lengthy chapters on ghost stories and witchcraft. However, only three of the ghost stories and thirteen of the witch stories are from Arkansas.

Reader's Digest. Into the Unknown. Pleasantville, N.Y.: Reader's Digest Association, 1981. This well-illustrated volume investigates the causes of mysterious phenomena that have taken place throughout the world. The book investigates the theories given for the Bell Witch's appearance (1778l) and for the construction of Indian mounds in Georgia and Louisiana (2737). A section at the end entitled "Miscellanea of the Unknown" contains a listing of significant terms, people, and phenomena relating to the occult.

Reneaux, J. J. *Cajun Folktales.* Little Rock: August House, 1992. Reneaux, a nationally acclaimed storyteller, states in the introduction that she has told the tales as she has heard them but "has added personal touches, twists, turns as the stories grew to be a natural part of [her] own life" (13). Still, the six ghost stories in this volume are a representative sample of Louisiana's signature ghost tales.

Rhyne, Nancy. *Tales of the South Carolina Low-Country*. Winston-Salem, N.C.: Blair, 1984. In the introduction, Rhyne states that she has supplemented the WPA stories about South Carolina with interviews that she conducted with informants whose names were provided by a storyteller named Genevieve Chandler. Unfortunately, like so many collectors, Rhyne provides little biographical information on her informants and no comparative data.

Roberts, Nancy. *Civil War Ghosts Stories and Legends*. Columbia: University of South Carolina Press, 1992. A former writer for the *Charlotte Observer*, Roberts moved to North Carolina rather late in life. These Civil War tales, gathered from both the North and the South, are rewritten versions of stories that Roberts has heard. She does not provide any comparative data or biographical data about the informants. The southern states in which the stories take place are Georgia, Maryland, Mississippi, North Carolina, South Carolina, Texas, and Virginia.

————. *Ghosts and Specters of the Old South*. Orangeburg, S.C.: Sandlapper, 1974. These ghost stories from Virginia, Florida, and North Carolina are written primarily for children. These well-known stories include "The Ghost of Captain Flint" (15) and "The Gray Man's Warning" (41).

————. *Ghosts of the Southern Mountains and Appalachia*. Columbia: University of South Carolina Press, 1978. These rewritten versions of folktales take place in Alabama, Georgia, Kentucky, Maryland, North Carolina, South Carolina, Tennessee, and West Virginia. No comparative data or biographical information about the informants is provided. The story entitled "Return of the Bell Witch" (12) features W. M. Eden, whose version of the tale appears in story 148 in this volume.

————. *South Carolina Ghosts: From the Coast to the Mountains*. Columbia: University of South Carolina Press, 1983. In the preface to the book, Roberts states that her stories are based upon actual events. She adds that the names of the informants have been changed to protect their privacy. No comparative data or biographical information about the informants is provided. The most famous stories included in this collection are "The Gray Man" (68) and "The Blue Lady of Hilton Head" (42).

————. *Southern Ghosts*. Orangeburg, S.C.: Sandlapper, 1979. Roberts's very slim volume is a good introduction to fourteen of the South's best-known ghost tales. Written in a pleasant style suitable for young readers, Roberts's book is very well illustrated. Included in this collection are "President Carter's Haunted House" (5), "The Brown Mountain Lights" (13), and "Railroad Bill" (24).

Saxon, Lyle. *Fabulous New Orleans*. New Orleans: Robert L. Crager and Company, 1950. In this volume, the man known as "Mr. New Orleans" presents some of the city's trademark tales and legends, many of which focus on well-known landmarks. Saxon's versions of the haunting of the LaLaurie House (202) and the life of Marie Laveau (237) are considered by many folklorists to be the most authentic accounts of these world-famous tales.

Saxon, Lyle, et al. *Gumbo Ya-Ya.* Gretna, La.: Pelican, 1987. First published in 1945, this lively collection of WPA material compiled by the Louisiana Writers' Project is now regarded as a classic of the genre. Although the book is highly readable, especially the lengthy chapter on ghost tales, all of the stories are rewritten summaries. The names of some of the informants are given, but many are simply referred to by such descriptive phrases as a "French-woman" or "a newspaper reporter." However, the book is well illustrated; the photographs accompanying the chapter on ghost stories are particularly interesting. The book also has a fascinating appendix on superstitions.

Solomon, Jack, and Olivia Solomon. *Ghosts and Goosebumps: Ghost Stories, Tall Tales, and Superstitions from Alabama.* Tuscaloosa: University of Alabama Press, 1981. This collection of ghost stories and superstitions was compiled from the Troy area by the Solomons and student collectors at Troy State University and Alexander State College. The Solomons have balanced the stories by the primarily white informants with life histories and narratives of ex-slaves, collected during the 1930s for the Federal Writers' Project. Although they did not provide any notes on the informants or comparative data, they did include a very good scholarly essay at the beginning and an annotated bibliography at the end. There is also a listing of Alabama folktales that are available in the Library of Congress.

Tackett, Sarah Jane Turnbow. *Alabama's Favorite Folk Tales.* Birmingham, Ala,: Seacoast, 1998. In this book, Turnbow has rewritten folktales taken from newspapers and individual informants. Sources are listed at the end of each story. Supernatural tales in this collection include "Willie Compton's Mining Tale" (15); "Midnight Ashes" (21); "Mysterious Tales from Bibb County" (29); "Sally Carter's Story" (55); and "The Creature" (105).

Taylor, L. B., Jr. *Civil War Ghosts of Virginia.* U.S.A.: Progress Printing, 1985. Taylor's collection of Civil War ghost stories, albeit not a scholarly work of folklore, is enhanced by the inclusion of photographs, drawings, and factual data. Taylor also includes statements by firsthand witnesses of the ghostly phenomena. This book should appeal to Civil War buffs as well as to lovers of ghostlore.

———. *The Ghosts of Richmond . . . and Nearby Environs.* U.S.A.: Progress Printing, 1985. Taylor's book of ghost stories is well illustrated but does not list its sources, although he does give the names of the people who recount their experiences with the supernatural. The book also contains fragments of ghost tales and stories about sites that no longer exist. Another interesting touch is a chapter on places that should be haunted, owing to the tragic events that occurred there, but are not.

———. *The Ghosts of Tidewater . . . and Nearby Environs.* U.S.A.: Progress Printing, 1990. A well-researched collection of ghost tales from the Tidewater region, this book is limited in its usefulness to the folklorist or the historian because of the absence of notes. Drawings and photographs help make the stories come alive for the reader.

Taylor, Troy. *Season of the Witch*. Alton, Ill.: Whitechapel Productions, 1999. This is one of the most comprehensive accounts of the Bell Witch of Robertson County, Tennessee, to appear in many years. Paranormal investigator Troy Taylor does a fine job assimilating the many versions of the story of the Bell Witch, beginning with the first book on the phenomenon, Richard Williams Bell's *Our Family Troubles* (1894). The book is enhanced by period illustrations and Taylor's photographs. The author's personal experiences in the Bell Witch Cave effectively bring this old story into the present day. The books included in the bibliography deal primarily with the paranormal aspects of the tale.

———. *Spirits of the Civil War: A Guide to the Ghosts and Hauntings of America's Bloodiest Conflict*. Alton, Ill.: Whitechapel Productions, 1999. Nationally-known ghost hunter Troy Taylor combines history and legend in this comprehensive collection. Unlike many books dealing with ghosts of the Civil War, Taylor does not restrict himself only to those states where battles were fought. Even though many of these stories are fairly famous, Taylor breathes new life into them by including his own experiences at the sites. Directions to the haunted locations and a complete bibliography are provided. General readers will find the book to be a fascinating introduction to the haunted history of the Civil War.

Time-Life Books. *Hauntings*. New York: Barnes and Noble, 1989. This very well illustrated "coffee-table book" is of limited use to the folklorist because it takes the stance that ghosts are real. However, the sections on the Bell Witch and the ghosts of Washington, D.C., provide the traditional accounts of the hauntings. The extensive bibliography will prove to be useful to anyone who is interested in "true" hauntings.

Vivano, Christy L. *Haunted Louisiana*. Metairie, La.: Tree House, 1992. The large print and beautiful drawings suggest that this little book was written primarily for a younger audience. Many of these stories, gathered from relatives, tour guides, and the Northwestern State University Library, are based on well-known historical figures, such as Jean Lafitte, Mark Twain, and Huey Long. The story entitled "The Loupe Garou" (23) is a variant of "Roo Garoo" (story 81).

Walser, Richard. *North Carolina Legends*. Raleigh: University of North Carolina Division off Archives and History, 1980. One of North Carolina's best-known collectors of folklore, Walser has written a book that is scholarly despite the fact that it appears to have been written for a general audience. He does not give much biographical information about his informants, but he does offer extensive comparative data on his tales. The drawings enhance the book's popular appeal.

Williams, Docia Schultz. *Phantoms of the Plains: Tales of West Texas Ghosts*. Plano: Republic of Texas Press, 1996. *Phantoms of the Plains* takes the reader on a tour of the haunted Indian forts, mesas, parks, and adobe dwellings of West Texas. Williams intersperses her first-person narrative with firsthand accounts of personal experiences with the supernatural. The appendix includes the names and biographical information of the informants but does not indicate which stories they are responsible for. This is not a folklore text in that it does not include comparative data on the tales or analyze the thematic elements. Still, the book is well organized and thorough. It is a fine introduction to the folklore of West Texas.

Windham, Kathryn Tucker. *Jeffrey Introduces 13 More Southern Ghosts.* Huntsville, Ala.: Strode, 1971. Rpt., Tuscaloosa: University of Alabama Press, 1988. Windham expanded her search for ghost stories beyond Alabama in this book because of her belief that there is something about the South that makes it a fertile breeding ground for ghostly tales. The best-known story is "Our Family Trouble" (73), which is the story of the Bell Witch from Tennessee.

———. *Jeffrey's Latest 13: More Alabama Ghosts.* Huntsville, Ala.: Strode, 1982. Rpt., Tuscaloosa: University of Alabama Press, 1987. The sequel to *13 Alabama Ghosts and Jeffrey* contains more artistic retellings of Alabama ghost stories. Except for the stories of the Boyington Oak (21) and the explosion of the James T. Staples steamboat (53), the tales in this volume are generally less well-known than the ones in the earlier book.

———. *13 Georgia Ghosts and Jeffrey.* Tuscaloosa: University of Alabama, 1976. All of these Georgia ghost stories have authentic historical backgrounds. However, Windham provides no comparative data or background information on the informants. The historical sites referred to in the amply-illustrated (twenty-six photographs and thirteen drawings) volume includes Andersonville prison (47), the Springer Opera House (35), Orna Villa (71) and Barnsley Gardens (125).

———. *13 Mississippi Ghosts and Jeffrey.* Tuscaloosa: University of Alabama Press, 1974. Unlike Windham's other volumes of rewritten folk tales, this book contains a map of Mississippi, which highlights the actual locations of her stories. Several of the stories provide the names of the informants and some biographical information. Most of the tales focus around some of the well-known antebellum homes scattered throughout the state.

———. *13 Tennessee Ghosts and Jeffrey.* Tuscaloosa: University of Alabama Press, 1977. This collection of rewritten texts includes Tennessee's most famous ghost story—the story of the Bell Witch—as well as ghost tales about such well-known historical events as the death of Merriwether Lewis and the Battle of Shiloh. Like all of her books, this one is very well illustrated.

Windham, Kathryn Tucker, and Margaret Gillis Figh. *13 Alabama Ghosts and Jeffrey.* Huntsville, Ala.: Strode, 1969. Rpt., Tuscaloosa: University of Alabama Press, 1987. Windham's artistic retellings of Alabama's most famous ghost stories, such as "The Face in the Courthouse Window (63) and "Huntingdon College's Red Lady" (97) have made this book a perennial favorite among children and adults alike since its first publication in 1969. The absence of comparative data and notes on the informants makes it clear that this book was intended primarily as entertainment.

Word, Christine. *Ghosts along the Bayou.* Lafayette, La.: Acadiana, 1988. These tales are based on personal interviews the author had with people who had had eerie experiences in Louisiana. Although this is not a scholarly folklore text in the strictest sense, Word does identify her informants and supplements her tales with lengthy quotations. The book is well illustrated with photographs and drawings.

Young, Richard Alan, and Judy Dockrey Young. *Ghost Stories from the American Southwest.* In *Ghastly Ghost Stories.* New York: Wings Books, 1993. It is no coincidence that this book was reprinted in a single volume with W. K. McNeil's *Ghost Stories from the American South.* Like McNeil's very fine book, the Youngs' collection of oral narratives begins with an excellent scholarly introduction and concludes with a notes section that reveals background information on the informants, motif numbers, and comparative data. An added bonus is a two-page section entitled "For Further Study," which includes the names of three oral history archives as well as the names of two resource providers for story materials in print.

Zweifel, Karyn. *Covered Bridge Ghost Stories.* Birmingham, Ala.: Crane Hill, 1995. Compiling an entire collection of covered bridge ghost stories is an excellent concept because bridges are the settings of many tales told by young people who like to frequent out-of-the-way places. The absence of comparative data and biographical information on the informants indicates that this book was written for a general audience. At the end of the stories, Zweifel provides detailed directions to each of the bridges. The southern states featured in this book are Alabama (three stories), Georgia (two stories), Mississippi, and Tennessee.

———. *Dog-Gone Ghost Stories: 13 Hair-Raising Tales of Unearthly Dogs.* Birmingham, Ala.: Crane Hill, 1996. Dogs are the most common type of animal ghost found in the South, and a collection of dog-ghost stories is certainly warranted. Most of the stories contained in this collection are adapted from tales gathered by folklorists such as Ruth Ann Musick and Margaret Redding Siler. Zweifel does not identify the state in which the stories are set or include comparative data and information on the informants.

* * *

İ п d e x

CPSIA information can be obtained
at www.ICGtesting.com
Printed in the USA
FSHW010905151220
76647FS